COMMUNICATING WITH
THE WORLD

THE INSTITUTE FOR THE STUDY OF DIPLOMACY concentrates on the processes of conducting foreign relations abroad, in the belief that studies of diplomatic operations are useful means of teaching or improving diplomatic skills and of broadening public understanding of diplomacy. Working closely with the academic program of the Georgetown University School of Foreign Service, the Institute conducts a program of research, publication, teaching, diplomats in residence, conferences, and lectures.

COMMUNICATING WITH THE WORLD

U.S. Public Diplomacy Overseas

Hans N. Tuch

Foreword by Marvin Kalb

An Institute for the Study of Diplomacy Book

ST. MARTIN'S PRESS
New York

© 1990 by the Institute for the Study of Diplomacy,
Georgetown University, Washington, D.C.

For information, write:
Scholarly and Reference Division,
St. Martin's Press, Inc., 175 Fifth Avenue,
New York, N.Y. 10010

First published in the United States of America in 1990
Second paperback printing 1993

Printed in the United States of America

ISBN: 0-312-04532-8
       0-312-04809-2 (pbk.)

Library of Congress Cataloging-in-Publication Data

Tuch, Hans N., 1924—
   Communicating with the world: U.S. public diplomacy overseas / by
Hans N. Tuch; foreword by Marvin Kalb.
      p. cm. — (Martin F. Herz series on United States diplomacy)
   includes bibliographical references.
   ISBN 0-312-04532-8   ISBN 0-312-04809-2 (pbk.)
   1. United States — Diplomatic and consular service. 2. Diplomacy.
I. Title. II. Series.
JX1706.T78 1990
327.2 — dc20   89-49579
                                      CIP

To my wife, Mimi, who lovingly and unselfishly shared my life and my experiences in public diplomacy and contributed to making my years in the Foreign Service meaningful, satisfying, and memorable.

Contents

Vignettes

Foreword

Marvin Kalb

Hans Tuch (who has always been known to his friends as Tom) has written a valuable book: valuable, first and foremost, to a new generation of Foreign Service officers beginning to grasp the essential lesson of the sad Vietnam experience — that a policy conceived in secrecy and implemented by deception, denied the popular support so essential in a democracy, will fail, no matter how honorable the original intent. The book is valuable also to the student of American foreign policy who has come to appreciate the fact that policy has at least two faces, one that remains private and the other that must be made public, and to the journalist, American or foreign, who is skeptical of any nugget of information that is officially volunteered or leaked rather than unearthed during independent pursuit of a story. (Why, after all, the journalist asks, would I be given a "fact" unless it serves the government's interest? If it serves the government's interest, then by definition it may be self-serving, perhaps even devoid of credibility, and thus lose its value to me.)

Tom Tuch understands the rules of the game. He was, for more than thirty years, one of the most professional public affairs officers I have ever met. I don't know where — maybe in Moscow, or Berlin, or Brasilia, or Bonn, several of the capitals in which he served so ably — but somewhere he learned

COMMUNICATING WITH THE WORLD

that the currency of public diplomacy is credibility, and that no matter how blunt the challenge, or how sensitive the information, he must never lie. He could dance and dodge, and Tuch has been quite adept at both, but he must never, as Harry Reasoner said years ago of Lyndon Johnson, be "less than candid." Once a PAO lies, he's finished. Journalists have a way of thinking that every lie is a big lie; they dismiss small lies, white lies, inadvertent lies, as simply lies, all these distinctions generally lost in the journalist's mind. There were many times when Tom Tuch could not tell the truth; but even on those occasions he did not mislead the press, not to the best of my knowledge. He steered reporters away from bad leads, and occasionally helped them with a few good ones.

He is, in this sense, the perfect author for this book. He has a gentle, winning personality, able to expand contacts and retain friendships. In the age of "winning the hearts and minds" of contested parts of the world that was once the urgent mandate of the United States Information Agency, Tom Tuch was a super envoy. He never met a person he couldn't befriend, nor a language he couldn't master. From Russian to German to Portuguese he fluttered, always fluent enough to enhance his role as a serious diplomat eager to understand the nuances of the country to which he was assigned, while representing the subtlest shifts of American policy with clarity and tireless dedication.

Communicating with the World: U.S. Public Diplomacy Overseas is, in addition to being valuable, an important book. At its core, it recognizes that diplomacy has changed radically from the time a hundred years ago when a British envoy in the Near East reported to the Foreign Office that the pasha had died and "What should I do?" Many months later, the time consumed in the envoy's query reaching London and the Foreign Office's response ricocheting back to him, a cryptic, oddly amusing message finally arrived at the British mission to the pasha's homeland. "First suggest burial service," was the Foreign Office's advice. "Then convey Her Majesty's deepest regrets."

What once took months now takes seconds. Technology has squeezed time for reflection out of old-fashioned diplomacy. Space has been obliterated. Now the diplomats have been forced to compete with the journalists to get their stories to the home office. It is an unfair contest. The diplomats are not paid to be quick, but often they learn about events in their own backyard from a bulletin on the radio or television, or from a call from a State Department colleague who has heard the same bulletin in Washington. Everyone is often dependent on the same sources of information, but not everyone, certainly not the journalist, is responsible for giving advice to the secretary of state or the president about what the United States should do. That is the diplomat's job.

It is a job made all the more difficult by the increasingly central role that the press plays in the process of decision making. Soviet President Mikhail Gorbachev uses the press with stunning effectiveness. He caresses the lens like a professional anchorman, knowing that its power can enhance his diplomacy. During a visit to Bonn, he picked up a child with flowers, and this picture of friendliness bounced off every corner of the globe and did more to bury the hatchet in Soviet-German relations than any agreement he signed with Chancellor Helmut Kohl. One of Gorbachev's spokespersons told me recently that before he briefs foreign reporters in the Soviet Foreign Ministry, he watches CNN in his Moscow office to learn what's happening in the world and what questions he can expect to field. David Gergen, who once worked in the Reagan White House, says that the president's famous zero-option speech, which laid the basis for the medium-range missile agreement he later signed with Gorbachev, was delivered at 2:00 PM, because the message was aimed at Western Europe and 2:00 PM in Washington was prime time in Paris, London, and Bonn.

Pollster Lou Harris estimates that there are now thirty million people in Western Europe who speak English and depend on American news organizations for their news. Before the democracy movement was crushed in Beijing, the students communicated their cry for freedom through Western cameras, unfurling slogans in English and French and propping up their own version of the Statue of Liberty symbolically to convey their sympathy for American values and their impatience with Communism. The images from Tiananmen Square, first of democracy and then of repression, ignited strong emotions throughout the world, accelerating the pace of politics in China and of diplomacy everywhere else.

It is a new world, linking technology, journalism, and diplomacy in a global loop of interdependence, and raising in virtually every trouble spot profound questions about American responsibilities, but also profound opportunities. Ronald Reagan, who throughout his presidency was on a first-name basis with the camera, referred to information as the "oxygen of the modern age," the power that "seeps through the walls topped with barbed wire. . . . [M]ore than armies, more than diplomacy, more than the best intentions of democratic nations, the communications revolution will be the greatest force for the advancement of human freedom the world has ever seen."

The best diplomacy these days takes advantage of the power of a free flow of information. Tom Tuch, in his book, focuses on public diplomacy and uses four case studies to amplify his points. They are, first, the start of U.S.-Soviet cultural relations in the mid-1950s; second, the practice of public diplomacy in Brazil; third, dealing with the successor generation in Germany; and, finally, the deployment of medium-range missiles in West Germany in the early 1980s. In each case Tuch plays a key role, but he is wise enough to know that more senior officials in Washington make the decisions. As an experienced public affairs officer in the field, Tuch can make a recommendation, he can offer advice, he can raise a cautionary flag; but his is an advisory role in a key corner of diplomacy — "only one piston in the foreign affairs engine," as he puts it.

Washington is beginning to understand the power and potential of public diplomacy, not propaganda but the unafraid exercise of ideas and information in the global marketplace. Tuch's book is helpful instruction for a secretary of state, a director of central intelligence and, yes, even a president.

Preface

Chinese villagers in Szechuan listen over their communal loudspeakers to the news of student demonstrations in Beijing in a Voice of America Chinese broadcast. A Peruvian Fulbright student is studying environmental economics at the University of Florida. Leading U.S. and Soviet cardiologists discuss new techniques of combatting heart disease via satellite television on USIA's Worldnet. Michael Novak of the American Enterprise Institute discusses American reaction to the Pope's encyclical with an audience in Brazil. A Stockholm newspaper editor writes an editorial about the INF treaty on the basis of the full text of Secretary of State George Shultz's news conference, supplied him through the USIS Wireless File. A teenager from Olathe, Kansas spends the year living with a German family and attending high school in Freiburg as a participant in the Congress-Bundestag Youth Exchange Program. A minister of education from Senegal travels around the southwestern United States for a month, visiting school boards, elementary and high schools, and universities as a USIA International Visitor. A nursing student from Cuernavaca checks out a book about obstetrical nursing in the Benjamin Franklin Library in Mexico City. An American exhibit guide explains American information technology in Russian to a group of exhibit visitors in Tashkent, as two thousand others stand patiently in line to enter the exhibition hall.

These are but a few routine examples of public diplomacy as practiced by the United States government. What public diplomacy is, why it is part of our foreign affairs process, how it is practiced by the U.S. government throughout the world, who the practitioners are, and whether it is effective — these questions are the subject of this study.

Most of this book is based on my thirty-five years of experience in practicing public diplomacy. And most of that experience has been in three distinct areas of the world—Germany, the Soviet Union and other Communist countries of Eastern Europe, and Brazil. Readers will understand that the majority of examples I cite to illustrate the practice of public diplomacy will involve my service in those countries; and they will forgive me, I hope, if I slight other areas, although I have tried to broaden my personal experience by consultation and conversation with colleagues experienced in public diplomacy whose service was in China and countries in Africa, the Middle East, and Asia with which I am not familiar.

In a book which includes the distillation of so many years in the Foreign Service, many contribute to the thoughts, ideas, and opinions that the author expresses. With my gratitude to all who will recognize their input to this manuscript, I mention by name only those who helped with the actual publication of the book: David Newsom, who encouraged its writing and saw to its publication; Margery Boichel Thompson, who edited it expertly and thereby improved it greatly; Gifford Malone, Mary Brady, and Terrence Catherman, who read it critically and gave me indispensable advice and valuable suggestions; C. B. (Cliff) Groce, Alan Heil, and Robert Gosende, who, by reading pertinent parts of it, helped me with ideas and corrected mistakes; Martin Manning, who checked the manuscript for factual and historical errors and supplied needed documents; Nina Parmee, who assisted with research and indexing; and to Jeffry A. Robelen, manuscript production coordinator, and Michael Snyder, principal manuscript "word processor." My thanks to all.

Finally, this volume is the first in the Martin F. Herz Series on United States Diplomacy, established by the Institute for the Study of Diplomacy to honor the memory of an exemplary scholar-diplomat who was the Institute's first director of studies.

Abbreviations and Acronyms

ABEA	Brazilian Association of American Studies
ABRAPUI	Brazilian Association of University Professors of English Language and Literature
AFS	American Field Service, former name of AFS International, a youth exchange organization
AmPart	American Participant [Program] (USIA)
BBC	British Broadcasting Corporation
BNC	binational center
BPAO	branch public affairs officer
CAMPUS	Central American Program for Undergraduate Scholarships (USIA)
CAO	cultural affairs officer [or cultural attaché]
CAPES	Brazilian government organization for foreign educational grants and scholarships
CDU	Christian Democratic Union (FRG)
CNPq	National Research Council (Brazil)
CP	country plan (USIS)
CSU	Christian Social Union (FRG - Bavaria)
CU	State Department Bureau of Educational and Cultural Affairs
DAAD	German Academic Exchange Service
DRS	Distribution and Records System (USIS)
E/YX	USIA Office of Youth Exchanges
E/AA	USIA Office of Academic Affairs
EUR/CE	State Department Office of Central European Affairs
Euronet	USIA television network, predecessor to Worldnet
FAPESP	São Paulo State Foundation for Research
FDP	Free Democratic Party (FRG)
FRG	Federal Republic of Germany [West Germany]

FSNE/FNE	Foreign Service national employee
FSO	Foreign Service officer
GAAS	German Association of American Studies
GAI	German-American Institute
GDR	German Democratic Republic [East Germany]
GOB	Government of Brazil
INF	intermediate-range nuclear forces
IREX	International Research and Exchanges Board
IUCTG	Inter-University Committee on Travel Grants
IV	International Visitor [Program] (USIA)
Komsomol	Soviet Communist Youth League
LASPAU	Latin-American Scholarship Program with American Universities (USIA)
MPAA	Motion Picture Association of America
NAPA	National Partners of the Americas
NATO	North Atlantic Treaty Organization
NSDD	National Security Decision Directive
NSF	National Science Foundation
PAO	public affairs officer
PPP	U.S. Congress - FRG Bundestag Youth Exchange Program
PRC	People's Republic of China
RFE	Radio Free Europe
RIAS	Radio in the American Sector (Berlin)
RL	Radio Liberty
SPD	Social Democratic Party (FRG)
USAID	U.S. Agency for International Development
USIA	U.S. Information Agency
USIAAA	U.S. Information Agency Alumni Association
USICA	U.S. Information Agency Communication Agency
USIS	U.S. Information Service
VOA	Voice of America
Worldnet	USIA's worldwide television network
YFU	Youth for Understanding, Inc.

Part I

The Practice of U.S. Public Diplomacy Abroad

"The achievement...of true understanding between any two governments depends fundamentally on the kind of relationship that exists between the peoples, rather than on foreign ministers and ambassadors."

— ARTHUR BURNS
(from a speech at the Overseas Club,
Hamburg, March 14, 1983)

1
Defining Public Diplomacy

Whether one dates its beginning to the Sermon on the Mount, the seventeenth century Pontifical Congregation for the Propagation of the Faith, the Declaration of Independence, President Truman's "Campaign of Truth," or the founding of the Murrow Center at the Fletcher School of Law and Diplomacy in 1965, public diplomacy has been around for a long time. It may not always have been accepted as an intellectual concept, as an academic discipline, or as a profession in which qualified Foreign Service officers engage. But as governments have come to realize that foreign relations can no longer be managed by traditional diplomatic practices alone, public diplomacy has become an imperative of a nation's international life.

As we launch into a discussion and analysis of the conduct of public diplomacy by the U.S. government's foreign affairs community, we need to start with a definition. What is public diplomacy?

I define public diplomacy as *a government's process of communicating with foreign publics in an attempt to bring about understanding for its nation's ideas and ideals, its institutions and culture, as well as its national goals and current policies.*

Public diplomacy differs from traditional diplomacy in that the latter involves conducting the relations among nations through the interaction of governments, foreign ministries in most cases. Traditional diplomacy often is — must be — a process requiring confidentiality and privacy. (Confidentiality in diplomacy by no means implies secret treaties or covenants. It merely means that there may have to be a confidential process for reaching an agreement.)

3

In contrast, public diplomacy is almost always, by definition, an open process. Publicity is its inherent purpose; the appeal is to the public: we want people to know and understand. The so-called Stanton Panel on Information and Cultural Relations[1] introduced its seminal 1974 report by stating, "Public diplomacy is a central part of American foreign policy simply because the freedom to know is such an important part of America." [2]

International relations changed so drastically and permanently in this century that traditional diplomacy alone could no longer manage the peacetime affairs of nations. Public diplomacy, attempting to communicate directly with peoples in other countries, came into its own as an indispensable component of international relations.

Why Public Diplomacy

A number of changes in the conduct of international relations since World War II have been particularly significant in making public diplomacy such a vital element in the foreign affairs process.

First, the communications revolution, which began shortly after the Second World War and continues today, makes possible the instantaneous transmission of information of all kinds across oceans and over mountains to the remotest areas of the world, disregarding national boundaries and penetrating into the tightest fortresses of thought control. Transistor radios, television, satellite transmissions, supersonic jet transportation, international computer link-ups, electronic data processing, and telefax enable people everywhere to receive and pass on information that may previously have taken days or weeks to reach them, if at all. It is no longer only nations' governments that know what is going on abroad; their citizens are able to obtain the same information at almost the same time — and act on it.

The second reason for the rise of public diplomacy follows on the first: The information now available to large publics everywhere directly affects the formation of public attitudes and the expression of public opinion. Thus, public opinion has become an important factor in international affairs, exerting influence on the decisions and actions of governments. One may remember the impression on the American public of nightly network television broadcasts from Vietnam in the sixties and seventies, or of more recent reportage of the brutal assault on Chinese students in Tiananmen Square.

The immediacy of wrenching images on television news increasingly influences policy, according to presidential press secretary Marlin Fitzwater, referring in particular to the impact of Chinese soldiers shooting students on the policy decisions of President Bush. "You wonder," said Fitzwater, "if Nixon and Kissinger could have opened up China if television had shown the atrocities of the Cultural Revolution."[3]

The impact of public opinion on the actions of governments is not limited to the democracies. Totalitarian governments also recognize the power of public opinion within their own realms, as they have known and exploited its power in the promotion of their policies in other countries. Unlike the democracies, however, they also fear the influence of public opinion, else they would not suppress it within their own domains and try to prevent it from being affected by anyone other than their own authorities.

The third principal factor in making public diplomacy a necessity of contemporary international relations was the proliferation in the post–World War II era of new states in the international arena — forty-seven of them between 1948 and 1964 — each with its own stake in the world of ideas, its own politics, economics, traditions, and culture, each interested in promulgating its policies and views to the rest of the world, each with a profile to show and a face to save. Using modern communications technologies — or demanding equal access to them from the industrialized world if they did not yet possess them — these newly emerging nations have become both practitioners and targets of public diplomacy.

Fourth, the ideological struggles that buffeted the world for over forty years required that the democracies be able to compete vigorously in the contest of ideas. We in the United States needed to be able to promote our views and values, our culture and our society, to peoples of other cultures, traditions, and ideologies, as in President Truman's "Campaign of Truth."

Finally, the most obvious yet elusive factor is that in the formulation of public opinion, perceptions are often as important as reality. If people believe something to be true, it is frequently the same, in political terms, as if it were true. In the United States, a free press allows for a variety of information, opinion, and ideas. But most of the world's people do not have ready access to multiple and independent sources of information. Thus, it is a function of U.S. public diplomacy to try to correct perceptions that cloud reality.

The problem that public diplomacy faces here is compounded by the tremendous cultural diversity in the world that makes it so difficult for people to grasp the profusion of information coming at them from everywhere and to form accurate judgments. At the same time, it is precisely the complexity of current international relations coupled with the emerging importance of public opinion that make it incumbent on people to be well informed and to understand each other's truths and realities.

Yet, even though we had learned to recognize that the image foreign publics receive of America is blurred by Hollywood fantasies, sensationalized by the mass media, distorted by the falsifications of our adversaries, and complicated by the size and diversity of our nation, conducting U.S. foreign propaganda activities was for a long time regarded by Americans and their representatives in Congress with some ambivalence.

Propaganda is not, as we will explain later, an entirely respectable word in our vocabulary, and disseminating it abroad was thought by some as merely joining others in a disreputable enterprise. Equally important, our concept of freedom has always compelled us to garner our information from various sources and to trust least of all what the government tells us.

Furthermore, the recognition that it was important for other peoples to understand us — our motives, our beliefs, our values — came late and reluctantly. In the past, we had not cared what others thought of us — they could take us or leave us.

But even when the necessity for the U.S. government to conduct public diplomacy was accepted, the Congress insisted on immunizing the American people from its own government's propaganda by limiting the government's activities to telling its story abroad. The distinction was clear: to this day, the U.S government's public diplomacy programs and products cannot by law be disseminated to the American public. (Exceptions must be approved by Congress and are rare.)

These reservations aside, the need for the United States to conduct public diplomacy is today hardly in dispute. It is equally important to recognize that public diplomacy is a communications process that works in both directions: as we convey information and promote understanding about us abroad, we can do so effectively only if we learn about and understand others, and communicate on the basis of that knowledge. As Arthur Goodfriend observed, if we intend to open the minds of others to American viewpoints, we first have to open our minds to theirs.[4]

Clarifying the Definition

Before discussing the practice of public diplomacy, a further word must be said about the meaning of public diplomacy. The definition of public diplomacy that was offered on the first page of this chapter is by no means acceptable to all, particularly not to some who served in the Reagan administration. This becomes evident when one examines the wording of the 1983 National Security Decision Directive 77 (NSDD–77), which describes public diplomacy as "those actions of the government designed to generate support for our national security objectives"; or when one reads the Reagan State Department's definition, which states: "Public diplomacy is 20th century public affairs adapting traditional approaches both domestically and abroad to take account of modern communications technology."[5]

I submit that both definitions—contradictory as they are, yet coming from the same administration—are erroneous and misleading. Supporting our national security objectives is indeed one element of U.S. public diplomacy and an important one at that, but it is by no means the only one. Significant economic, political, social, and cultural interests are also important elements of U.S. foreign policy that are promoted through public diplomacy efforts. Further, neither the Department of State nor anyone else in the U.S. government practices "diplomacy"—traditional or public—with its own citizenry.

One of our most distinguished diplomats, Philip C. Habib, explained the difference between public diplomacy and public affairs succinctly when he wrote:

> The word diplomacy means "outside" and has nothing to do with the American people....Gaining the support of the American people for U.S. policy initiatives is entirely different from attempting to pursue the interests of the United States in the foreign arena. That is what diplomacy is all about—the representation of the national interest abroad.[6]

The confusion surrounding the meaning of public diplomacy is the principal reason for discussing its definition in some detail. As Habib makes clear, it does not include informing or persuading our domestic population regarding foreign policy, as the Reagan State Department appeared to think; nor does Congress appropriate resources to conduct the nation's public diplomacy for this purpose.

Furthermore, the confusion in terminology handicaps the U.S. foreign policy process. In conducting public diplomacy abroad we try to achieve understanding of America — its values, traditions, and institutions — as a psychological foundation for our second objective — achieving understanding of specific foreign policies. We do this by addressing and communicating with foreign audiences whose history, culture, social processes, and language we must study so that we can project our policies to them in understandable and acceptable ways.

In conducting a public affairs program in the United States, the Department of State tries to gain support for the administration's foreign policies by addressing a domestic audience with which it is familiar. The two processes are not the same in concept, intent, audience, or method. Confusing the terms is therefore likely to harm the desired outcome of both.

The "founding" definition of public diplomacy, some say the coining of the term, is often attributed to Edmund Gullion, a former American diplomat who was dean of the Fletcher School of Law and Diplomacy when the Edward R. Murrow Center of Public Diplomacy was established there in 1965. The Fletcher catalogue described public diplomacy as "the role of the press and other media in international affairs, cultivation by governments of public opinion, the non-governmental interaction of private groups and interests in one country with those of another, and the impact of these transnational processes on the formulation of policy and the conduct of foreign affairs."[7]

This definition is, however, too broad, again because it goes considerably beyond the concept of the usually accepted meaning of "diplomacy." The Fletcher definition describes the entire international and intercultural communications process, of which public diplomacy is an important, but only one, element.

The reader may ask, why get hung up on the phrase "public diplomacy" if it causes so much confusion? Why not avoid that circumlocution and speak plainly and unambiguously about propaganda or, if that term causes discomfort, talk about political advocacy and intercultural communication, or even simply refer to information and cultural activities in the context of the foreign affairs process?

Propaganda is a perfectly appropriate term if used in its original and correct meaning. Its origin is the seventeenth century Sacred Congregation for the Propagation of the Faith, a Vatican institution to educate priests who were going abroad to serve the Church.[8] If one thinks of propaganda in terms of disseminating ideas and information, there is no problem in using this word to describe the U.S. government's information and cultural activities abroad. But in the English language — at least in America — propaganda has acquired a pejorative meaning, referring to the deliberate spreading of lies and false information. (In 1967, perhaps because of this pejorative sense, the Vatican came up with a new name: Congregation for the Evangelization of People.)

The Soviet Union, in projecting its revolutionary ideology abroad, institutionalized foreign propaganda activities in the 1920s, both overtly, through radio, publications, and exchanges, and covertly, through their affiliated Communist Party organs in foreign countries. But it was Nazi Germany's Propaganda Ministry that is probably responsible for giving propaganda its bad name in this country, as Josef Goebbels, who came to personify the word, used it to disseminate his stream of untruths, hate, and distortion. For the general public, propaganda has consequently become a concept with highly negative connotations that, most will agree, are unsuitable for the characterization of the government's legitimate information and cultural activities.

Referring to information and cultural activities without fitting them into an overall concept — such as public diplomacy — is also not the answer. Public diplomacy is more than just those activities, as Gifford Malone fully recognizes while disagreeing with the use of the term.[9] It includes the very important "learning experience," or, if you will, the so-called two-way street (to repeat): If we strive to be successful in our efforts to create understanding for our society and for our policies, we must first understand the motives, culture, history, and psychology of the people with whom we wish to communicate, and certainly their language.

This requirement to understand others is indispensable to public diplomacy, and it is part of what makes public diplomacy an important tool of our foreign policy process. While our information and cultural activities abroad are generally accepted by the American foreign affairs establishment as an often useful and sometimes necessary aspect of the U.S. foreign relations process, the second principal function of public diplomacy — the gauging of public opinion abroad and the consideration of these public attitudes and perceptions — is not sufficiently recognized as an integral element in the formulation and execution of U.S. foreign policy. How will our foreign policy initiatives be perceived by peoples of other cultures and traditions? How can we formulate and explain them so that they will be understood?

Too often in our recent history have we launched initiatives abroad or declared a new policy without sufficient consideration of how this initiative or that policy will be seen by diverse peoples in disparate regions of the world; and the support and acceptance of our initiatives and policies have suffered accordingly. David Hitchcock has provided an example of this shortcoming of our foreign policy process.

From his long experience in public diplomacy and understanding of Japan, Hitchcock explains how difficult it is to persuade both U.S. and Japanese policymakers that one reason for their apparently insurmountable confrontation on economic issues is that each side views problems only from its own cultural perspective. Each has had great difficulty in solving mutual differences because each has been blind to the other side's way of thinking and acting: The United States wants the Japanese to treat it fairly. "Fairness" is the principle on which it insists. The Japanese, on the other hand, want a smooth and harmonious process. "Harmony" is their main objective. Both sides need to take these psychological and cultural differences into consideration before they can accommodate each other.[10]

Public diplomacy, in its attempt to affect the attitudes and opinions of foreign publics, involves the entire communications spectrum, modern communications technology as well as such other methods of intercultural communication as cultural and educational exchanges, libraries, publications, and people (among them professionally qualified Foreign Service officers). And it includes our own "learning experience," because we must understand the hopes, fears, and hang-ups of other peoples if we are going to be successful in persuading them to understand us.

If public diplomacy is to be effectively employed in promoting our national foreign policy interests, we must first agree on its meaning. The chapters to follow will examine its potential and limitations.

NOTES

1. Panel on International Information, Education and Cultural Relations, established in 1973, headed by Dr. Frank Stanton, former president of CBS.

2. "Stanton Panel Reports," in U.S. Advisory Commission on Information, 27th Report, July 1974 (Washington: U.S. Government Printing Office, 1974) v–viii.

3. As quoted in Maureen Dowd, "White House," *New York Times*, 11 Aug. 1989.

4. Arthur Goodfriend, *The Twisted Mind* (New York: St. Martin's Press, 1963), 141.

5. Office of Public Diplomacy, Department of State, in *State*, Jan. 1988, 53.

6. In Richard Starr, ed., *Public Diplomacy: USA versus USSR* (Stanford, CA: Hoover Institution Press, Stanford University, 1986), 283.

7. *The Fletcher School of Law and Diplomacy, Tufts University, 1975–76*, Medford, MA, 48.

8. Pope Gregory XV, 1628, quoting Mark XVI: "Go ye into all the world and preach the gospel to every creature." He founded the Sacred Congregation for the Propagation of the Faith. Propaganda: propagating ("the faith").

9. Gifford D. Malone, *Political Advocacy and Cultural Communication: Organizing the Nation's Public Diplomacy* (Lanham, MD: University Press of America, 1988), 1–11.

10. David Hitchcock, USIA's director for East Asian and Pacific Affairs and former PAO in Tokyo, speaking at the Association of Asian Studies regional conference, Georgetown University, 21 Oct. 1989.

2

The Origins and Development of U.S. Public Diplomacy

Having attempted to define public diplomacy and place it within the context of the overall foreign affairs process, we turn to the *practice* of public diplomacy by the U.S. government, assessing first the impact of history, personalities, and legislation on current policies and practices.

Throughout America's post–World War II history, there have been debates, differences of view, confusion, and abrupt changes of direction as to what constitutes the U.S. practice of public diplomacy, what it should be expected to accomplish, and what it cannot accomplish. Witness merely the current confusion about the definition of public diplomacy, described in the previous chapter. Since 1948, according to the late Lois Roth, thirty-one U.S. government studies have dealt with U.S. government propaganda, information, and cultural programs.[1] Articles, symposia, and books on the subject abound.[2]

The focus of this study will be the *conduct* of public diplomacy in the context of U.S. foreign operations abroad, not the organization or location of public diplomacy within the federal government. To bring some perspective to the current practice of public diplomacy by our diplomatic missions around the world, one must understand how it has been affected by congressional enactments, executive branch policymakers, and international events.

Throughout the relatively short history of public diplomacy, its practitioners — primarily Foreign Service officers (FSOs) trained and experienced in this specialized field of diplomacy — have had to cope with a number of basic issues that remain controversial and largely unresolved. Perhaps they cannot be resolved definitively. Yet, the dynamics of the debate have given public diplomacy its forward thrust and kept its practitioners engaged in the dialectics of their profession.

These are the basic issues:

— Should U.S. public diplomacy address itself to mass audiences or to the elites in other countries?

— Should U.S. public diplomacy concern itself with long-term objectives, creating a climate of understanding for the United States, or should it concern itself with short-term objectives, such as gaining acceptance for intermediate-range nuclear forces (INF) deployment in Europe?

— Should U.S. public diplomacy use primarily "fast" media, namely, information programs involving press, radio, and television; or should it work through the "slow" media — cultural and educational exchanges, books, libraries, exhibitions?

— Should U.S. public diplomacy be primarily concerned with countering communist ideology, or should its principal objectives be to promote democracy?

— Should U.S. public diplomacy represent the policies of the incumbent administration, or should it reflect American society in its diversity?

A succession of U.S. administrations has usually pulled or pushed America's public diplomacy in one or another direction, viewing these alternatives as mutually exclusive. Only too rarely have they been regarded as complementary approaches requiring a rational balance. The fault lies partly in the lack of a clear idea on the part of most administrations, including that of Ronald Reagan, of what public diplomacy could and should achieve, or in exaggerated expectations of its potential.

Among those who directed public diplomacy within the U.S. government and those who predominated in legislating its policies and resources, most have favored one or another direction as dictated by their own experience, political predilection, and dedication to having their ideas prevail. Thus, the problem for the professionals in the field — who, since 1953, have been the FSOs and domestic employees of the U.S. Information Agency (USIA) — is an absence of a permanent consensus as to what U.S. public diplomacy consists of and what direction it should take. Such a fluid situation, while frequently confusing, has, however, provided opportunities to try new ingredients in the bubbling public diplomacy cauldron, making it possible for public diplomacy to adjust more readily to changing world conditions, altered requirements of U.S. policy, and new ways to promote American interests. There also have been periods and instances of chaos. That is why it is useful to touch on some of the events, personalities, and congressional actions that have had a decisive impact on the conduct of contemporary U.S. public diplomacy.

The Dawn of Public Diplomacy

The U.S. government's first involvement in foreign information activities came during World War I when President Woodrow Wilson created the Committee on Public Information (named the Creel Committee for its chairman, George Creel), with the mandate to make U.S. war aims widely known throughout the world. The Creel Committee was abolished in 1919.

Not until 1938, in response to the danger posed by German cultural imperialism and Nazi efforts at aggressive political subversion in Latin America, did President Franklin D. Roosevelt revive foreign information and cultural activities by creating the Interdepartmental Committee for Scientific Cooperation and the Division for Cultural Cooperation in the Department of State. The subsequent assignment of cultural affairs officers to some Latin American posts to organize exchange programs marked the beginning of cultural relations with foreign countries.

United States public diplomacy following World War II can be attributed to two basic sources: the Cold War and the U.S. occupation of Germany, Austria, and Japan.

In the first month following the end of the war, President Truman had abolished the Office of War Information, the wartime information and propaganda agency, after dispersing its functions to other bureaus.[3] At the same time, he directed the Department of State to formulate permanent plans for the U.S. conduct of public diplomacy (although he did not use that term at the time). As he explained it, "The nature of present-day foreign relations makes it essential for the United States to maintain informational activities abroad as an integral part of the conduct of our foreign affairs." He said the United States would "endeavor to see to it that other peoples receive a full and fair picture of American life and of the aims and policies of the United States Government."[4]

The president put teeth into this directive in his famous "Campaign of Truth" speech in April 1950:

> The cause of freedom is being challenged throughout the world today by the forces of imperialistic Communism. This is a struggle, above all else, for the minds of men. Propaganda is one of the most powerful weapons the Communists have in this struggle. Deceit, distortion, and lies are systematically used by them as a matter of deliberate policy.
>
> This propaganda can be overcome by truth — plain, simple, unvarnished truth — presented by newspapers, radio, newsreels, and other sources that the people trust....
>
> We know how false these Communist promises are. But it is not enough for us to know this. Unless we get the real story across to people in other countries, we will lose the battle for men's minds by pure default....
>
> We must make ourselves known as we really are — not as Communist propaganda pictures us. We must pool our efforts with those of other free peoples in a sustained, intensified program to promote the cause of freedom against the propaganda of slavery. We must make ourselves heard round the world in a great campaign of truth.[5]

The Voice of America (VOA) radio network, which had had its start in February 1942 as a World War II propaganda medium, became the most active U.S. government instrument to carry this campaign forward. Organized into language services, VOA broadcast to all areas of the world, but particularly to the Communist countries in Europe and Asia. In the early 1950s, VOA was joined in its anti-Communist crusade by Radio Liberation, later changed to Radio Liberty (RL), broadcasting to the Soviet Union in Russian and several other indigenous Soviet languages, and by Radio Free Europe (RFE), broadcasting to the Communist countries of Eastern Europe in their respective languages.

These broadcasters had differing structures based on differing missions. The Voice of America was the official U.S. government radio, part of the State Department until 1953, when it was incorporated within the newly created U.S. Information Agency. Its broadcasting mission at the time was to express U.S. policy and U.S. life in the context of the Campaign of Truth.

Radio Liberty and Radio Free Europe, in contrast, were designed as surrogate radio networks, broadcasting to the populations of the "enslaved nations" as though they were domestic stations supplying information and news denied their audiences by the Communist authorities. Initially, RFE and RL were financed by the U.S. government in secret. Since 1973, however, RFE/RL, now one radio network, is operated overtly by the Board of International Broadcasting and financed through congressional appropriations. Its mission, however, remains essentially the same.

The important thing to recognize is that the missions of VOA and of RFE/RL were separate from the beginning, although they were both instruments of the worldwide information campaign that the U.S. government conducted against Communist psychological aggression.

The other principal foundation stone of U.S. public diplomacy was the government's effort, in the years following the Allied victory, to reorient and reeducate the peoples of the defeated totalitarian nations of Nazi Germany, Austria, and Japan toward democracy. These programs, between 1946 and 1954, involved the U.S. government for the first time in extensive and long-range cultural, educational, and social programs abroad.[6] Activities concerned with cultural and educational exchanges, publishing, libraries and cultural centers, secondary schools, universities, and social reforms were introduced and, in some cases, imposed, in order to bring to the peoples of these defeated nations a new democratic way of life and democratic institutions.

The extent and importance accorded this program are demonstrated by statistics. Between 1949 and 1954, over ten thousand Germans came to the United States on official exchanges — as leaders, trainees, university students, or teenagers. During the same period, over eight hundred U.S. specialists were sent to Germany to teach, train, and consult. During the three-year period 1950–1952 alone, one thousand Germans in the leader category were invited each year to come to the United States. Altogether, 13,354 persons participated in the U.S. government's German Exchange of Persons Program between 1947 and 1954.[7]

As a rationale for this effort, Henry Kellermann cites a 1949 statement by the acting secretary of state:

> There is fundamental agreement within the Department...that the United States cannot afford to spend billions on economic reconstruction without a valiant effort in the field of education and cultural relations. It has been the basic principle underlying this Government's policy for Germany that "the reeducation of the German people is an integral part of policies intended to help develop a democratic form of government and to restore a stable and

peaceful economy."...The Department has recognized...that the task of educating the German people away from authoritarianism and aggression and toward democracy and peace remains the hardest and longest of all our responsibilities in Germany and, in the long run, the most decisive.[8]

This sensible and sensitive policy of coordinated political, economic, and public affairs objectives vis-à-vis Germany, as well as Austria and Japan, appears to be unique in the annals of our diplomatic relations — a view supported by Kellermann.[9] It served U.S. interests then, and one can state without exaggeration that the beneficial result is still reflected today in the close and stable U.S.–German partnership.

Both the administration and the Congress recognized at the time that the liberated countries of Europe, prostrate as they were on the day of victory, also needed support and assistance, not only to revive economically, but to be intellectually and culturally reinvigorated so that a strong and viable Atlantic alliance could be established. Assistant Secretary of State William Benton is said to have played a pivotal role during the late 1940s in giving cultural and information programs prominence in the conduct of U.S. foreign affairs.[10]

The Fulbright Act of 1946,[11] named for its originator, Senator J. William Fulbright of Arkansas, legislated the exchange of students, researchers, and academicians. It led the way to other exchange efforts, including exchanges of youths, professionals, trade unionists, and artists, all designed to enrich the lives of both Europeans and Americans and to provide a firm foundation for a strong, democratic, interdependent Atlantic community.

From these two separate sources — the Cold War and reconstruction of Germany, Austria, and Japan — have sprung the policies and programs of U.S. public diplomacy, as well as the principles at issue cited earlier.

To a significant degree, contemporary U.S. public diplomacy has also been dictated by legislation. The initial law legitimizing public diplomacy, so to speak, was the United States Information and Educational Exchange Act of 1948, known as the Smith-Mundt Act, designated "an act to promote the better understanding of the United States among the peoples of the world and to strengthen cooperative international relations."[12]

To implement these purposes, the Act provides for assistance to schools, libraries, and community centers overseas and authorizes "the preparation, and dissemination abroad, of information about the United States, its people and its policies through press, publications, radio, motion pictures, and other informa-

tion media, and through information centers and instructors abroad." The Act
also created the U.S. Advisory Commission on Information "to formulate and
recommend policies and programs for carrying out the intentions of the Act."

It should be remembered that the Smith-Mundt Act was promulgated when
all U.S. foreign information and cultural activities were still part of the Department of State. The Act later became the operative legislation for the U.S.
Information Agency (USIA) when it was created as a separate agency in August
1953 as a result of Reorganization Plan #8. USIA consequently became the U.S.
government instrument for the conduct of public diplomacy, a mandate it holds
to this day.

Various committees, as detailed by Lois Roth,[13] had examined U.S. overseas
information efforts at the start of the Eisenhower administration and had made
conflicting recommendations as to how public diplomacy should be organized
within the U.S. government. Most suggested that it should be conducted from
within the Department of State. It seems facetious but appears to be true that
the creation of USIA as a separate and independent agency was a consequence
of Secretary of State John Foster Dulles's distaste for operational matters. He
desired his department to be concerned with policy and not with the management of foreign operations. Such was his influence at the time that his views
prevailed: USIA was established as a separate agency of the executive branch,
and its director was invested with most of the responsibilities for conducting
overseas information activities that under the Smith-Mundt Act had been
invested in the secretary of state.

As the new agency was established, two major problems arose that were to
have a profound effect on the U.S. government's conduct of public diplomacy
for years to come: One was Senator Joseph McCarthy's debilitating accusations
of Communist subversion on the part of a number of public diplomacy professionals. Among the senator's "victims" was Reed Harris, the highly respected
acting administrator of the information program. He resigned in well-justified
protest when confronted with, but unable to do anything about, the senator's
irresponsible and unjustified charges against USIA employees, including
several working for the Voice of America. Another example of the ignominious
activities of McCarthy and his staff was the trip in the spring of 1953 of the
senator's "junketeering gumshoes" (as they were justifiably memorialized),
Roy Cohn and David Schine. Senator McCarthy had a prolonged effect on the
morale of many public diplomacy professionals, who had felt abandoned by
their superiors in defending their integrity and loyalty.

Roy Cohn's Descent on the Libraries of Europe

In the spring of 1953, I was director of the America House (U.S. Cultural Center) in Frankfurt, which, because of its extensive library of American books and periodicals, became a target of the Roy Cohn-G. David Schine anti-Communist crusade in Europe. As the only American official at the America House and a relatively junior officer, I was eager to be supported by a more senior Foreign Service officer in what I anticipated could become an ordeal. Both my consul general and his deputy were conveniently off on an Easter vacation. Fortunately, Henry Dunlap, who was in charge of all the America Houses in Germany, called from Bonn and offered to come to Frankfurt to be at my side, suggesting that what I needed was a witness to everything that would be said. I gladly accepted.

Cohn and Schine arrived shortly after lunch with a gaggle of reporters, creating a commotion in the normally subdued reading-room atmosphere of the cultural center. Cohn immediately asked where I had hidden the Communist authors in the library. I replied that, to the best of my knowledge, there were no Communist authors in the library. He then asked where I kept the Dashiell Hammett books. I led him to the shelf holding *The Maltese Falcon* and *The Thin Man*. He turned to the reporters and announced triumphantly that this was proof that there were indeed Communists represented in the American library.

In the periodicals section, Cohn asked where the anti-Communist magazines were. I pointed out those that I considered anti-Communist, showing him the Jesuit periodical *America, Business Week*, and others, including *Time* and *Newsweek*. He dismissed *Time* by saying it was [a swear word] to him. When he discovered we did not have the *American Legion Monthly*, he declared that we obviously had no anti-Communist magazines.

Just before departing—the visit lasted over half an hour—Cohn and Schine were stopped by a reporter who read them the reference to "junketeering gumshoes" that had just come over the wires. Both appeared angry and wanted to know who had made the statement.

Finally, a young United Press reporter, Marshall Loeb, asked Cohn, "Sir, when are you going to burn the books here?" Cohn replied that was not his purpose in coming to Europe. Loeb persisted, saying his office had sent him to watch the two investigators burn books, "you know, just as the Nazis did in 1933." Cohn got really angry at this and berated the reporter, to which Loeb calmly replied, "Mr. Cohn, if you aren't going to burn any books here, you don't interest me," and walked away.

The other problem was that Senator Fulbright did not permit "his" exchange program to become part of USIA. He insisted that all educational and cultural exchange activities remain within the State Department, often citing two reasons for his views: He did not want to have academic exchanges become "tainted" by what he called a government propaganda operation, and he was afraid that the exchange programs might be politicized if they were managed by the Information Agency.

Senator Fulbright did not realize then, and apparently to this day has not accepted, that in American embassies abroad it has always been USIA employees—the public affairs officer, the cultural attaché, and their staffs—who administer educational and cultural exchange programs. No one, to the best of my knowledge, has ever accused these public diplomats of "tainting" the programs through their association with USIA. As counselor for public affairs in Brasilia, I myself served as chairman of the U.S.–Brazilian Fulbright Commission. I never heard anyone in that country or in the United States express the view that my USIA connection compromised my direction of academic exchange programs in that country.

The division of cultural exchange functions between the State Department and USIA complicated the management of these activities in the field, for the officers operating them had to respond to USIA direction for library, English teaching, exhibit, and speakers programs, and to State supervision for their exchange-of-persons activities. As a field officer responsible for managing these cultural and educational programs, I always had difficulty understanding the senator's rationale and felt that he was mistaken in his convictions in this regard. Yet, he was powerful in the Congress, and his views prevailed until 1978, during the Carter administration, when cultural and academic exchanges were transferred from State to USIA. It is true that some USIA directors have had, at least initially, little understanding for either the role or the importance of cultural and educational exchanges in the intercultural communications process, and they may have influenced the senator's strong views on the subject all these years.

There are also some among my former colleagues who still believe that there is something immoral about throwing educational and cultural activities into the same hamper with the U.S. government's information programs, that educational and cultural exchanges are somehow antithetical to the foreign relations process and our foreign affairs goals. Clearly, international educational and cultural programs should not ever be used to further an administration's short-term objectives. Granted, administrations have occasionally tried to use such programs to achieve immediate political goals, most often in a negative way by denying the opportunity for exposition or examination of ideas or opinions that were unpopular with the nation's current leadership; but in my experience, these aberrations always quickly came to public attention and were criticized and corrected. They should not be permitted to compromise the legitimacy of expending public funds for educational and cultural activities that will benefit the nation in the long term by providing an opportunity to have our country and our society better understood abroad and, at the same time, by permitting our citizens to acquire knowledge about other peoples and nations.

Our publicly funded cultural and educational exchange programs serve our national interests and long-term foreign policy objectives. This is entirely legitimate. As part of our public diplomacy efforts, these programs will not compromise but advance the independence and freedom of intellectual and academic pursuit in this country.

The Eisenhower Administration

President Dwight D. Eisenhower promulgated a mission statement for the newly created agency, known as the U.S. Information Agency (USIA) in Washington and U.S. Information Service (USIS) abroad. In his statement, Eisenhower instructed the agency "to submit evidence to peoples of other nations by means of communication techniques that the objectives and policies of the United States are in harmony with and will advance their legitimate aspirations for freedom, progress and peace."[14]

The objective was to convey information. As mentioned earlier, during the 1950s, USIA's policy and programs were conducted along two different tracks. One was the anti-Communist — the Cold War — track. The tone of USIA's output was at times propagandistic and simplistic, reflecting the techniques of American advertising. Theodore Streibert, USIA's first director, came from the advertising industry.[15] Though a competent manager, he gave scant attention to whether and how the American message might be received by audiences abroad. Selling "People's Capitalism" became the slogan labeling the agency's promotional task, with little regard to how the term "capitalism" might strike peoples living in other societies. (The Advertising Council, the trade organization of the advertising industry, became a valued adviser to USIA management at that time.)

The Voice of America was regarded by many as strident in its anti-Communist output. Some of its staffers had come to VOA as refugees from the captive nations of Eastern Europe with recollections of the terror they had experienced. They often permitted their emotions to color their broadcasts. Others, cowed by McCarthy, declined to criticize the virulent tone of some broadcasts lest their patriotism be questioned.[16]

On an entirely different track of USIA programming were the cultural and information activities that had had their genesis in the military occupation of Germany, Austria, and Japan. Following the Smith-Mundt Act, USIA introduced other library, publications, exhibits, and speakers programs. Alongside the academic exchanges managed by the State Department Bureau of Educational and Cultural Affairs, these were the agency's principal public diplomacy tools.

In Germany, for instance, USIA maintained sizable cultural centers, known as America Houses (in German, *Amerika Häuser*), with extensive library collections, exhibitions, speakers programs, English teaching, concerts, theater groups, and outreach activities. In cities where the entire cultural infrastructure had been devastated as a result of the war, the America Houses served literally as community centers until the indigenous cultural and artistic entities had been rebuilt. Then the America Houses, now highly respected institutions, converted themselves over time into outlets of information and cultural expression about the United States. Library collections were reduced and specialized, lectures and conferences focused on America, and exhibits concerned themselves with American artists and themes.

As my first Foreign Service assignment, I served as a director of such an America House, first in Wiesbaden and then in Frankfurt, from 1949 to 1955. The Frankfurt center had a library of about 45,000 volumes and 300-odd periodicals, and a staff of some forty-five librarians, programmers, artists, English teachers, and administrative personnel. We had such Americans as Thornton Wilder, historian John Hope Franklin, and pianist Leon Fleischer lecturing and performing for us, and we sponsored such attractions as the Juilliard String Quartet.

One of the veterans of the U.S. Military Government's efforts at reorientation and reeducation in Germany, Michael Weyl, put it this way: "We tried to educate the Germans to adopt...democratic educational practices and introduce educational reforms, but we did not want to foist these upon them....The America Houses served as educational reference libraries." [17]

The significance of the libraries is confirmed by a German researcher who wrote in 1984:

> The principal impact of the America Houses was...in influencing and changing the view of America among the German people. Through the medium of the library it was possible to persuade many Germans to regard America positively and often admiringly.

The same researcher noted that one could not "underestimate" the success of the America Houses in introducing Germans to a new open-shelf library system, which "made libraries attractive institutions." [18]

The two tracks—the Cold War and the reorientation program in the former Axis countries—came together fairly early. In 1947, according to Weyl, who was then cultural affairs officer in Stuttgart,

> ...reeducation and reorientation became the major preoccupation of Military Government...Americans were appointed to run these American libraries, [and] we got many more resources. There was a major shift in policy. We were in a confrontational situation vis-à-vis the Soviets, who were clearly engaged in an expansionist policy. We had the responsibility toward the occupied nations, our former enemies, who, we realized, had to be made into friends and allies. That brought the two strands...together and brought lots of resources to work focused on reorientation....It was a dual mission; they complemented each other. [19]

Another of USIA's major overseas activities in the mid-1950s was a series of Atoms for Peace exhibits, launched to support and advance a specific foreign policy objective, the peaceful use of the atom. This project, according to W. Phillips Davison, was handled well by the new agency. Information officials participated in full staff discussion regarding the release of news about the plan, which was announced first by the president at the United Nations General Assembly, "a major forum." The president's statement "was couched in language that was easily understood,...the plan had already been discussed with the leaders of England and France, [and] the U.S. Information Agency was prepared in advance to make the President's words known to audiences around the world." [20]

In addition, USIA published a number of periodicals, among them the widely respected *Problems of Communism*.[21] In 1956, the first exchange of publications with the Soviet Union began with the publication of *America Illustrated*, in exchange for the Soviet magazine *USSR*, later to be replaced by *Soviet Life*.

With Nikita Khrushchev's tenuous attempts at creating a thaw in the winter of Soviet orthodoxy after the 1955 Geneva summit conference, the direction and tone of some of USIA's programs also changed. Largely responsible for altering course and tone was another USIA director, George V. Allen, who replaced the briefly serving Arthur Larsen in November 1957. Allen, a man whose background and experience differed from those of his predecessors, was a senior career diplomat. He had been American ambassador to India, Iran, and Greece, assistant secretary of state for Near East and South Asian affairs, and, significantly, assistant secretary of state for public affairs before the creation of USIA. He was a prominent member of the foreign affairs establishment who respected, and was respected by, his fellow Foreign Service officers.

Such mutual respect made itself felt in practical ways. I was serving in Moscow as press and cultural attaché at the time under Ambassador Llewellyn Thompson, the experienced and highly regarded Soviet expert. We were preparing for the first major American National Exhibition in Moscow in August 1959, to be designed and operated by USIA, under the auspices of the first U.S.–Soviet Cultural Agreement, concluded the year before.[22] As one might imagine, there were many negotiations, hitches, and close calls that had to be managed locally, not the least of which was Vice President Nixon's attendance at the opening, together with Khrushchev. Two men who thought along similar lines, aware of each other's objectives and problems — Thompson on the spot in Moscow and George Allen running USIA in Washington — in large measure made the first major U.S. public diplomacy project in the Soviet Union the success that it became.

Ambassador Thompson understood well the opportunities and limitations faced by public diplomacy of this sort in the Soviet Union. He saw new possibilities at that time of reaching out to the Soviet public and making an attempt to communicate with them directly through the medium of cultural exchange: publications, exhibitions, students. He favored these exchanges, labored at them, gave those of us directly responsible for carrying them out his support, counsel, and personal involvement. He saw in this public diplomacy effort an opportunity for advancing American policy vis-à-vis the Soviet Union.

George Allen, in turn, was able to direct an adjustment in USIA's tone and output in response to these new realities of our international involvement. Both he and Thompson understood what might be achieved through public diplomacy, although at the time neither used the term or probably had ever heard of it.

Allen also worked a major change of tone in the Voice of America. He and others in USIA believed that VOA should strive to become an international broadcast medium, transmitting to the world comprehensive, accurate, and objective news and information about the United States and international events. His intent was to gain international acceptance for VOA as a respected source of information like the BBC, which had established its reputation for unbiased accuracy during World War II. VOA had the technical capability and journalistic expertise to become a significant and credible medium of international news and information. It would take almost twenty years, however, before VOA could claim a reputation competitive with that of the BBC in at least some areas of the world. And there are many who insist that even today VOA ranks second behind the BBC in worldwide effectiveness. VOA will be discussed in greater detail in Chapter 5.

One other innovation on which George Allen insisted was that VOA, like the BBC, broadcast in English around the clock, in order further to establish itself as a widely available, consistent, and authoritative voice of information from the United States.

The Kennedy Years

It was during the Kennedy years that USIA came into its own, both within the U.S. government and around the world. Major credit is due to Edward R. Murrow, who was appointed director in 1961. Renowned as the epitome of journalistic professionalism, this most prestigious of American broadcast journalists brought to the job an unmatched reputation for integrity and honesty. Merely through his presence, he lent the agency a new level of acceptance within the bureaucracy.[23]

Not only was Murrow an accomplished practitioner of public diplomacy; he *lived* it. Throughout his public life he was the great communicator who, through his personality, his integrity, and his skill as a conveyor of information, inspired confidence in the truthfulness of his message. One thing is certain: He inspired a generation of Foreign Service officers engaged in public diplomacy. His thoughts on the subject were best articulated in an interview with Edward P. Morgan, another respected Washington journalist. Morgan quotes Murrow as saying in that interview:

> It has always seemed to me the real art in this business is not so much moving information or guidance or policy five or ten thousand miles. That is an electronic problem. The real art is to move it the last three feet in face-to-face conversation.

Murrow thought of public diplomacy as an art — the art of getting the message from the loudspeaker to the mind of the foreign listener, or from the book into the consciousness of the foreign reader. A novel thought — public diplomacy as an art — from a superior artist in the field! And the importance he attributed to personal contact, the direct relationship between the purveyor of information and his target, finds an echo throughout this book.

Murrow's direction of USIA was more spiritual, inspirational, and substantive than managerial. For the managerial side, he relied on his able deputy, Donald M. Wilson, a former *Life* correspondent who was close to Robert F. Kennedy, the president's brother; and on Thomas H. Sorensen, a USIA career Foreign Service officer, who was elevated to deputy director for policy (he was the brother of Theodore Sorensen, the president's close advisor).[24]

Murrow's personal introduction to the perils of public diplomacy came even before his Senate confirmation when the press reported that he had asked the BBC not to broadcast his earlier CBS TV documentary, "Harvest of Shame." When his alleged interference with the free flow of information hit the American media, he immediately acknowledged his mistake publicly.[25]

The one time that Murrow personally took to the microphone again was when the Soviets broke the 1958 atmospheric nuclear testing moratorium in late summer of 1961. Although he advised the president not to reply in kind to Khrushchev's provocation,[26] he himself was so incensed that he unilaterally ordered all VOA transmitters targeted on the Soviet Union to broadcast his personally written commentary condemning the Soviet action. For him, this was the appropriate moment to use all available media to transmit an unmistakable message to the Soviet bloc over the heads of their rulers.

In January 1963, the Kennedy administration issued a new presidential statement for USIA that altered the agency's mission significantly.[27] Whereas USIA's earlier task had been merely to *inform* foreign audiences and to *explain*

U.S. objectives, the new mission of USIA was "to help achieve United States foreign policy objectives by...influencing public attitudes in other nations." This represented a recognition that information alone was not enough and that USIA must employ persuasion to affect foreign public attitudes. The statement also specified the means that USIA was to employ in influencing attitudes: radio, libraries, books, press, motion pictures, television, exhibits, English teaching, and, perhaps most important, personal contact. (Cultural and educational exchanges, which were not included, remained with the State Department as part of its arsenal of communication media.)

Even more significant than this expansion of USIA's mission was the second new way in which the agency was to help achieve foreign policy objectives, namely, by "advising the President, his representatives abroad, and the various departments and agencies on the implications of foreign opinion for present and contemplated United States policies, programs and official statements." The president thus recognized that policymaking needed to include consideration of foreign attitudes, and that determining these attitudes was part of the public diplomacy function of USIA.

The presidential statement further specified:

> The advisory function is to be carried out at various levels in Washington and within the Country Team at United States diplomatic missions abroad. While the Director of the United States Information Agency shall take the initiative in offering counsel when he deems it advisable, the various departments and agencies should seek such counsel when considering policies and programs which may substantially affect or be affected by foreign opinion.

This recognition of the advisory function was to give USIA and its public diplomats a significant new responsibility in the foreign affairs process. As Murrow once put it, "I want to be in on the take-offs — not only on the landings."

Reflecting on his stewardship of USIA on its tenth anniversary, Murrow noted some lessons from the past:

> Foremost among them is our new relationship with the White House and the Department of State. Representatives of [USIA] join the other personal advisers of the president in discussions of policy while it is being formed. We are therefore no longer mere publicists grinding out our appointed quota of press releases. We have become psychological advisers to the president

and, in turn, to each ambassador in his individual country team. Further, through continual contact with the communications systems and networks of foreign countries, USIS officers have become specialists in conveying a message from the United States to another people. Theirs is the knowledge of the structure and technique of communication. They are most effective when this fact is understood.[28]

The first major legislative initiative concerning public diplomacy since the Smith-Mundt Act of 1948 was the Mutual Educational and Cultural Exchange Act of 1961, known as the Fulbright-Hays Act.[29] It consolidated various educational and cultural exchange activities that had previously been contained in other acts, including the original law establishing the Fulbright academic exchange program. The new Act also authorized other cultural and athletic exchanges and U.S. representation in international festivals and exhibitions; the interchange and translation of books, periodicals, and other educational materials; the establishment and operation of cultural and educational centers to promote mutual understanding; and the fostering and support of American studies abroad. Although at that time most of the academic and cultural exchange-of-persons activities were still located in the State Department's Bureau of Cultural and Educational Affairs (CU), Executive Order #11034 of June 25, 1962, delegated to the director of USIA responsibility for participating in the planning and execution of many of these programs, which were carried out abroad by USIA Foreign Service officers.

Also during the Kennedy years, USIA finally came to grips with the Third World. A number of new nations in Africa, Asia, and the Caribbean area had gained independence and begun to play a role in international relations — if not always individually, then collectively as the emerging Third World. Initially U.S. interests in these new countries had been primarily related to economic development. Growing awareness of their increasing political strength prompted efforts to deal with them on a political, psychological, social, and cultural level.

Perhaps, in retrospect, our approach was too impulsive, indiscriminate in terms of what we could accomplish, and, in some cases, amateurishly counterproductive. At any rate, USIS operations were launched in practically every new country with which we had established diplomatic relations. USIA's focus, as a result, was expanded from one involving our principal allies in Europe and Asia and our adversaries in the Communist world to one that included the new nations of the Third World and our interest in their democratic development.

Public Diplomacy in the 1960s and 1970s

Legislation, policies, and programs concerning public diplomacy, as mentioned earlier, have been materially affected by USIA's directors — their personalities, ideologies, managerial styles, political convictions, and relationships with their presidents. Already cited were the examples of Theodore Streibert, George V. Allen, and Edward R. Murrow. USIA directors, all presidential appointees, have often been able to exert a greater influence on the policy, content, and style of their agency's programs and modes of operation than their counterparts in other departments of the executive branch. The Foreign Service officers working for USIA in the field were perhaps more conscious than the Washington-bound bureaucracy of the abrupt changes in policy and operations that occurred from one director to the next. That this could happen repeatedly was, perhaps, because USIA was still regarded by many as a temporary government agency that — unlike some older agencies — had no solid foundation in tradition, legislation, or, above all, a domestic constituency.

Congress from the outset forbade USIA to distribute its products and publicize its programs domestically for fear that administrations might use the agency to propagandize the domestic population. American citizens living outside Washington consequently had little knowledge of USIA's policies and activities, and less about public diplomacy in general. Public awareness of the agency's programs was sporadic at best, usually limited to vague ideas about VOA and USIA's battle against "the Communist menace." Congressional approval of what USIA was doing was often generated by what support USIA directors could muster from important committee chairmen in both houses or by what encouragement they could garner through their relationship with the president. The force of their ideological convictions and the degree of their political sophistication were additional factors in the quality of leadership that USIA directors brought to their job.

It was during the second half of the 1960s that USIA experienced a major upheaval as it came to play an increasingly larger role in the U.S. involvement in Vietnam.[30] There is no conclusive evidence whether USIA sought this role during the time when Carl Rowan was the agency's director (1964–65), or whether these new responsibilities were thrust upon the agency by an administration that intensified U.S. participation in the war and poured ever greater physical and psychological resources into the conflict.

USIA's role in Vietnam was fourfold: (1) In conducting an enlarged information and cultural program and (2) in serving as U.S. mission spokesmen for the international press, USIS officers fulfilled their traditional and mandated responsibilities. (3) In getting deeply involved in psychological warfare against enemy troops and (4) in supporting, at times even supplanting, the Vietnamese Ministry of Information in its job of educating the indigenous population about Vietnam's war aims, USIS officers assumed responsibilities and engaged in activities not normally included under the rubric of public diplomacy.

There had been previous instances of USIA involvement in what one might consider domestic political and psychological operations of foreign governments, for example, in Central America and Iran, but never to such an extent as in Vietnam. Fully one-tenth of USIA's human and material resources were engaged in Vietnam in the latter years of the sixties and early seventies. This not only stretched the agency's personnel system to the extreme — finding, training, and deploying such a large number of qualified officers within a short period of time — but it also, and more importantly, deprived USIA activities in other vital areas of the world of qualified personnel and adequate material resources.

Whether this extraordinary effort in Vietnam was justified is not at issue here. But the precipitous and drastic reallocation of personnel and resources, the expansion — some say distortion — in Vietnam of USIA's traditional mandate, and the agency's preoccupation with Vietnam over an extended period of time skewed public diplomacy efforts in other parts of the world to the detriment of our foreign policies.

Leonard Marks, USIA director from 1965 to 1968, was committed to the agency and its mission. He was an able manager who enjoyed good relationships with the president, the secretary of state, and members of Congress. Ideologically he was a centrist, who was able to serve both Democratic and Republican administrations in high positions with equal effectiveness. His expertise is in communications law, yet he showed real understanding for long-range cultural programs and demonstrated his interest after leaving USIA by setting up a private foundation through which he has supported libraries and book collections at USIS posts overseas. One of his lasting, if unsung, accomplishments was his success in having USIA's career officers integrated into the career

Foreign Service (improving, no doubt, their status and role within the Establishment).

Frank Shakespeare, USIA director from 1969 to 1973, was an entirely different personality from his predecessors. He had been a broadcasting executive with extensive managerial background in the media. His handicap, in this writer's view, was the heavy ideological baggage he carried with him into his new office. His was a fervent, almost visceral, opposition to Communism, and his overriding motivation was to defeat Soviet aggression. USIA was his tool in this mission.

Shakespeare disagreed vigorously with what in his view was developing into a policy of détente and accommodation vis-à-vis the Soviet Union. He instructed his USIA officers in Washington and in the field to continue the hard anti-Soviet line in their programming. He prevailed with *his* policy for USIA, at least insofar as nobody in the White House or the State Department reined him in. The rumor went around that Henry Kissinger, then national security adviser, never paid much attention to what USIA was doing because he did not think it of any importance.[31] As a field officer in charge of an important USIS post in Europe, I frequently felt that heat and confusion as I was trying to cope with two divergent policies.

James Keogh's directorship of USIA from 1973 to 1976, during the second Nixon administration and the Ford administration, was relatively tranquil for the agency at a time of turmoil in the country. Keogh's tenure encompassed the end of the war in Vietnam and the Watergate scandal and its aftermath. It was not an easy time for the Voice of America, a government news operation, to function with journalistic independence. By every indication, however, VOA cut its journalistic teeth during that time, becoming a creditable, internationally recognized source of news and information. Its coverage of both Vietnam and Watergate was adjudged by many of its listeners abroad as independent, comprehensive, and accurate. In the view of VOA staffers in 1976, Keogh had not caved in to the pressures to muzzle VOA, and, in the tradition of the true journalist he had been—executive editor of *Time* magazine—had permitted VOA's writers, editors, and reporters to perform their tasks as they saw them.

The latest reorganization of USIA—and the resulting redirection of U.S. public diplomacy—came in 1978 during the Carter administration. That reorganization mandated two major changes that became basic to the agency's current operations. First, it transferred to USIA the functions previously carried out by the State Department Bureau of Cultural and Educational Affairs (CU), thereby consolidating all public diplomacy activities of the U.S. government in one organization, renamed at that time the U.S. International Communication Agency (USICA). Second, the reorganization for the first time stressed an additional mandate, that of the mutuality of public diplomacy — the learning, as well as the informing, experience. For some Cold War–schooled hard-liners, mutuality was a strange new concept, alien to their experience. For them, adapting to this new concept and accepting it was difficult and, in some respects, traumatic.

Both of these developments were so important to the future practice of public diplomacy as it was to be carried out by the agency's Foreign Service officers in the field that it is worth quoting here a portion of President Carter's memorandum of March 13, 1978,[32] to USICA Director John Reinhardt, the first career Foreign Service officer to head the organization since George Allen.

> In transmitting Reorganization Plan No. 2 of 1977 to the Congress, I said that the principal function of the Agency should be to reduce the degree to which misperceptions and misunderstandings complicate relations between the United States and other nations. In international affairs, as in our personal lives, the starting point of dealing effectively with others is the clearest possible understanding of differing points of view. The fundamental premise of the International Communication Agency is that it is in our national interest to encourage the sharing of ideas and cultural activities among the people of the United States and the peoples of other nations.
>
> It is in the general interest of the community of nations, as well as in our own interest, that other nations and other peoples know where this great country stands, and why. We want them to understand our values, our institutions — the vitality of our culture — and how these relate to their own experience. We must share our successes, and look for help in learning from our failures. We must make available to people of other nations facts they would not otherwise learn about ourselves and our views.
>
> It is also in our interest — and in the interest of other nations — that Americans have the opportunity to understand the histories, cultures and problems of others, so that we can come to understand their hopes, perceptions and aspirations. In so doing, the Agency will contribute to our capacity as a people and as a government to manage our foreign affairs with sensitivity, in an effective and responsible way.

The president's memorandum goes on to outline five main tasks for the practitioners of public diplomacy:

1. To encourage, aid and sponsor the broadest possible exchange of people and ideas between our country and other nations....

2. To give foreign peoples the best possible understanding of our policies and our intentions, and sufficient information about American society and culture to comprehend why we have chosen certain policies over others....

3. To help insure that our government adequately understands foreign public opinion and culture for policy-making purposes, and to assist individual Americans and institutions in learning about other nations and their cultures.

4. To assist in the development and execution of comprehensive national policies on international communications, designed to allow and encourage the maximum flow of information and ideas among the peoples of the world....

5. To...conduct negotiations on cultural exchanges with other governments, aware that the most effective sharing of culture, ideas and information comes between individual people rather than through formal acts of governments.

Finally, the memorandum calls upon the agency's public diplomats to observe the following guidelines:

— Since all the Agency's activities bear a relationship to our foreign policies and interests, you will seek guidance on those policies and interests from the Secretary of State.

— You will be responsible for maintaining the scholarly integrity and nonpolitical character of the exchange program within your agency, and for maintaining the independence of Voice of America news broadcasts....

— The Agency will undertake no...covert, manipulative or propagandistic [activities]...[It] can assume...that a great and free society is its own best witness, and can put its faith in the power of ideas.

I cannot think of a better credo, rationale, and explanation for the conduct of America's public diplomacy. One can only wish that others who directed the U.S. government's public diplomacy had read it and taken it to heart. Even if they did not, one can still hope that future managers of the U.S. foreign policy process will consider this document, accept it, and adhere to it.

There was nothing in President Carter's memorandum about the new agency's organization or the functions of its various offices and services. Its new name, U.S. International Communication Agency, was considered necessary to reflect the amalgamation of the State Department's cultural and educational exchange functions with those of USIA, and thus to imply a broader mission and to give the mutual communication process greater recognition. The new name did not stick and was changed back to U.S. Information Agency in 1982. One reason was that, abroad, the U.S. Information Service — USIS — was a widely accepted name for the people and facilities that represented the broad range of U.S. government public diplomacy activities. (Furthermore, when translated, "communication" had a different meaning in several foreign languages, including the local postal and telecommunication services.)[33]

The Reagan Years

A retelling of public diplomacy's trials and tribulations over the years would not be complete without a few paragraphs on the management and influence of Charles Z. Wick, whose tenure as director during most of the eight years of the Reagan administration was the longest since the agency's inception. Wick probably did not read President Carter's memorandum. He certainly did not subscribe to it, at least not initially. His concept of public diplomacy was quite simple: to build the image of the president around the world, and to be the flag bearer for what he considered Reagan's principal foreign objective, the fight against aggressive international Communism. His main instrument was to be television, the one medium he deemed to be an effective weapon in this war. He also favored radio and championed expansion of the Voice of America.

Public diplomacy as a profession or discipline did not appear to interest Wick, although he readily adopted the term for promoting his personal vision of his task. Initially, the value of educational and cultural exchanges was foreign to him. It was only congressional insistence and public pressure — primarily from the academic community — that forced him to restore previously curtailed resources for these activities. Once convinced that exchange programs were a congressional priority, he became their champion, without, however, diminishing his enthusiasm for the power of television.

Wick was persuaded that a new cooperative program between government and the private sector to sponsor teenage youth exchanges between the United States and the industrialized democracies would constitute another feather in the president's cap and might strengthen the bonds with the Atlantic Community and Japan that seemed to be sagging. It was Wick's superb sense of public relations and knack as a fund-raiser that brought about President Reagan's International Youth Exchange Initiative, launched at the Versailles Economic Summit in 1982.

Director Wick was able to increase the agency's budget substantially, in the first instance for technical modernization of the Voice of America and for the new Worldnet television technology. New funds were also designated, significantly, for cultural and educational exchanges. Some officers in the field felt that USIA management had created an imbalance, with substantial increases in Washington personnel for new program initiatives and reductions of personnel and resources at USIS posts abroad. This led them to question the cost-effectiveness of some of the new Washington-generated activities in terms of their country-specific public diplomacy objectives.

Partly as a result of his mercurial management style, partly as a consequence of *his* perception of what public diplomacy was all about, partly because of his extraordinary personal ties to the president, and partly because of his long tenure that strengthened his clout within the bureaucracy, Wick's influence within the agency and his long-term impact on USIA's style and operations cannot be underestimated. His direction of the agency will come up in later chapters discussing specific USIA programs with which he has been identified, particularly Worldnet, the agency's innovative worldwide television network.

NOTES

1. Lois W. Roth, "Public Diplomacy: 1952–1977," *The Fletcher Forum*, Vol. 8, No. 2 (Summer 1984), p. 353.

2. A perceptive 1988 study is Gifford Malone's *Political Advocacy and Cultural Communication*, op. cit. Another discussion of the subject is contained in three articles in the April 1988 *Foreign Service Journal*: Hans N. Tuch, "The Endless Debate"; Gifford Malone, "Equal But Separate"; and Robert Chatten, "Wrong Division," pp. 30-43. See also David I. Hitchcock, Jr., *U.S. Public Diplomacy*, Significant Issues Series (Washington, D.C.: Center for Strategic and International Studies, 1988). An excellent academic introduction to, and analysis of, public diplomacy in the context of foreign affairs is W. Phillips Davison, *International Political Communication* (New York: Frederick A. Praeger, 1965).

3. Executive Order 9608, 31 Aug. 1945, *Department of State Bulletin*, 2 Sept. 1945, p. 307, citing 10 *Federal Register* 11223.

4. "Termination of O.W.I. and Disposition of Certain Functions of O.I.A.A.," Statement by the President, *Department of State Bulletin*, 2 Sept. 1945, 306.

5. Address on Foreign Policy at a Luncheon of the American Society of Newspaper Editors, 20 April 1950, *Public Papers of the Presidents — Harry S Truman, 1950*, 260–64.

6. For a detailed account of the U.S.–German cultural exchange program from its postwar beginning in 1945 to 1954, see Henry J. Kellermann, *Cultural Relations as an Instrument of U.S. Foreign Policy: The Educational Exchange Program between the United States and Germany 1945–1954* (Washington, D.C.: Department of State Publication 8931, International Information and Cultural Series 114, March 1978), 3–252.

7. Ibid., Appendix, 261, 264, 276.

8. Ibid., 79.

9. Interview with Henry Kellermann by author on 30 Jan. 1989, for Oral History Project of the USIA Alumni Association.

10. William R. Tyler, retired U.S. ambassador, in an oral history interview conducted by Charles Stuart Kennedy, Foreign Affairs Oral History Program, Georgetown University, Washington, D.C., Interview I, 17 Nov. 1987, 37–56. The Tyler interviews contain an enlightening discussion of the need for and beginning of U.S. cultural and information activities in Western Europe, particularly France, after World War II. As public affairs counselor at the embassy in Paris, 1948–52, Tyler observed no special distinction between his information and cultural activities and his political activities. "Toward the end of my time," he said, "I was acting almost as a political officer, . . . [using] information and cultural resources in order to promote the objectives and interests of U.S. policy." (Interview II, 1 Dec. 1987, 1–2.)

11. Public Law 584 — 79th Congress (Chapter 723 — 2nd Session), S 1636.

12. Public Law 402 — 80th Congress (Chapter 36 — 2nd Session), H.R. 3342.

13. Roth, "Public Diplomacy: 1952–1977," op. cit.

14. Statement by the President, The White House, 28 Oct. 1953; and "Directive-Approved by the President for the Guidance of the United States Information Agency," 28 Oct. 1953, *Public Papers of the Presidents of the United States — Dwight D. Eisenhower, 1953*, Office of the Federal Register, National Archives and Record Service (Washington, DC: U.S. Government Printing Office, 1960), 728.

15. For a list of USIA Directors see Appendix 1.

16. One of my jobs while serving as policy officer for the Voice of America Munich Center in 1957 was to help change the overly harsh anti-Communist tone of VOA's output to the Soviet Bloc. I did so mostly by writing commentaries and news analyses in a tone I thought appropriate, rather than changing the writings of others. On one occasion, when I offered my commentary to one of the language services in substitution for one written by that service's chief, he told me bluntly that he regretted that Senator McCarthy had not been able to finish his campaign and get rid of all the Communists in USIA.

17. Interview with Michael Weyl, 16 June 1988, Bethesda, MD, recorded for USIA Alumni Association Oral History Project. For the views of an Austrian scholar, who was exposed in his early years to USIS programs and activities in Vienna (1946–50) that appear to have had a considerable influence on him and his contemporaries, see Reinhold Wagnleitner, "From Cold War to Cool War: U.S. Cultural Influence in Austria after World War II," paper presented to the Society for Historians of American Foreign Relations Conference, Washington, D.C., 10 June 1988; and idem., "Propagating the American Dream: Cultural Policies as Means of Integration," *American Studies International* XXIV, No. 1 (Apr. 1986), 60–84.

18. Angela Möller, *Die Gründung der Amerika-Häuser 1945–1949: Ein Beitrag zur Geschichte Amerikanischer Kultur-und-Informationspolitik in Deutschland*, MA dissertation (unpublished), Ludwig-Maxilians-Universität München, Social Science Faculty, Munich, 1984, 159 [translated by author].

19. Michael Weyl, interview, op.cit.

20. Davison, *International Political Communication*, 168.

21. *Problems of Communism* is one of only two USIA products — the other being *English Teaching Forum* — that Congress has permitted to be distributed within the United States.

22. See case study, chapter 9.

23. I missed meeting Murrow for the first time on September 17, 1944, as he covered the 101st Airborne Division's landing in Holland from a C-47 plane flying alongside the one out of which I jumped. But I was fortunate to work with Murrow while he was director of USIA. Some of us at the time, when asked where we were employed, used to reply that we were working for Ed Murrow, rather than mentioning USIA, and found recognition and acceptance quicker and easier.

24. Thomas Sorensen is the author of *The Word War: The Story of American Propaganda* (New York: Harper & Row, 1968).

25. A. M. Sperber, *Murrow: His Life and Times* (New York: Freundlich Books, 1986), 628–31.

26. Ibid., 660.

27. Memorandum for the Director, United States Information Agency, from John F. Kennedy, The White House, 25 Jan. 1963.

28. *Foreign Service Journal*, July 1963 (reprinted in *Foreign Service Journal*, July/August 1988).

29. Public Law 87-256, 87th Congress, H.R. 8666, 21 Sept. 1961.

30. The discussion on USIA's role during the Vietnam War is based in part on an interview with Daniel P. Oleksiw, conducted for the USIA Alumni Association (USIAAA) Oral History Project. Mr. Oleksiw, a retired Foreign Service officer, was USIA assistant director for the Far East area, 1966–70, and in that capacity directed the agency's program and activities in Vietnam.

31. This rumor was substantiated by Richard Monsen, who served as head of a USIA office supporting Henry Kissinger's National Security Council (NSC) Review Group, on which the USIA director held a seat. In an interview on August 22, 1988 (taped for the USIAAA Oral History Project), Monsen said he noted that after a while no meetings of the review group were being scheduled by Kissinger. He inquired and was told by an NSC staffer confidentially that Kissinger had wanted, but was unable, to get rid of Shakespeare from the review group, so he formed another committee without Shakespeare to do the review group's work. He did not abolish the original review group but left it without work or meetings.

32. The White House, Memorandum for Director, International Communication Agency, 13 March 1978.

33. The Reagan administration's reversion to "U.S. Information Agency" was popular with the agency's employees, especially FSOs overseas, most of whom had never liked the other name. Too many had had to explain repeatedly that the International Communication Agency — ICA — had nothing to do with the Central Intelligence Agency — CIA.

3
Practicing Public Diplomacy

Most of what has been discussed in the preceding pages serves as background, foundation, mystique, and rationale of the practice of public diplomacy as it is currently conducted. Public diplomacy cannot, of course, make bad policy good. Nothing can. Edward R. Murrow underlined this truism when he said, "Skillful propagation of poor policy would merely intensify error."[1] However, public diplomacy, intelligently applied, can enhance the attainment of a foreign policy objective and make foreign policy more comprehensible, even acceptable, by improving knowledge and understanding of our society, our purposes, and our values. How, one may ask, does public diplomacy accomplish these purposes?

It begins with the practitioners of public diplomacy — the U.S. Information Agency's career Foreign Service officers (FSOs), who are specially trained and qualified for this profession. They are on a parallel track with the State Department FSOs, who are trained and qualified for economic, political, or consular work. Practitioners of public diplomacy should meet four qualifications, attained through education, training, and experience: First, they must have a solid foundation in the history, institutions, and culture of America and the American people. Second, public diplomats must know the purpose and substance of the policy that is to be represented and promulgated. Third, FSOs specializing in public diplomacy must have an understanding of the people in the country to which they are assigned — their traditions, their culture, and their psychology. And finally, they must be competent communicators, knowledgeable in the methods of conveying "the message."

One of public diplomacy's earliest academic professionals, W. Phillips Davison, put it this way: "Public diplomacy combines the skills of the traditional diplomat with those of the specialist in mass communication and the social researcher. The diplomat formulates the ideas that he would like to have communicated to a foreign public, the social researcher studies the intended audience, and the communications specialist chooses the most appropriate media and composes the messages." [2]

Foreign Service officers who specialize in public diplomacy are among the structural spokes of an embassy wheel, even though their Washington base and employers are the U.S. Information Agency. They are part of what is often referred to as the embassy's "country team," headed by the ambassador, the chief of mission. It is the conviction of most professionals that public diplomacy cannot function unless this integration of USIS into the embassy organization is accepted by Washington, by the chief of mission, and by the USIS staff. Only through such integration and coordination can U.S. policy be implemented and executed effectively, using all the resources and expertise available to the U.S. government in a particular country.

It is also a truism that no matter how experienced and talented the USIS staff, public diplomacy cannot function effectively unless the ambassador too is familiar with its application and its potential, and unless the ambassador regards the conduct of public diplomacy as one of his or her responsibilities. The ambassador is, by the very nature of the position, also a public diplomat.

This is so important that it warrants some detail here, because even today some ambassadors, both career and noncareer, fail to understand public diplomacy and are therefore unable to appreciate and use it in their missions. (They may also be confused by the different meanings and interpretations currently given to public diplomacy, as described in chapter 1.)

During my Foreign Service career, I worked with three ambassadors, two career and one noncareer, who fully understood the need for public diplomacy and its potential for their mission. The first of these was Llewellyn Thompson in Moscow, whose affinity for public diplomacy has already been described in the previous chapter. The second was John Hugh Crimmins, with whom I served in Brazil from 1972 to 1975. Commanding linguistic and area expertise as well as managerial capabilities, he used his personnel resources as though he were playing a violin, knowing exactly when and how to bow his political, economic, development aid, military, and, above all, public diplomacy strings to produce perfectly pitched and rhythmic harmony in the orchestration of his embassy's mission. He understood, for instance, the importance of relating to the Brazilian media at a time of pervasive censorship, which, however, principally concerned the control of internal information while being relatively liberal toward the reporting of international affairs. Crimmins and his USIS staff were therefore constantly in communication with selected editors, reporters, and columnists. From them they learned what was going on in Brazil, and through them they conveyed to the Brazilian public information about U.S. policies and actions vis-à-vis Brazil and the rest of the world, information that Brazilians, as traditional U.S. allies, needed to have.

A third ambassador who understood and valued public diplomacy was a noncareer appointee, Arthur F. Burns. The noted economist, educator, and counselor to presidents was seventy-eight years old when he began an entirely new career as U.S. ambassador to the Federal Republic of Germany. In his eagerness to grasp his new responsibilities, his intellectual openmindedness and basic understanding of how best to devote his energies and talents persuaded him that one of his principal tasks would be that of a communicator and bridge builder: a communicator of American ideas, ideals, and policies; and a bridge builder especially to young Germans, who, for various reasons, had been alienated from America, a country so important to their democratic existence and security. The so-called successor generation became his particular target, and he worked diligently with his USIS staff to reach them and communicate with them.[3]

Together with his public affairs advisers, Burns, an astute public diplomat, decided that in spite of the many invitations he received, he should limit his major speeches to two a year so as to attain maximum impact and not "devalue the currency." The audience and host organization for each appearance were thus carefully selected for optimum exposure. The subject of the speech was chosen in consultation with the senior staff for its intellectual substance and timeliness. It was then crafted over a period of at least a month, researched, edited, and honed to Burns's standard of perfection so that it could stand as an important statement, to be published, commented upon in the press, and summarized in such widely read publications as the *Reader's Digest*, thereby enjoying a wide resonance in Germany and beyond.

As Burns's public affairs officer, I recognized early on what an asset he was for our public diplomacy. If I were to give a speech, for example, to an audience of eighty-five members of the Stuttgart Chamber of Commerce, it might later be reported briefly in two local newspapers, and that would be it. If, on the other hand, I helped Dr. Burns with one of his major addresses, time-consuming as that might be, I knew that the impact and echo of his words would be infinitely wider and deeper and therefore much more effective in advancing our public diplomacy goals. Burns was a magnificent resource in this regard and willingly lent himself to this task throughout his service in Bonn.

Then there are some others. I know of one high-profile ambassador in the Johnson administration who thought of public diplomacy as publicity in the United States for himself. He directed his USIS staff to provide daily U.S. media coverage of his activities in the country of his assignment so that his American public would remember him while he was abroad. When his USIS officers did not do the job to his satisfaction, he prevailed on Washington to recall them. None of this did him any good: He later ran for high public office and was defeated. One must surmise that U.S. public diplomacy suffered during his mission—to the detriment of U.S. foreign policy in that particular country.

Another example, perhaps an extreme one, was the noncareer ambassador in a small but not unimportant island capital who claimed to know all about public diplomacy because he had been a successful businessman. He outfitted his staff in colorful clothes, which he required them to wear, entertained lavishly on his private yacht, and gave copies of pornographic videocassettes to those he wished to please. He set back public diplomacy—indeed, diplomacy—several generations.

And, as a final example, there is the senior career Foreign Service officer, a former ambassador, who asked a colleague incredulously, "Do you really believe in this public diplomacy stuff?" Such diplomats are becoming rarer, however. Some thirty years ago it took some of them an equally long time to recognize that economic specialization had become a similarly important element in their diplomatic universe.

For public diplomacy to work as an effective instrument in the foreign affairs process, there has to be sympathetic and informed interaction between the chief of mission and the USIS staff, because the chief of mission is responsible for all U.S. government activities in his host country, including the conduct of public diplomacy. This axiom is sometimes inadequately understood at first by the politically appointed Washington management of USIA, even though practically every administration has reinforced these ambassadorial responsibilities by a presidential letter. Conversely, a career officer in the field is occasionally denied support from his Washington superiors when he is confronted by unreasonable or even illegal demands from a politically appointed ambassador who does not know or understand the responsibilities of the USIS officer. In either case, rare as it may be, the USIS officer might find himself in jeopardy not of his own making.

If the USIS staff responds to the ambassador's oversight responsibility and the chief of mission understands the practice of public diplomacy, the foundation for their interaction has been laid. This interaction then extends to the other sections of the embassy. Nowadays these often include, besides the traditional political, economic, and consular sections, a variety of U.S. agencies represented in our larger missions: Commerce, Agriculture, Treasury, Defense, Justice, Customs, Drug Enforcement, AID, Peace Corps, and others. They all have important foreign affairs roles to play. They therefore also affect the conduct of public diplomacy and, in turn, are affected by, or even depend on, public diplomacy for the implementation of their particular programs.

The head of the USIS mission in a U.S. embassy is usually the public affairs officer — the PAO — or sometimes counselor or minister of embassy for public affairs, depending on the size and importance of the post. The PAO supervises the two principal public diplomacy activities: the information/media programs, usually under an information officer/press attaché, and the educational/cultural programs and exchanges, usually under a cultural officer or attaché.[4] The embassies of most other countries keep these activities quite separate, under a press attaché or counselor and a cultural attaché or counselor, respectively. Public diplomacy as practiced by the U.S. government, however, suggests that information/media programs and educational/cultural programs and exchanges both serve to make the United States and its policies understood by foreign publics and to advise policymakers (in this case the ambassador) about public attitudes and perceptions. The programs are not only interrelated but also interactive, depending on each other for reinforcement and support.

Some refer to information activities as the "fast" media, designed primarily to "advocate" immediate or short-term policy objectives, while educational and cultural programs are the "slow" media whose purpose is to bring about long-term understanding of the United States and its society. That is an oversimplification. Good public diplomacy uses those methods and techniques of communication — "fast" or "slow" media, information or cultural programs—that are appropriate and potentially effective vis-à-vis specifically selected audiences on a given theme or subject.

It should be noted that the role of spokesman in an American embassy is traditionally assumed by the public affairs officer or the press attaché. Since it is a USIS responsibility to deal with the media in a foreign country, it is natural that the spokesman's duties fall to the PAO or some other USIS officer. This responsibility also leads to a relationship between the USIS officer/spokesman and American journalists stationed in or visiting the country, since the latter look to the spokesman, the professional press officer, as a contact and for assistance in dealing with the embassy. Thus, while USIA's products and programs are by law unavailable to the American public, the U.S. media working abroad usually look to the USIS officer/embassy spokesman for official U.S. pronouncements and unofficial information and advice. In legal terms, this might be an anomaly. In practice it works.

Experience over the last twenty-five years has demonstrated that a rational approach to public diplomacy requires two periodic processes: audience determination and subject selection. The first involves what is known as an "institutional analysis," and the second is called the "country plan."

The Institutional Analysis

Institutional analysis for the selection of audiences is necessary because the U.S. government's resources are limited. We cannot afford the level of communication activities needed to target the entire population of a country, a wasteful approach in any case. Only segments of a country's population take an interest in, and have influence over, their government's policies, including its relationship with the United States. The old question whether U.S. public diplomacy should address itself to mass audiences or to selected individuals and groups is therefore almost moot since the resources for mass appeals do not exist.

I say *almost* moot because one medium that can address mass audiences cost-effectively is radio—the Voice of America. Because of its importance as a communications medium, because it deals with mass audiences, and because of its location in Washington rather than in the field, we will discuss the Voice of America as well as its television sibling, Worldnet, in separate chapters.

An institutional analysis should be conducted periodically, perhaps every six years and certainly whenever there is a major social or political change in a country. By this means, the USIS mission attempts to identify the individuals and groups that constitute the most significant audiences or participants in the two-way communications process for the conduct of public diplomacy programs. We must determine who are the opinion leaders and molders in the society — the "gatekeepers," in the academic jargon of sociology. They are the people with whom we wish to communicate, to have a dialogue if possible, so that they can digest and understand our "message," perhaps be persuaded by it but at any rate pass it along in the process of formulating public opinion. Beyond these current molders of public attitudes, we also want to identify potential gatekeepers, those likely to become influential in the opinion-forming process in the future.

Conducting an institutional analysis takes time and effort. Those who do the study must usually rely on local expertise — foreign national USIS colleagues or outside sources — since the American officers by themselves lack intimate knowledge of the intricacies in the communications network within a foreign society.

It is not enough to say that the press is an important target group. We must determine which newspapers, periodicals, or radio and television outlets are important to us in relation to the subjects and themes we wish to convey. Using an American analogy in determining the newspaper to be selected as our target, we would probably choose the *New York Times* over the mass-circulation *Daily News* as the paper read by the opinion makers in our society. But that is not enough. In order to communicate effectively we must find the correspondent, columnist, or editor within the publication who is most likely to respond to our communications as a partner in dialogue on a given subject. At different times we may thus select different individuals working for the same important publication, depending on the subject matter we wish to address. And then we may go back and include in our list a particular reporter or editor working for the *Daily News* or *New York Post* because we know him or her to be influential with a certain audience on a specific subject.

Selecting individual gatekeepers in the academic community works along similar lines. Which faculties in which universities would be considered the most useful targets for public diplomacy programs? Within faculties, which professors? Which students have the potential for future leadership based on their academic performance and student activities? If the church is an influential element in the society, which church? If it is the Roman Catholic Church, is it the traditional hierarchy or the worker-priests with whom we should communicate, or both? In a democracy, the political sector normally plays a major role in the molding of public attitudes. But we cannot be in touch with all members of the parliament and thus must decide which committee chairmen and which members of the opposition are our most likely dialogue partners — dialogue partners not only of the PAO, the information officer, or the cultural attaché, but of the ambassador, the political counselor, the commercial officer, or the agricultural attaché.

In Moscow, until recently, few people who were not members of the Communist Party (with the exception of selected dissidents) would have been on the list of potential embassy contacts. Unless one were a party member, one would have had little influence in the workings of that society. That has obviously changed. Quite suddenly *glasnost* and *perestroika* have opened the country to the ideas and influence of many people not previously associated with the party *nomenklatura*.

Upon completion of the institutional analysis, the USIS post usually has two lists compiled (nowadays frequently on a computer): one, the primary contact list of individuals with whom the concerned embassy officers will maintain an active and fairly constant communications relationship, for they are our most valuable and potentially effective dialogue partners; and a secondary contact list of individuals, groups, and organizations with whom we wish to be able to communicate but who for various reasons are not as intensively cultivated. They may live far from the capital, making contact difficult except by mail or at infrequent intervals; they may have influence in areas that involve our interests only intermittently; they may not wish to be in frequent contact with us; or it may be imprudent for us to be too closely associated with them. They would constitute a secondary focus for our contact activities.

Having made a record of these two groups, an inner and an outer circle of contacts, it is then the PAO's responsibility to monitor staff use of the contact lists in the communications process. The "distribution and records system" (DRS), as it is called by the U.S. Information Agency, is an effective management tool in determining individual responsibility on the part of those participating in an embassy's public diplomacy program, in maintaining and updating contacts and target groups, and in measuring the cost-effectiveness of public diplomacy activities conducted by the post.

The Country Plan

The country plan is an effective and now generally applied system by which each USIS post annually determines the themes and subjects for its public diplomacy program, their treatment, their targets, and the method of conveying them.

The country plan preparation begins within the embassy with a round of consultation by the PAO on the foreign policy issues that are appropriate for public diplomacy treatment. This is where the interaction with the ambassador and the other members of the country team, mentioned earlier as most important, occurs in practice. The public diplomacy issues are almost always identical with the overall embassy objectives, although they are usually fewer in number since some issues of concern to the embassy do not normally lend themselves to public diplomacy treatment, for example, visa regulations, intelligence analysis, agricultural reporting, or military sales.

The PAO then prepares a crucial introductory essay describing the bilateral communications climate that affects the relationship between the United States and the country of assignment. This essay is primarily for the benefit of USIA management in Washington, but it also provides the PAO the opportunity to outline the rationale for the entire public diplomacy program for the coming year. In the essay the PAO describes the barriers, problems, and opportunities affecting the communications process in the country. Such items as censorship, literacy, freedom of the press, internal political processes and divisions, public attitudes toward the United States, cultural differences, and societal anomalies are set forth.

This essay then leads to a listing of the specific public diplomacy objectives and issues requiring attention, in order of importance. Finally, the country plan suggests the methods and media deemed most useful and cost-effective in addressing these issues vis-à-vis the post-selected target audiences, then lists the support required from Washington to carry out the recommended program.

In the 1986 country plan prepared for the Federal Republic of Germany,[5] to illustrate, two major objectives were singled out: (1) to explain to the German public that the United States was committed to achieving nuclear arms control and that the NATO double-track decision on INF deployment was in the alliance's political and security interests; and (2) "to persuade particularly the younger generation of Germans that the ties that have been established between our two societies...are beneficial for both countries and...necessary for the preservation of our democratic systems and peace."

Public diplomacy, it is clear from this country plan, involves both a relatively short-term issue of an immediate foreign policy nature and long-term concerns that engage our respective societies. How these objectives were addressed by the USIS Bonn staff is detailed in two of the case studies presented in Part II.

Before the country plan is forwarded to Washington, it must be approved by the ambassador. That is a sine qua non and reflects the presidential letter of authority, mentioned earlier, that charges the ambassador with the direction of all civilian U.S. government programs in the country of assignment. It is another step in the process of coordinated interaction with the chief of mission. Without the ambassador's knowledge, concurrence, and participation, no public diplomacy effort is going to work.

The country plan is then sent to USIA in Washington for its consideration, critique, and approval. A dialogue often ensues between the USIS mission (the post) and the responsible USIA area directorate in Washington. The country plan is analyzed, additional post justifications are requested, and proposals are defended. The most difficult discussions are about allocation of Washington resources needed by the post to carry out its country plan. The post often requests funds for exchange visitors, for the Fulbright program, for English-teaching and American studies materials, for speakers, and for publications in amounts greater than Washington can provide. Compromises are struck.

Normally, there is relatively little disagreement on the country plan's objectives and issues, because Washington knows that they were carefully worked out by the post with the agreement of the ambassador. There are occasional exceptions to this, but usually only when a USIA director has a particular hobbyhorse that he insists on riding, even in unfamiliar territory. Frank Shakespeare, as mentioned earlier, considered doing battle against the Communist menace the prime objective of his agency. He would therefore cast a suspicious eye on any of his PAOs who did not mention this objective as a principal country plan concern. In Brazil in 1971, fighting the Communist menace hardly needed to be a primary objective for public diplomacy inasmuch as the ruling right-wing military dictatorship was as militantly anti-Communist as Frank Shakespeare. The PAO, however, a realist, inserted this objective near the top of his country plan to avoid confrontation with the director and to obtain the agency's otherwise unlikely quick approval.

Another, more recent, example was Director Charles Wick's preoccupation with television, which he considered the agency's most powerful public diplomacy weapon. In some respects, of course, television is a highly effective medium, as the chapter on USIA's Worldnet program will show. But when, against all professional advice in Washington, Wick conjured up a television extravaganza like "Let Poland be Poland," he was convinced beyond any doubt that such a show was the most dramatic method of condemning the rape of Poland's emerging democracy in the fall of 1981. There was no one who could persuade him that Frank Sinatra and his show business friends might effectively combat Soviet subversion in Peoria but not in Bonn, Brussels, Bologna, or Bordeaux.[6]

These are indeed aberrations in the current practice of public diplomacy. The country plan exercise is an efficient and rational approach to projecting a pragmatic plan for carrying out a public diplomacy program. As a public affairs officer, I always considered the country plan as a "contract" which, once approved by the agency's management in Washington, bound the post to carry out the program delineated in the plan and committed USIA to providing the necessary guidance and support. The agency could measure the post's performance against what had been agreed upon in the "contract." If an unforeseen development warranted a change in the country plan during the year, the post could always propose alterations for consideration in Washington, even, as sometimes happens, on an emergency basis.

The Program

U.S. public diplomacy programs around the world differ in substance and method by target country and society. It has been my experience that discrete approaches to public diplomacy are required depending upon whether it is practiced in the industrialized democracies, in developing countries, or in the politically denied areas of the world.

In the latter — primarily the Communist countries but also some right- and left-wing dictatorships — there is the immediate problem of whether it is possible to communicate with the public at all. Often it is not. Totalitarian regimes try to control all foreign access to their populations. They control the domestic media; they control entry into and exit from the country; they try to control the very thoughts their people think. And they rule by fear of punishment if their control is violated. Such control is necessary and logical for the existence of dictatorships: totalitarianism can perpetuate its rule only by keeping citizens isolated from any information other than what its rulers permit to be disseminated. Totalitarian regimes make every effort to prevent public opinion on any issue, domestic or foreign, from forming independently.

This type of closed society exists today in absolute terms in only a few countries of the world. But it did exist for all practical purposes both in the Soviet Union until the late fifties and in China until the mid-seventies. In China, the U.S. government did not even have official representation to observe and report, to say nothing about communicating with the Chinese people. In the Soviet Union we had an embassy, but its personnel and their activities were severely circumscribed, making it impossible to conduct any kind of public diplomacy program there. Analogous situations exist today for the United States in such countries as Iran, Cambodia, Vietnam, North Korea, and Albania.

Our only possibility of communicating effectively with a country's population under these circumstances is by short-wave radio. For the United States, that is the Voice of America. If the technical facilities are available, radio can be a powerful medium of communication — albeit in only one direction, not allowing for dialogue.

Until the chairman of China's State Radio and Television Authority told us on his first visit to the United States in the fall of 1979, VOA's management had no idea that VOA broadcasts to the People's Republic of China were heard by millions of Chinese all those years when we had no other access to them. That same official related quite unabashedly that the only way to learn English was from the VOA English-language broadcasts (which were not jammed), and that many Chinese had kept up with international news and happenings by regularly listening to VOA (in spite of the jamming of the Chinese-language broadcasts), even to the extent that they could recite the names of VOA correspondents and other radio personalities.[7]

The importance of the VOA for the Chinese people appears not to have diminished even under the less restrictive conditions that prevailed in the People's Republic during the May 1989 student demonstrations. As *New York Times* correspondent Sheryl WuDunn reported from Beijing:

> When the streets here swell with protestors, people all over China tune in the Voice of America. During the turmoil of recent weeks, people in offices,

factories and schools throughout China have clustered by the radio to listen
to the latest episodes in the saga of student protest. At Beijing University,
students huddle around posters that report the latest Voice bulletins, and the
other day, hundreds of students crowded around a dormitory window
listening to a dispatch....During times of unrest, China's news organizations
tend to be silent about what many Chinese are most interested in, sending
waves of...listeners to [VOA].[8]

And because of its 60 million or so listeners in China, WuDunn reports, "the
Voice at times seems to have a greater effect on local politics than do China's
own news organizations."

According to Congressman Stephen J. Solarz of New York, the same
observation seemed to be true even as Chinese authorities resumed jamming
VOA broadcasts in the first days of June 1989 during the brutal suppression of
the students' quest for freedom. Discussing the massacre of Chinese citizens by
army troops on the PBS McNeil-Lehrer NewsHour on June 5, he noted that the
Chinese public, especially in times like these, depended on VOA for news of
what was happening in that country, and he complimented the U.S. radio
network for its "magnificent" coverage.

Until 1956, VOA was practically the sole source of information from
America for the Soviet population. It was heavily jammed in Russian and other
Soviet languages in which VOA broadcast, but reports from all over the Soviet
Union indicated that many Soviet citizens managed somehow to hear the *Golos
Ameriki* (identified by its stirring theme, "Columbia, the Gem of the Ocean,"
later changed to a more playful "Yankee Doodle"). Like the Chinese, Soviet
authorities have never jammed VOA's English-language broadcasts, which
were thus easily available, especially to some among the English-speaking
intelligentsia.[9]

In 1956, an agreement was concluded between the United States and the
Soviet Union permitting reciprocal distribution of the U.S. Russian-language
monthly, *Amerika*, and the Soviet English-language periodical, *USSR* (later
changed to *Soviet Life*). The glossy, attractively printed *Amerika*, which
resembled *Life* magazine, provided the first window into the life of Americans
for Soviet citizens. The periodical immediately became so popular that it was
virtually unavailable except through a black market arrangement with news
kiosk sellers.

Amerika Magazine in the Soviet Union

It was part of my job at the American embassy in Moscow in the late fifties and early sixties to monitor Soviet distribution of *Amerika* and to counsel the editors in Washington about content. Every month on the day the journal was to be distributed, I set out to check the newsstands in Moscow to see that copies of the periodical were indeed delivered and on sale. I saw lines forming immediately when Soviet citizens noted the distinctive journal disappearing under the counter of newsstands, to be produced reluctantly and secretively by the sellers only for favorite customers — who often had made prior arrangements to obtain the magazine, usually at a price considerably higher than the 50 kopeks printed on the cover.

Unfortunately, their counterpart journal, *Soviet Life*, never became very popular in the United States, and sales lagged. As a matter of strict reciprocity, Soviet authorities returned to the American embassy each month the same number of "unsold" copies of the 50,000 print run of *Amerika* as the number of *Soviet Life*'s left unsold in the United States. These leftover copies of *Amerika* were stored in the basement of Spaso House, the American ambassador's residence, and their quantity became a critical mass when the rate of return of *Soviet Life* reached 20,000 per month.

We in Moscow did everything to encourage distribution of *Soviet Life* in the United States so as to avoid returns of *Amerika*. And we used ingenuity to distribute the returns, for we knew the magazine's popularity. Ownership of a copy of *Amerika* signified being "with it," and each copy passed through many hands, one of the reasons we insisted that it be printed on good stock.

I remember several times taking copies on airplane trips and depositing them ostentatiously in the pocket in front of my seat. Within minutes they would all be gone, with the first request usually coming from the flight attendant who, after reading it in the back of the plane, passed it into the cockpit.

In this era of *glasnost*, *Amerika* seems as popular as ever. Circulation has been reciprocally increased, and "returns" have been miraculously eliminated.

In 1958 the door to public diplomacy was opened wider with the conclusion of the first U.S.-Soviet cultural agreement. It marked the beginning of a more normal, if not relaxed, relationship with the Soviet Union, highlighted by Khrushchev's visit to the United States in 1959 in what was then called the "Spirit of Camp David." To illustrate the application of public diplomacy in a relatively closed society, the case study in chapter 9 explains in greater detail how U.S. public diplomacy tried to make an impact in the Soviet Union.

The developing world offers an entirely different challenge for public diplomacy. A public diplomat serving in one of the newly emerging African countries, for example, must adopt a different approach to his or her task. First, one must ask how large a "public" there is—how many people outside the government or ruling circles are there with whom it is worthwhile to communicate? What is the literacy rate, and how high is the educational level of the population? Can USIS or the embassy reach the leadership of the country through a program directed to the public, even if that public is small?

Depending on the answer to these questions, two alternatives appear to be available to U.S. policymakers: to assist, through information programs and educational and cultural exchanges, in the development of a social and political infrastructure that will lead over time to the emergence of an educated and politically interested public; or to decide not to conduct a full-fledged USIS program because the audience does not exist or the country will not in the foreseeable future be important enough in our scheme of things to warrant a public diplomacy program.

A complicating factor in considering these alternatives is the Third World's preoccupation with economic and technological development. Thus, it is not USIS but rather the U.S. Agency for International Development (AID) that can best respond to the urgent needs of these societies. Long-term cultural and information programs, while seen by U.S. policymakers as important in developing a mutually beneficial relationship, are often regarded as of secondary importance by the leaders of these nations in maintaining their countries' independence and viability. Technology transfer and training are the immediate priorities of these leaders, so that any USIS program would have to be adapted to such national priorities.

During the sixties and seventies, the United States tended to establish a USIS presence in practically every capital where it maintained a diplomatic mission. A proliferation of USIS posts resulted (staffed sometimes by only one American officer and an untrained foreign national staff), with inadequate prior thought being given to what informational and cultural activities could profitably be conducted in the particular country and how a public diplomacy program could serve U.S. foreign policy interests. On occasion a contributing factor in establishing a public diplomacy presence was the desire of an American ambassador to have a larger staff and greater program resources, more as a matter of prestige than for policy reasons. USIA frequently reasoned in similar terms: it wanted to be represented everywhere.

Parkinson's Law applied. The opening of a USIS post was often followed by the establishment of a library (providing legitimacy for the PAO as its director) without sufficient consideration as to whether books and periodicals were the best means of communicating in that society. Perhaps it would have been more useful in some cases to establish an English-teaching facility and supply it with teaching personnel and materials. Or, in cases where assigning a USIS officer was not justifiable, it might have been sufficient to appoint an ambassador with training and experience in public diplomacy, who could address the subject where warranted. USIA could have supported the chief of mission with program materials and advice. This alternative was never adopted, however, and in most developing countries a discrete USIS program, in some cases a very limited one, is conducted as an element of our diplomatic mission.

A PAO serving in a developing country should think in terms of programs and resources applicable to prevailing conditions in that country. Is a library really useful? A cultural center may well be a viable instrument of communication, perhaps not so much for its book collection as for a meeting place for English teaching, discussion groups, or film and video showings. An exchange program might most effectively concentrate on helping develop an educational infrastructure. It could provide teacher-training grants in the United States or academic study opportunities on the undergraduate level. Similarly, public diplomacy programs might serve to build a media infrastructure — certainly an important element in a democratic society — by providing study and training opportunities locally or in the United States for young journalists. The Voice of America, for instance, with very limited resources, provides such training for radio journalists as part of the USIS programs in a number of African countries. If, as observers seem to agree, this VOA project develops African correspondents and editors well trained in the modes and methods of Western journalism, would an increase in resources for this program be an appropriate way of strengthening our communication efforts in that part of the world?

From the perspective of USIS country objectives, VOA frequently plays yet another vital role in Africa: It serves as an important regional information medium in areas with widely dispersed, largely illiterate populations, where there is no adequate communications infrastructure, but where everyone owns a transistor radio. Possibly even more significant, VOA has filled a cultural void by linking African societies of different histories, traditions, and creative impulses through its special programs on African culture. In the absence of indigenous African cross-cultural resources, for instance, VOA broadcasts a program, "Conversations with African Writers," to acquaint Africans with their own literary heritage and current creativity and with those of their neighbors. Similarly, there are VOA programs featuring African music and a series dealing with African scientists.

A PAO serving in one of the industrialized democracies in Europe or Asia will project U.S. public diplomacy objectives entirely differently — again, however, in the context of the particular society. The PAO must reach the important gatekeepers, since it is impossible to be in touch with a mass audience of literate and media-saturated citizens so many of whom have a say in expressing public attitudes and exerting influence on their respective governments.

In this type of situation, the PAO's target audience may include young people, the so-called successor generation, who, research shows, form their political opinions and their prejudices while still in high school. Or the concentration might be on postgraduate students and young instructors rather than undergraduates, since local facilities for the latter are adequate. The PAO might also suggest that it is more cost-effective to employ television, USIA's Worldnet, for instance, than to get VOA to enter a radio-saturated market in which it would be difficult to compete with a variety of well-established radio stations of different political and cultural hues. The PAO might recommend against radio and in favor of television, furthermore, because he knows that it would be expensive, time-consuming, and technically difficult for VOA to build an audience in such an environment and to hold it.

Clearly, public diplomacy programs vary according to prevailing conditions in different societies. Public diplomacy's objectives and audiences, as well as the applicable communications tools, should be determined accordingly. Based on my own experience both in the field and in Washington, in public diplomacy, where local situations and conditions are so important to the successful pursuit of U.S. objectives, U.S. policymakers should rely on the judgment of the officer on the spot. Just as an ambassador is most often the best person to determine and represent the U.S. interest in a given country, the PAO is in the optimum position to define the kind of program that can best support USIS objectives there, to select the target audiences, and to decide what specific communications tools to employ. This admittedly subjective view is based on the assumption that the field officer is qualified, experienced, and proven.

That, in turn, presupposes that the USIA Foreign Service career personnel system is oriented toward developing area expertise, a prerequisite in public diplomacy. Over the years the pendulum has swung widely on this point. Some USIA directors have been field-oriented; during their terms of office, PAOs abroad and the geographic area directors in Washington were the dominant and dominating personalities in the agency. At other times USIA directors have favored the Washington program managers, those who directed academic and cultural exchange activities, television, press operations, or in some instances, the management moguls in charge of budgets, equipment, and personnel. The majority of the latter during recent years were noncareer officials.

In public diplomacy, however, where knowledge of the language, the culture, the political ambiance, the history, and traditions of a country are such important elements for the potential success of our efforts, the man or woman in the local hot seat abroad ought to be recognized as the operational linchpin by those who direct the U.S. Information Agency. When that is not the case, aberrations, mistakes, waste of resources, and activities counterproductive to U.S. foreign policy interests are too likely to occur.

NOTES

1. In Alexander Kendrick, *Prime Time: The Life of Edward R. Murrow* (Boston: Little Brown, 1969), 465.

2. W. Phillips Davison, "Mass Communication and Diplomacy," in *World Politics: An Introduction*, ed. James N. Rosenau, Kenneth W. Thompson, and Gavin Boyd (New York: The Free Press, 1976), 399.

3. Hans N. Tuch, *Arthur Burns and the Successor Generation* (Lanham, MD: University Press of America, 1988), 1–12.

4. In discussing the work of USIS missions, this discourse consciously uses a shorthand style of referring to the public affairs officer (PAO) without also specifying the cultural affairs officer (CAO) and the information officer (IO). This omission is not meant to denigrate the work or the importance of these two vital public diplomats (and their staffs) who together with the PAO constitute a USIS mission.

5. For excerpts from the USIS 1986 country plan for the Federal Republic of Germany, see Appendix 2.

6. "Let Poland Be Poland" was a USIA-produced 90-minute television program that tried to use the techniques of American political propaganda — featuring popular entertainers and actors — to rally foreign public sentiment against the Polish Communist regime. It was transmitted by satellite from New York and was supposed to be simultaneously telecast at prime time by as many European and other TV stations as possible. To many professional USIA officers it became a prime example, a metaphor, for the well-meant yet wrong-headed and wasteful attempts by inexperienced policymakers to use inappropriate methods to promote foreign policy objectives.

7. One surprise that greeted the large press party accompanying President Ford to Beijing in 1975 was a crowd of Chinese who rushed to the press plane, all asking to meet Philomena Jurey. Who *was* Philomena Jurey, many of the correspondents wanted to know. She turned out to be the long-time VOA White House correspondent, practically unrecognized in the United States but the best-known American journalist in China.

8. *New York Times*, 9 May 1989.

9. I once asked Aleksander Ginsberg, the former dissident activist, how many people in the Soviet Union he thought listened to VOA. He blandly replied that he did not know anyone in the USSR who did not listen to VOA, and then launched into a lengthy critique of what he did not like about VOA's Russian broadcasts.

4
The Methods — The Media

This chapter ties together the elements that constitute the whole of U.S. public diplomacy: the environment, the objectives, the audience, and, finally, the methods. It does not catalogue all, but rather discusses some, of the media and methods of conducting public diplomacy programs in terms of the environment in which they are practiced, the objectives they are to achieve, and the targets they are to address or involve.

The Wireless File

In any list of USIA products ranked by ambassadors or PAOs according to usefulness, first place often goes to the Wireless File, a compendium of authoritative U.S. government statements and information electronically transmitted daily to USIS posts around the world from USIA in Washington. Called the Wireless File because it used to be transmitted from Washington by radio and received on teleprinters, the name persists as an in-house generic term at USIA. Locally in the field, it is known by various names, among them Embassy Daily Bulletin, USIS Bulletin, USIS News and Information, or *Amerika Dienst*. Current state-of-the-art technology has developed a system whereby the file is computerized in Washington, and USIS posts throughout the world can call all or any part of it up at any time on their computer screens via satellite transmission.

The Wireless File typically contains full texts of presidential speeches and statements; White House, State Department, and congressional press releases; texts of briefings and press conferences; commentary from the U.S. press; and USIA-written interpretive and explanatory articles bearing on U.S. foreign relations, administration policies, or matters of bilateral interest. The Wireless File provides both an information service and a news service for the press. Most ambassadors and other embassy officers value it for providing timely and authoritative information needed in their work. In Bonn it was distributed daily within the embassy and to opinion leaders in the government, the parliament, and the media in the capital and throughout the country. Federal Chancellor Helmut Schmidt, for instance, found it so useful that he sent a driver to the embassy at 6:30 every morning for his personal wire service copy, not wanting to wait for delivery several hours later of the printed USIS-distributed bulletin. His successor has continued the practice.

No self-respecting editor in the Federal Republic of Germany would ever print a Wireless File article in his paper. After all, it is a foreign government hand-out. Yet USIS officers in Bonn would get urgent calls from editors all over Germany if the file, nowadays transmitted to them electronically, was late in arriving. They used it regularly for authoritative background information and as a help in writing and editing their articles and editorials. They valued it for the full texts of statements and speeches, rather than having to rely on the partial and pre-edited versions customarily transmitted by the commercial wire services.

In many other countries, especially those in the Third World, the Wireless File is so highly respected for accuracy and authority that its material serves as what the profession calls "hard copy"—authentic source material—for many daily papers and weekly periodicals. Even in as sophisticated and highly regarded a newspaper as the *Estado de São Paulo*, Wireless File stories were reprinted verbatim during my time in Brazil in the early seventies, often with Brazilian names as bylines, implying they were written by the paper's own correspondents in Washington. During a time of heavy government censorship such a story perhaps had a better chance of escaping the censor's scissors than others with a São Paulo dateline.

Thus, whether as information for internal embassy or external use or as a source for news and features in the foreign press, the Wireless File as a state-of-the-art communications medium retains its viability around the world.

The early history of the Wireless File and controversy about its function in the late 1940s and early 1950s serve as illustration of the reservations some in Congress and the public had at the time about the U.S. government's involvement in information activities. The Congress early on prohibited domestic distribution of USIA products and has sustained that prohibition over the years, with very few exceptions. There were also a number of influential Americans who feared that the U.S. government's foreign information programs might interfere and unfairly compete with private American enterprise in other countries and who maintained that at any rate the private sector could do a better job. The U.S. wire services were initially quite suspicious of the Wireless File, fearing that it might compete with their ability to sell their services to potential customers abroad. A prohibition was instituted against out-of-embassy distribution of the international and domestic news summary that was a daily feature of the file. That summary was restricted to internal informational use.

Over the years, concern about the Wireless File and other USIA products diminished as commercial organizations recognized that these products were not in competition with those of the private sector. As a matter of fact, both AP and UPI now sell their services to USIA (to VOA for operational use, to other USIA elements in Washington and abroad for internal information) and consider the agency a good customer.

Press and Publications

The Press and Publications Service of USIA, which produces the Wireless File, also publishes a number of periodicals. Some, like *Amerika*, are geographically oriented; others, like *Economic Impact*, specialize in particular subjects. In certain countries and with certain audiences, these well-edited, highly professional publications contribute significantly to public diplomacy. The magazine *Topic*, for instance, a slick picture monthly published in English and French versions, has been a popular medium of information in a number of African countries that have nothing comparable in their own media catalogue. The quarterly *Dialogue* aims at a sophisticated, rather intellectual audience. It most often reprints articles from American publications that would appeal to a similar readership in the United States. This periodical was considered so highly prestigious in Brazil that USIS published a Portuguese edition, *Dialogo*, in order to satisfy a particular Brazilian audience it was trying to reach.

Some years ago, the PAO in Moscow persuaded USIA to translate *Dialogue* into Russian and try distributing it in limited numbers, even though it was not covered under the U.S.–Soviet Cultural Agreement, as *Amerika* was. It was purely an experiment, and a costly one, since USIA had no idea whether the embassy staff would be able to distribute it at all. The PAO was convinced that the publication would be popular with Soviet intellectuals, especially since there was no other product with which to reach the Soviet intelligentsia nor many opportunities to communicate with them. The experiment worked, and to this day each issue of *Dialogue* is translated and distributed in the Soviet Union.

In the Federal Republic of Germany, where an audience for *Dialogue* was clearly present, USIS decided not to publish a German edition and also not to make much use of the English edition. German readers to whom this publication would have appealed had access to the American publications in which the articles originally appeared or to German publications that covered similar ground. USIS Bonn thus felt that as good as this publication was and as targeted as it appeared to be in certain countries for certain audiences, it was not a cost-effective public diplomacy instrument in Germany.

Problems of Communism and *English Teaching Forum*, mentioned earlier, are two other highly respected USIA periodicals that appeal to special audiences, scholars and English teachers respectively, and that enjoy worldwide readership.

Occasionally USIA launches publications to fill a specific need. *Economic Impact* came into being in 1973 because economics was deemed particularly relevant to U.S. foreign policy in many areas of the world at the time. It remains a subject of major interest in most USIS programs today.

USIS posts, with support from Washington, may also publish a single pamphlet or start a periodical for a specific purpose with a particular audience in mind. In the Federal Republic of Germany USIS began two such publications in the early eighties, one a newsletter about American labor and one, the *American Studies Newsletter*, designed for English and civics teachers in German high schools. In the latter case, the *Newsletter* filled the long-term need of providing the country's 20,000 English language and American studies teachers with information on currently available teaching materials to help them improve and increase their teaching about the United States. Many teachers had complained about the unavailability of just such a resource, forcing them to rely on British materials. USIS Bonn considered this a priority need in its efforts to enhance knowledge about America among German high school students, an important goal in its country plan. After considerable research and with assistance from the USIA English-teaching staff in Washington, the publication was launched. Various German state ministries of education provided support by taking on the distribution of the *Newsletter*, a significant contribution in view of the otherwise prohibitive mailing costs. The periodical, incidentally, was printed in USIA's own printing plant in Manila, saving USIS Bonn the commercial printing costs.

The labor newsletter was a cooperative venture between USIS Bonn and the embassy's labor counselor. Such a specialized and limited-circulation publication in German would serve a useful purpose, they concluded, namely, to help increase and improve U.S. contacts with trade union officials and members, who in Germany constitute an important target group for U.S. public diplomacy.

Exhibitions

Exhibitions used to constitute a major public diplomacy medium. In 1955 a two-year project to develop Atoms for Peace exhibits all over the world resulted from President Eisenhower's 1954 United Nations General Assembly speech promoting the peaceful uses of nuclear energy as a major U.S. foreign policy objective. This theme, it was thought, lent itself to public diplomacy development since it was meant, at least in part, to capture the minds of people who had been exposed only to the fear of the atomic bomb. One of the countries in which this exhibition became a popular success was Japan, where it traveled to various cities for over two years. It was cosponsored by the Yomiuri newspaper chain, whose founder and publisher believed that the Japanese should be exposed to this sensitive theme as therapy for its national trauma. The exhibit, consisting of actual equipment, instrumentation, descriptive materials, and mock-ups, explained advances in nuclear power production, transportation, and the medical uses of the atom.[1]

The worldwide success of this theme exhibit motivated USIA's management in 1956 to engage in another major exhibit venture, on U.S. space exploration. That effort was curtailed, however, after the Soviet launching of Sputnik in 1957 showed the world how much ahead of the United States the Soviets were in this endeavor.

By far the largest and most comprehensive USIA exhibit in the 1950s was the American National Exhibition in Moscow in the summer of 1959. It was one of the products of the first U.S.–Soviet Cultural Agreement of 1958, which included a reciprocal Soviet exhibit mounted in New York at the same time. The U.S. exhibition in Moscow was a huge organizational, architectural, and budgetary venture that was planned, designed, and coordinated by the agency and assisted by a number of major U.S. corporations with commercial, or at least promotional, interests in the Soviet Union.[2] The exhibition featured the latest in U.S. home and entertainment technology (including an RCA color television studio), science, fashions, American family living (a model one-family house), consumer products, photography (Edward Steichen's "Family of Man"), and art. The centerpiece was a Buckminster Fuller geodesic dome that contained a gigantic seven-screen film projection depicting a 24-hour period in the lives of typical Americans living in various parts of the United States. The dome also held an IBM computer—new at the time—that answered thousands of questions about America posed by Soviet visitors. The exhibition is remembered in this country primarily as the locale for Richard Nixon's famous "kitchen debate" with Nikita Khrushchev.

Arts and Artifacts—Khrushchev at the American Exhibit

In conducting Nikita Khrushchev through a preview of the 1959 American National Exhibition in Moscow before its formal opening, Vice President Nixon led him first to the RCA color television studio, where a videotaping of the two in conversation was demonstrated. (This was for the Soviets such a new technological development that the video head was locked up nightly in an embassy safe to protect it from anticipated theft.) While the two talked for the video cameras, Khrushchev became increasingly aggressive, but Nixon remained restrained. As they emerged from the studio, Nixon told his embassy escorts that as the host he felt he should be polite, but added: "What gives with him? If he starts that again, I'll let him have it."

The next stop on the tour was a walk-through of the model of a "typical" American one-family home. As they stopped to look at the kitchen, Khrushchev again started the polemics, and this time Nixon gave tit for tat. Every time it looked as though they were going into a real "clinch," they backed off, laughed, embraced, and went at it again.

They were surrounded by a crowd of American photographers and reporters who were snapping pictures and scribbling furiously. To the best of this writer's knowledge, there is no verbatim record of this "kitchen debate,"only what the newsmen pieced together either directly or from the interpreters. The bout lasted close to twenty minutes—a fascinating confrontation that was a pure, if historic, accident.

When Nikita Khrushchev returned for a second visit to the exhibition, his interpreter got lost in the crush of the crowd that surrounded the chairman as he viewed the display of American art. As the U.S. cultural and press attaché escorting him, I was corralled into amateur interpreting duty. All went well as Khrushchev examined the nineteenth and early twentieth-century American paintings. When he came upon a work by John Marin and I explained its title, "Sea and Sky," Khrushchev remarked, "It looks as though someone peed on the canvas." Stuttering, I translated, "The Chairman said it appeared to him that a little boy had made a puddle on the canvas." Khrushchev inquired, and was told, how his comment had been interpreted, whereupon he admonished, "Please interpret the Chairman correctly." I said, "It looks as though someone peed on the canvas."

Khrushchev's comments grew increasingly critical as he viewed the works of contemporary American artists, culminating in an angry outburst — perhaps calculated, perhaps real — upon seeing the large female nude statue by Gaston Lachaise (from New York's Museum of Modern Art) that was the centerpiece of the sculpture garden. He shouted, in Russian, "Only a pederast could have done this." And he rushed off, followed by his entourage.

It is difficult to measure the impact — in public diplomacy terms — of such a major and expensive effort. In my judgment, it more than paid off. For hundreds of thousands of Soviet citizens, many coming from afar, it was their first glimpse of America, their first personal contact and conversation with Americans — the fifty-odd Russian-speaking American exhibit guides. Not only did they see something of life in America, but they also enjoyed themselves, sampling Pepsi for the first time, having their hair coiffed and their faces made up by Coty beauticians, swaying with the music at the fashion show, getting their first look at color television, seeing the inside of a typical American one-family home. And many remembered the experience for a long time. On a visit to Moscow fifteen years later, I met a man on the street, still wearing on his lapel the American National Exhibition emblem (*znachok*), who told me that his visit to the exhibit in 1959 was a lifelong memory, a pleasant memory, since it was his first look at America.[3]

During the sixties and early seventies, USIA was the principal organizer or coordinator of overseas U.S. government exhibitions at world's fairs, at international trade fairs, at theme exhibitions, and art shows. At the end of the 1970s, however, large-scale exhibits lost their popularity as public diplomacy media. They required a long lead time — for planning, preparation, and building — but made a relatively fleeting impact in most places; they were very expensive; and they were considered by some more of a "show-the-flag" prestige event rather than one making a substantive contribution. Most USIA managers came to the conclusion that other programs were more cost-effective in meeting public diplomacy objectives.

One exception is the series of traveling exhibits on specific themes that continue to be sent to the Soviet Union (and some of the Eastern European countries), especially to the more remote provincial cities in that vast land. They are rightfully regarded as excellent media of communication in societies where other methods of acquainting people with America are impossible or severely restricted. These exhibits have featured such varied subjects as American architecture, education, recreation, graphic arts, and information technology. It should be noted that the effectiveness of these shows is considerably enhanced by the presence of Russian-speaking American guides. They constitute the human connection to the Soviet citizens whose first contact with any American is often at these shows. Some would even claim, perhaps in slight exaggeration, that the main justification for the exhibits is that they provide a place for Soviet visitors to interact with these young Americans. The guides certainly do make a substantial contribution in the communications process, which they could not do without the exhibits. It was mainly the presence of the American guides — and their effectiveness — that caused the Soviets to oppose further exchanges of exhibits, and the United States to insist on their continuance, every time the Cultural Agreement came up for renewal.

Cultural and Information Centers

The idea of cultural and information centers as the focus of U.S. public diplomacy activities emerged in large measure from the occupation of Germany. There were twenty-seven such cultural centers, the *Amerika Häuser*, in the Federal Republic of Germany and Berlin in 1951.[4] As mentioned earlier, the *Amerika Haus* had served the purpose of reorientation and reeducation as part of U.S. efforts to rebuild a democratic society in Germany in the postwar era. Similar centers had also been part of the occupation in Japan and Austria.

This institution became the model for U.S. cultural and information centers in other countries, where they were gradually introduced as elements of public diplomacy programs. The nucleus of these cultural/information centers was usually a library of American books and periodicals, nowadays including videotapes, microfilm, and microfiche. In and around the library various events were scheduled — lectures, discussions, seminars, musical performances, play readings, exhibits, and English-teaching programs.

The number of *Amerika Häuser* in Germany was drastically reduced after 1950, since they were no longer needed as local community centers when the German cities rebuilt their cultural infrastructure. Many were closed because of budgetary reduction and redirection of public diplomacy resources to other countries. Those that remained were restructured to provide up-to-date information about the United States and evidence of contemporary American cultural creativity. Some of those that had to be closed were adopted by German local, state, or federal authorities and renamed German-American Institutes. These continued to receive some support from the U.S. government, usually in the form of the director's salary, library materials, and programs. As of 1989 there were seven *Amerika Häuser* and five German-American Institutes, the latter without substantial U.S. government subsidy since 1986.

The advantages and disadvantages of the centers in Germany are largely representative of those that USIA faces in maintaining similar institutions in other countries. One major advantage of a U.S. cultural center is that in most countries it is recognized as a legitimate institution, openly and visibly representing American society and its culture. It is the place in the community to which local citizens look for information about the United States and for examples and expression of American cultural achievements. Besides having a library and offering lectures, concerts, exhibits, and film and videotape showings, the center is the natural meeting place for personal encounters between American public diplomats and members of their target audiences.

A U.S. Foreign Service officer who directs such a cultural center does not have to peddle USIS books, tapes, and study grants out of an office in the embassy, but instead functions within an institution widely recognized as representing American culture and information. It is a place to which local citizens can freely come and in which they are welcomed hospitably. Its visibility, its openness, and the quality of its programs provide its American director and staff the legitimacy and prestige they need to do their public diplomacy job.

Cultural centers also sometimes represent liabilities. They are expensive and relatively inflexible investments in plant and overhead. Instead of inviting members of the target audience to hear an American speaker at the center, might there be a local organization to cosponsor the event and thereby bring the speaker to his or her "natural" audience? An American exhibit, say, on native Indian art, might find a more receptive audience if it were displayed in a local museum rather than at the center; or a panel discussion on the question of human rights, for instance, might find more sympathetic participants if it were held on neutral ground and not at the U.S. center. In times of political tension, local citizens may not want to be seen entering a U.S. information center; they might be more comfortable meeting with an American visitor in a private home. In some situations, the authorities might even make it difficult for local citizens to gain access to these centers and libraries. These American institutions, conspicuous as they are, have also been known to serve as convenient targets for protest demonstrations and even for terrorist acts, thereby contributing to increasing tensions between the United States and the host country.

The advantages and handicaps of maintaining U.S. libraries and centers can be weighed only on a case-by-case basis. They require careful consideration by USIA, the embassy, and the local public affairs officer. Before deciding to close a center, the PAO must consider whether there are alternative outlets for USIS programs and, more important, whether the closing might signal, or be perceived as, a withdrawal of American interest, a lessening of a U.S. commitment to the bilateral relationship, or, indeed, as a sign of defeat vis-à-vis those who would wish us to retreat from the scene.

Similarly, a PAO must consider the purpose, the pros and cons of a new center before establishing it. Is there a significant audience for the center? Are there alternatives for establishing a library, for instance, a university library that might welcome a separate American collection, find free space for it, and make it available to its faculty and students? If so, is the library accessible to non-university visitors? Should the library have any special subject concentration to respond to a particular public diplomacy objective? Should it include a videocassette collection, or should it perhaps concentrate on videotapes to the exclusion or limitation of reading material? Would the cassettes be available only on the premises or could they be lent out like books (assuming that the local videocassette recording system is compatible with the tapes available in the USIS library)? Is the center needed for other USIS programs, or would the director schedule programs in the center only because it has space and facilities that would otherwise go unused? Are the programs—lectures, English teaching, exhibits, concerts—viable public diplomacy tools in the country? Is the center accessible to the visitors that constitute the target audience, or are security requirements such that the center must be located at a distance from its natural audience and be so protected for reasons of security as to appear to discourage access? Will the center's establishment constitute a political statement of respect, friendship, or development support, or will it merely be a red flag for those opposing the American presence?

These are issues and questions that must be considered in the context of the overall relationship, the political/cultural environment, and the U.S. government's long-term public diplomacy objectives in the country.

Binational Centers

The German-American Institutes were a cooperative venture between the U.S. government (USIS/Bonn) and German private and government entities, undertaken to continue activities previously carried out unilaterally by the United States. The concept of binational centers, of which the German-American Institutes are an example, goes back many years. Binational centers (BNCs) started in Latin America, some before World War II, and continue today as important manifestations of interest in American culture, language, and society on the part of foreign communities. Some of these BNCs (with local names like Casa Thomas Jefferson, Biblioteca Benjamin Franklin, Instituto Brazil-Estados Unidos, or São Paulo Alumni Association) are entirely privately operated by a local foreign entity. Most of them, however, have as their governing body some form of official and/or private U.S. and foreign association with the purpose of furthering bilateral cultural cooperation and, most often, English-language teaching (which produces the main source of revenue).

The extent to which these BNCs can be considered as serving U.S. public diplomacy objectives depends entirely on their local organization and the support they receive from the USIS post in the country. USIS recognized and cooperated with over a dozen in Brazil alone, for example. In a BNC that is locally and privately organized primarily for the purpose of teaching English, with little or no financial support from the U.S. government, the USIS post might be able to offer assistance in the form of English-teaching materials, a modest book collection, and copies of the USIA publication *English Teaching Forum*, but our influence in terms of projecting specific public diplomacy objectives would be limited. If, on the other hand, the BNC is an institution that desires and receives substantial U.S. recognition and support—by paying the salary of an American director, maintaining a library, providing programs and exhibits — then the possibility exists of having these institutions serve long-term U.S. public diplomacy goals.

As a specific example, during my last assignment in the Federal Republic of Germany, from 1980 to 1985, USIS Bonn supported four BNCs — the German-American Institutes in Heidelberg, Nuremberg, Tübingen, and Freiburg — by paying the directors' salaries, maintaining a library of American books and periodicals, and providing speakers, performers, and occasional exhibits. The German side paid the rent, utilities, and salaries of the foreign national staff. The U.S. contribution was about 40 percent, the German (local, state, and federal) contribution about 60 percent. A local board of directors, on which USIS officers were represented, guided the operation of the Institute. Occasionally activities took place which, had it been a USIS-operated *Amerika Haus*, would not have been considered worthwhile. For a 40 percent contribution, however, USIS received an estimated 80 percent value. That, we felt, was a good investment, especially in times of budgetary stringency when we found the financial responsibility of operating our "wholly owned" *Amerika Häuser* a heavy burden.

Some readers may wonder why such mundane thoughts about budgets and finance are expressed in a discussion of the practice of public diplomacy. They are, however, necessary and important elements in a public affairs officer's management responsibilities. Each USIS post must justify vis-à-vis Washington (USIA and Congress) the cost-effectiveness of all public diplomacy activities in its jurisdiction. The exceptions to the PAO's financial responsibility are the Voice of America and Worldnet programs, which are operated and budgeted from Washington.

For the information of the reader, Appendix 3 contains an illustrative example of the budget of a medium-size USIS post (Colombia). A further example of how BNCs fit into USIA's overall public diplomacy operations and of how they may be financed is presented in the case study on USIS Brazil in chapter 10.

Libraries. The USIS library as an instrument of public diplomacy is not confined to its collection of publications and other materials. Usually the core of a U.S. or binational center, the library is not a passive institution waiting for passersby to come in to check out a book, read a magazine, or view a videotape. The well-trained USIS librarian uses the library to communicate with specifically targeted audiences. The library staff does this, for instance, by compiling a list of articles in periodicals on a subject of interest and sending it out to alert potential readers. This, unsurprisingly, is called the Article Alert List. Librarians will even send out the articles themselves to selected recipients if they believe the subject and the addressees are sufficiently important.

Similarly, bibliographies and book announcements are sent to selected audiences, inviting them to become familiar with the pertinent publications. USIS lecturers and symposia are supported with bibliographies and book exhibits on the subject under discussion.

USIS librarians, furthermore, interact with other libraries in the country — those associated with universities, government departments, or communities — and serve as founts of information on American subjects for these indigenous institutions. Again, the USIS or binational center library often represents the cultural bridge which, by its very presence, tends to enhance U.S. credibility and which, at the same time, conveys a sense of prestige to the local community.

Book Translations

USIA's book translation program has had its ups and downs over the years. Interestingly, the Soviet Union considers the translation and distribution of books abroad one of its most important public diplomacy activities. In a number of countries, particularly in Latin America, PAOs have found that American publications relating to country plan objectives are excellent public diplomacy tools when translated into the native language and sold through commercial channels. (See the case study on Brazil in Chapter 10.) The relatively modest expense for USIA involves paying the U.S. publisher for translation rights and buying a certain quantity of the resulting books, which are placed in USIS and BNC libraries and used for presentation to target group members. This form of subsidy usually provides the incentive to a local publisher to translate and publish desired books.

The book translation program has been particularly successful in Latin America, where there is a wide market for Spanish and Portuguese translations of American books. The program is also popular in French-speaking African countries. It would normally not be applicable in Western Europe, where publishers are able to translate and sell American books of significance on their own. Some USIS posts may still find it useful to purchase certain books in translation, for placement in USIS libraries and for direct presentation, when they are deemed useful in promoting a country plan objective.

Teaching the English Language

English-teaching programs, which are frequently conducted as part of American cultural and binational center activities, have been a focus of the U.S. Information Agency and of USIS posts around the world for many years. Much discussion and some controversy have centered on whether the teaching of English is an effective tool of public diplomacy. Since at least the 1950s, there has been agreement that English-teaching programs could be highly useful if they were targeted on designated audiences and if they conveyed information about America and its culture as a component of the teaching process.

The binational centers, especially those in Latin America, continue to concentrate on English-teaching programs, which often receive generous support from the USIS post in the country. USIS-operated American cultural centers also conduct English-teaching programs, but usually only when they meet the agreed criteria.

In highly developed countries, USIS posts may not find it necessary or even useful to be directly involved in English teaching, although they frequently assist in improving English-teaching programs in local schools and universities. As already mentioned, the *American Studies Newsletter* developed by USIS Bonn serves the twenty thousand teachers of English and civics in the Federal Republic of Germany. More important, the quarterly *English Teaching Forum*, published by USIA in Washington, enjoys the respect and popularity of teachers of English around the world.

The teaching of English in many countries has traditionally stressed British English taught with an emphasis on British civilization and culture. An aim of USIA and its USIS posts abroad has been to promote the teaching of American English as a conduit for conveying information and ideas about the United States. Besides the *English Teaching Forum*, USIA makes available to USIS posts professional experts in the teaching of American English to foreigners. They advise local institutions that train English teachers, and they assist instructors in BNCs and USIS cultural center English-teaching programs, through consultations, workshops, and seminars.

The Voice of America has featured English-teaching programs for many years, primarily in its foreign-language broadcasts. According to the Chinese broadcasting official mentioned earlier, almost all Chinese who had known some English before normalization of relations with the United States had learned it via VOA.

While accompanying Vice President Nixon to Siberia in 1959, I met several young Russians on the street in Novosibirsk who spoke to me in English, slowly and with a deep baritone intonation that I immediately recognized as an imitation of the voice of Willis Connover, the VOA disk jockey. Because of the popularity of his regular jazz music programs, Connover had by then become the best-known contemporary American in the Soviet Union. The young Soviets told me that they listened to him nightly and had learned their English from his broadcasts. Connover was pleased to learn that his influence in the Soviet Union extended beyond his music broadcasts to the way young Soviets communicated in the English language.

A regular daily feature of VOA's worldwide English broadcasts since 1959 has been a program called "Special English." Using a vocabulary of only two thousand English words, the program broadcasts news and features spoken at a cadence slower than normal, thereby making the content easier to understand for people not having English as a first language. "Special English" has become among the most popular VOA programs, and many credit it with helping them learn English.

Teaching English via television, which was a BBC monopoly for many years, has been the subject of recent research and development by USIA. A cooperative project with the McMillan Company of twenty-six half-hour programs is being readied for marketing abroad. It appears to be a natural for television stations, Worldnet programming, and VCR use in many countries.

American Participants (AmParts) Program

USIS-invited American speakers, discussants, and conference participants have for a long time been an effective medium for conveying pertinent and timely information and ideas abroad. An extension of the personal contact work done by USIS and other embassy officers, these qualified Americans (in the bureaucratic language widely known as American Participants, or AmParts) are invited by public affairs officers to appear before selected audiences to discuss subjects of importance to public diplomacy. These Americans, often from academia but also frequently from private industry, the media, and public life, are chosen as experts to provide a better and wider perspective on a subject than anyone in the official U.S. mission is able to do. The audience for these guests might be two or three important editors invited to lunch at the PAO's home, a group of businessmen at a seminar at the local Chamber of Commerce, a group of party politicians at the USIS cultural center, a university faculty, or a class of students — depending upon the particular American expert, the subject matter to be discussed, and the current interest and pertinence of the issue to the specific audience.

U.S. public diplomacy has made good use of this human resource. Besides their own specific expertise, these speakers represent the diversity of American thought, bringing to American public diplomacy a variety and richness of ideas and information that American public diplomats by themselves could not provide. These speakers personify a democratic society in action, whether they speak on administration policy; conduct responsible discussions of U.S. objectives; lecture on American poetry, literature, art, or sociology; or participate in a symposium on the delivery of health services. In Bonn the use of expert American speakers was a major aspect of the public diplomacy program because we were certain that they made a substantial contribution to the fulfillment of short-term and long-term goals of the country plan.

One reason these American experts made themselves available for USIS programming in Germany is that most of them felt that they themselves could learn and gain through the contacts we could make for them, which were usually better than they could make on their own. Speakers like William Griffith of the Massachusetts Institute of Technology, Dom Bonafide of the *National Journal*, Sidney Jones, undersecretary of commerce, Charles Wolf of the Rand Corporation, or David Gergen, then of the American Enterprise Institute, among many others, found that a good way for them to be in touch with people they wanted to meet was to permit themselves to be programmed by USIS. During any one year in the 1980–85 period, the USIS AmParts program in the Federal Republic of Germany benefited by the contribution of over one hundred invited experts.

I dwell in some detail on the American Participants Program as a valuable public diplomacy resource because it has generated considerable controversy at times, most recently during the Reagan administration. There was the revelation in 1983 of a list of names — dubbed "the blacklist" by the press — of potential speakers whom USIA management found unsuitable for participation in USIS programs for a variety of reasons, apparently including reasons of a partisan political nature. The manner in which the agency handled the speaker review process and its alleged political purpose created a furor that smudged at least temporarily the spotless reputation this program had enjoyed over the years.

Fortunately, USIA took corrective action quickly when the injurious aspects of the controversy came to light. Some of us in the field were as surprised as the general public about the existence of the "blacklist," because we had not, to the best of our knowledge, been affected by it. I told one inquiring CBS correspondent that no speaker requested by USIS Bonn had ever been turned down by USIA's management. (Some of them, of course, had turned down the invitation for their own reasons.)

American speakers, to summarize, are a valuable public diplomacy resource in two principal respects. First, when it comes to developing a broad understanding of the American society and institutions, they make significant contributions by demonstrating the diversity of responsible views in a democracy and, by their presence, give evidence of the openness of the American society. Second, in a foreign policy context, AmPart speakers are invited for the specific purpose of enabling USIS to address an issue that a post has determined to be of importance in its country plan.

Here I cite an actual example (one that is described in detail in the case study in Chapter 12). During the 1981–84 period it was a principal USIS country plan objective in the Federal Republic of Germany (FRG) to help convince the German public to accept deployment of intermediate-range nuclear missile forces (INF) as an element of NATO defense policy in the interest of all Alliance members. The FRG government faced a great deal of opposition, especially from the so-called peace movement that opposed deployment of INF weapons on German soil. They brought forth every argument against deployment, exploiting the media, mounting demonstrations, and taking advantage of all means available in the democratic political process to succeed in their opposition. In such circumstances it is logical that USIS Bonn would also want to employ all available resources, including the American Participants program, to support this specific policy objective. Obviously invitations to speak did not go to anyone opposed to this objective, and potential participants were free to accept or refuse the invitation to assist. American experts such as Richard Burt, Joseph Coffey, Helmut Sonnenfeld, David Abshire, Gale Mattox, Amos Jordan,

Angela Stent, and Gregory Flynn, among several others, made outstanding contributions to the attainment of this particular public diplomacy objective.

Educational and Cultural Exchanges

The Fulbright Academic Exchange Program was established in 1946 under legislation introduced by former Senator J. William Fulbright and subsequently updated in the Fulbright-Hays Act of 1961. By 1988, the program had involved more than 167,000 "Fulbrighters"—over 58,000 students, teachers, and scholars from the United States and 109,000 from abroad. In the words of the legislation, the purpose of the program is "to increase mutual understanding between the people of the United States and the people of other countries." Senator Fulbright himself put it this way:

> Perhaps the greatest power of educational exchange is the power to convert nations into peoples and to translate ideologies into human aspirations. I do not think educational exchange is certain to produce affection between peoples, nor indeed is that one of its essential purposes; it is quite enough if it contributes to the feeling of a common humanity, to an emotional awareness that other countries are populated not by doctrines that we fear but by individual people—people with the same capacity for pleasure and pain, for cruelty and kindness as the people we were brought up with in our own countries.[5]

The senator's ideas about educational exchanges, simply but eloquently expressed, are echoed in President Carter's March 1978 charge to USIA Director John Reinhardt, quoted in Chapter 2: that the agency's public diplomacy should strive "to reduce the degree to which misperceptions and misunderstanding complicate relations between the United States and the peoples of other nations."

The worldwide recognition of the Fulbright program indicates that it has served immeasurably to increase and improve U.S. understanding of foreign societies and understanding of America on the part of peoples in other countries. Edward Shils, the eminent University of Chicago sociologist, refers to the "community of knowers" that has been generated by the Fulbright program and labels it "the greatest migration of knowledge since the fall of Constantinople."[6]

Academic exchanges—students, teachers, university faculty and researchers—constitute the bulk of the official U.S. educational exchange program. Currently about 4,700 grants are given annually to Americans and foreigners. In advanced, industrialized countries, the Fulbright programs concern themselves almost exclusively with postgraduate studies and research, university teaching, and high school teacher exchanges. Originally, nearly all the funding for these programs came from the United States. Beginning in the 1960s, however, the budget for the Fulbright program in these countries has been shared and in some cases more than matched by the partner governments. The program is normally jointly administered by a bilateral Fulbright Commission that also sets the policy for the program and selects and places participants. In the United States the independent Board of Foreign Scholarships supervises the program and insures its scholarly integrity and nonpolitical character, while USIA provides the U.S. budget contribution and administers the program worldwide.

A near-perfect example of the Fulbright program's efficiency and effectiveness is the one administered by the US–FRG Educational Commission, which over the past thirty-odd years has become truly binational, with the program planning, execution, participation, and funding shared by the two countries. Since the late sixties, considerably more than half of the annual $4 million budget, up to 75 percent at times, has come from the German side. The West German government has always seen the long-range value of this program from its own perspective and has supported it to the extent of making up the difference during the years when the U.S. government was unable to match its half share of the budget, the largest of any Fulbright program in the world.

There is little doubt that the United States has been profiting from its investment in Fulbright exchange programs, even in such cases as the U.S.–West German example, where the program is planned and executed entirely bilaterally. The U.S. government has always taken care to be well represented on bilateral Fulbright commissions, with the public affairs officer, the cultural attaché, or in some cases even the deputy chief of mission representing the ambassador, as chairman or co-chairman of the commissions. This insures that in deciding on priorities, allocating budgets, and administering the program, each commission protects the long-term interests of the United States and, where there is sharing of funds, of both partners.

In many foreign countries where the Fulbright program is the best-known educational exchange activity, it continues to draw upon a deep well of affection and respect toward the United States. It often also plays a significant role in our political relationship with other countries, since the commissions provide a regular forum for discussion benefiting both parties. Within these political relationships, the Fulbright program represents our national commitment to a constructive activity that enables us better to comprehend the multicultured world in which we live, and others to appreciate one of our greatest national assets, the U.S. system of higher education.[7]

In the industrialized democracies, the Fulbright program traditionally has given funding priority to educational exchanges on the postgraduate level, because privately arranged exchange opportunities or adequate local facilities already existed on the undergraduate level. In a number of countries in the developing world, however, the greater need has been for study opportunities in the United States for those who had little or no opportunity for university training at home. The Hubert Humphrey Fellowship Program, begun in 1979, reaches beyond the traditional academic community, as USIA explains it, to bring outstanding midlevel professionals in public service from developing nations to the United States for a year of university study and work-related practical experience in such diverse fields as agriculture, public health, and public administration. During the 1987–88 academic year, there were 147 Humphrey Fellows from sixty-nine countries in the United States.[8]

Similarly, in 1986 USIA inaugurated a scholarship program for talented Central American and Caribbean students from non-elite socioeconomic backgrounds. Known as the Central American Program for Undergraduate Scholarships, or CAMPUS, this program is intended to give an opportunity for university study to potential future leaders in these countries who lack any other chance for a higher education. Its objectives are to improve the range and quality of educational alternatives for Central Americans especially in fields where there are skill shortages. This program's ultimate aim, like that of other educational exchange programs, is to build solid and lasting links between America and other countries.[9]

With this ultimate aim constantly in mind, USIA's educational and cultural exchange programs must be frequently reviewed and adjusted for new opportunities like the Humphrey Fellowships and CAMPUS. It is the responsibility of the public affairs officer to state his country objectives, analyze his audience, and recommend programs that fit into the bilateral communications climate. The variety of exchange programs that USIA administers and the new ones it starts are intended to accommodate the requirements of individual country plans.

In the early 1980s, PAOs serving in Germany and other West European countries came to realize, as noted earlier, that in these advanced, highly industrialized societies young people usually tend to form their political views, opinions, and prejudices before they enter universities or start a profession. These PAOs determined that if USIS were going to be successful in reaching and affecting the attitudes of the potential leaders of the successor generation in these countries, we would have to do so *before* they graduated from their respective high schools. A number of public affairs officers gave high priority in their country plans and in other communications with Washington to addressing the successor generation by communicating with them at the teenage level through youth exchanges.

Initially these proposals met with some resistance because the conventional wisdom had it that teenagers were too young to gain anything through these "kiddie exchanges," as they were skeptically called. But continued lobbying in Washington, including with some influential and interested members of Congress, succeeded in promoting the idea of long-term (ten months to a year) teenage exchanges. Concentrating on home stays, high school attendance, and community involvement, these exchanges were regarded as a potentially effective way of bringing about greater knowledge and better understanding among the young people of our respective societies. USIA Director Wick projected these ideas during the Reagan administration into the President's International Youth Exchange Initiative, thereby launching the U.S. government into a major new program in the field of public diplomacy.[10]

Such a major initiative as the international youth exchange program cannot be realized by USIA and its officers in the field alone. It requires the cooperation and participation, as well as the expertise, of such experienced and recognized private not-for-profit organizations as Youth for Understanding and AFS International, with their networks of thousands of volunteers in this country and abroad.

Yet another form of cultural exchange is USIA's program for International Visitors (IV). This program permits a USIS post, in close coordination with other members of the country team, to select a number of current or emerging leaders in various walks of life — government, politics, media, education, science, labor, or other key fields — to visit the United States on a travel program and schedule of their choice to gain in-depth perceptions of America and Americans through direct, person-to-person contact.

Most public affairs officers consider this program one of their most valuable assets. It is a relatively costly undertaking, designed as it is for an individual (or a small group of people sharing interests and backgrounds) for visits lasting between three and six weeks. (The minimum per capita cost for such an international visitor is $6,000.) The PAO and his embassy colleagues therefore go about the selection process carefully, relating their nominations directly to country plan objectives, the target audience, and the prevailing communications climate. The invitee is free to travel anywhere in the United States, with or without an interpreter/escort. Before departure, the USIS staff helps the foreign visitor plan an itinerary that will result in profitable exposure to the United States, its culture and its people, and that will accommodate the traveler's professional and personal interests. A frequent byproduct of this program is that Americans who come in contact with the visitor come away with new insight and knowledge about the visitor's home country or profession.

It is a matter of record and evidence of the program's effectiveness that over the years hundreds of former International Visitors have risen to important positions in their countries. USIA reports that, as of August 1987, 99 current and former chiefs-of-state and over 660 cabinet-level ministers around the world had participated in these U.S. government-sponsored exchange programs.[11]

In my own recent experience, only one selection for this program turned out to be what I would call a failure on our part in that the young and rising politician chosen did not appear to have learned anything about America during his trip. His eyes seemed to be closed to his experiences, and the prejudices that he had brought along on his visit seemed, if anything, to be reinforced. We did not, however, misjudge his potential: In the intervening five years he has become one of the leaders of the current opposition party in the Federal Republic of Germany.

One case that looked like another possible selection failure was that of a young member of the German Bundestag who had arrived in Washington and, unbeknown to USIS Bonn, had his wife and baby son in tow. Since the wife insisted on accompanying her husband on all appointments, program arrangements were totally dependent on the availability of baby sitters. USIA was quite unhappy with what appeared to be USIS Bonn's lack of care in selection and predeparture briefing, giving the whole trip the appearance of a frivolous vacation. There was a happy ending, however: The politician has risen to a significant position in one of the state governments, and even now, seven years later, speaks frequently about the educational experience of his trip and his appreciation for the opportunity to make lasting contacts with American counterparts.

Evaluating the long-term effectiveness of the International Visitor program, Winston Lord, U.S. ambassador to the People's Republic of China from 1985 to 1989, gave it high marks:

> Every American working in China faces the task of how to bridge the gap of misunderstanding and misinformation arising from the long hiatus in our bilateral relationship and the vast differences in our societies. The quiet success of the International Visitor program is one of our greatest allies in this challenge....Every IV returnee I have met is deeply impressed with America...not only our material achievements but especially the personal warmth and hospitality of American families who receive them in their homes....This effort has produced an impressive array of better informed individuals...who are taking increasingly important roles in government, academic, media, education, and economic circles.[12]

Public diplomacy objectives are often pursued through other cultural and educational initiatives. In some countries it is possible to establish or support the introduction of American studies programs at universities where previously the emphasis might have been on British literature, language, and history. For example, through the Fulbright program it was possible to bring to a Brazilian university that had expressed a desire to establish an American studies program a U.S. scholar in American studies who helped to organize and teach courses in the discipline. At the same time, two Brazilian scholars from the same university were invited to pursue American studies at a U.S. university. Upon their return these Brazilians were then able to take over the newly established discipline from the visiting U.S. professor. Both the home university of the U.S. professor and the U.S. institution that had hosted the Brazilian scholars remained in contact with the Brazilian university and provided support to its American studies program. The American university that had hosted the Brazilian scholars also benefited by their presence in improving its Brazilian studies program.

Similarly, by working closely with the German Association for American Studies over a period of several years, USIS Bonn was able to further two of its public diplomacy objectives. First, by persuading the association to broaden its membership to include high school teachers of American studies, it helped the latter to expand their American studies teaching in secondary schools (part of USIS Bonn's efforts, previously mentioned, to expand contact and communication with the teenage successor generation). Second, USIS encouraged the association to move away from its earlier preoccupation with the esoterica of American literature and language; to devote more attention to teaching and studying American history, political science, sociology, economics, and law; and to develop an interdisciplinary approach to American studies at German universities and, to some extent, secondary schools. To assist the membership of the association in doing this, USIS helped set up American Studies Resource Centers at a number of universities in the Federal Republic. These, complemented by the libraries of the seven America Houses and the USIS-published *American Studies Newsletter*, provided information, materials, and advice to teachers of English language and American studies in the FRG's secondary schools.

Still another method of pursuing U.S. public diplomacy objectives with educational exchange programs is through the expertise and facilitative assistance a USIS post can often provide in establishing and maintaining affiliations between U.S. and foreign universities. While this type of privately financed educational partnership has been going on for many years between American and European institutions of higher learning—there are over fifty such affiliations between U.S. and German universities—USIA's Universities Affiliation Program was expanded to Africa and became worldwide in 1983. Supported by grants from USIA in those cases where U.S. private and foreign resources are not sufficient, cooperative programs have been set up between domestic and foreign colleges and universities, usually involving exchanges of faculty, students, and staff. Partnerships between American institutions and those in the developing world have focused on exchanges in the social sciences, humanities, communication, and education. Since the expanded program's inception, 155 grants have been awarded to American institutions and their affiliated foreign partners.[13]

Performing arts are the final public diplomacy arrow in USIA's cultural and educational exchange quiver to be mentioned here. In the fifties and sixties the State Department sponsored and organized tours of major American performing arts groups around the world, such as the tour of the Boston Symphony to several European capitals, accompanied by a State Department cultural affairs officer as escort/impresario, in the early fifties. The New York Philharmonic, the Robert Shaw Chorale, the Cleveland Orchestra, the New York City Ballet, the University of Michigan Concert Band, the touring company of *My Fair Lady*, and the Dave Brubeck Quartet were among many such outstanding performing arts groups that were officially sponsored and at least partially financed by USIA to represent America's cultural excellence and artistic achievements abroad.

Beginning in the sixties, however, it was no longer necessary for the U.S. government to finance and manage such tours in Western Europe, where private sponsors were fully capable of doing so. The State Department therefore began concentrating its limited performing arts resources in areas where no funding alternatives existed and where such cultural events would make a particular impact in public diplomacy terms. The Soviet Union, Eastern Europe, and some of the countries in the developing world, particularly in Africa, continued to be targets for U.S.-sponsored performing arts groups, especially those that were able to demonstrate current creative achievements in the area of music, theater, and ballet.

Local USIS posts are often asked and are usually able to lend facilitative assistance to visiting American performing arts ensembles and individual artists — even those the agency does not support financially — thereby enhancing the impact of the visits. The Cleveland Orchestra, for instance, in planning a Latin American tour in 1978 with only minimum official U.S. financial help, nonetheless required local assistance in some cities where PAOs believed such appearances would contribute to USIS country plan objectives. A number of PAOs were able to assist in raising the necessary local financial contributions and also in providing publicity and arranging encounters for some of the Cleveland musicians in schools and conservatories. The orchestra and its musicians did much thereby to enhance the U.S. cultural image in cities like Rio de Janeiro and São Paulo, which otherwise would not have had the opportunity to hear one of the world's finest musical organizations.

Personal Contact

Most professional public diplomats would agree with Edward R. Murrow's dictum that the most important element of the communications process is person-to-person contact — "the last three feet." As someone professionally involved with public diplomacy, I have always been convinced that in the communications process the dialogue is only as good as its participants. Our Foreign Service public diplomats, who are the lead actors in the cross-cultural communications process, are our most valuable and indispensable resource. We could not function without their talent to create, to articulate, and to communicate.

A public affairs officer has three major responsibilities: as a manager of a USIS country program (including policy, organization, staff, and budget); as an advisor to the ambassador, the country team, and Washington headquarters on public attitudes in the country, as well as on ways of making U.S. policies understandable and acceptable to a foreign public; and as a communicator who personally participates in the communication process as interlocutor, dialogue partner, speech maker, or briefer. As program managers, PAOs must avoid bogging down the USIS staff in organizing and managing public diplomacy programs — becoming impresarios of the communications process — to the detriment of their responsibilities as individual communicators. Because PAOs and their embassy colleagues cannot be expert communicators in all fields required in the public diplomacy process, USIS posts often draw on the American Participants program for assistance.

Among the PAO's most effective instruments in this personal communication process are the USIA Foreign Press Centers, of which there are currently three — in Washington, New York, and Los Angeles. These press centers, staffed by experienced public diplomats, respond to requests for professional assistance from resident or visiting foreign correspondents. Where a PAO may find it difficult to make personal contact with a busy newspaper editor or television producer to talk about a specific issue, the PAO's colleague in one of the USIA Foreign Press Centers in the United States may more easily have a conversation with the U.S.-based correspondent of the respective publication or TV network while helping the correspondent get an interview with a policymaker or an invitation to a press briefing, while clarifying a particular question, or while providing useful information. That correspondent's reports, in print, on radio, or on local television, would very likely be featured by his or her editor or producer with greater prominence, and be regarded as more authoritative, than anything the USIS officer might have provided the editor on the latter's home turf. The PAO will therefore often call upon the Foreign Press Centers to help arrange interviews, tours, and personal contacts for resident foreign journalists. And in the case of visiting journalists, the PAO would advise the press center of their coming and outline their specific journalistic interests and concerns, suggesting interviews, visits, and briefings.

The three press centers and their staffs do much more than substitute for overseas public affairs officers as interlocutors with foreign journalists. In effect, they serve as surrogate USIS posts for the foreign journalists in the three cities where they are located. Equipped with a reference library, wire service tickers, the Wireless File, television monitors, and conference rooms, the press centers and the officers staffing them communicate with this particular target group. They organize briefings with administration spokesmen, political personalities, and others who have something significant to communicate, whether in foreign affairs, science, culture, economics, trade, or social issues. They organize study and reporting trips for groups of foreign journalists from one country, or of journalists with similar interests from several countries, to such places as "Silicon Valley," Santa Fe, Des Moines, Appalachia, or Atlanta to help them cover such topics as, respectively, high technology, opera and Indian art, farm issues, anti-poverty programs, and the American political process as demonstrated through a political convention.

Foreign journalists stationed in or visiting the United States, especially those not representing major media organizations and therefore frequently lacking the requisite access and resources, appreciate the special service the press centers provide and use them as an "office-away-from-office." In all these ways, the press center staffs enhance the communication process between the foreign journalist gatekeepers, their American dialogue partners, and their respective reading, listening, or viewing public back home.

It is not possible or even useful to categorize the various communication activities described in this chapter as serving chiefly long-term or chiefly short-term public diplomacy ends. Some of the programs work interactively in that they are useful both in the long term and in the short term when conducted together. Yet it is possible to generalize that educational and cultural exchanges, American studies and book publication programs, libraries, and exhibitions would normally not be geared to short-term foreign policy objectives. Their purpose is to assist in achieving basic knowledge about the United States and understanding of the way our society thinks, works, lives, and acts. Only on a firm foundation of such knowledge and understanding can we succeed in making our immediate or short-term objectives understood and possibly accepted. These short-term public diplomacy objectives are, in turn, best served by information programs employing the fast media—press, radio, television— as well as the American Participants program and, of course, the personal contact work of the Foreign Service public affairs professionals.

Picture, if you will, an American Participant speaker, armed with helpful printed information materials, who addresses a symposium or has an electronic dialogue with an audience whose members have experienced the United States either as former teenage exchangees, as students and scholars, or as International Visitors. Such coordinated interaction—call it orchestration—of some of these so-called long-term and short-term communications media can be particularly effective in achieving public diplomacy objectives.

NOTES

1. See Henry A. Dunlap and Hans N. Tuch, *Atoms at Your Service* (New York: Harper & Brothers, 1957). The book covers ground similar to the contents of the USIS exhibit.

2. The principal designer of the American National Exhibition was a USIA officer, Jack Masey, who later also designed the U.S. pavilion at the Montreal World's Fair in 1967. He currently heads a major design firm in New York.

3. In spite of the pervasive anti-American propaganda over the years, many Soviet citizens retain positive memories of the United States for a long time: Travelling around the Soviet Union in the late fifties, I met any number of people who told me that they felt close to Americans, not only because of the World War II alliance but because of the wonderful things Herbert Hoover had done in 1922, saving many Russians from starvation with his food package aid program.

4. Office of the U.S. High Commissioner for Germany, 10th Quarterly Report on Germany, January 1–March 31, 1952. In addition, the report notes that there were 135 reading rooms, which were branches of these twenty-seven America Houses. Together they had a monthly attendance of over one million.

5. J. William Fulbright, "Education for a New Kind of Industrial Revolution," USIA/IPS "Byliner" No.F-67-73, March 1967.

6. In Mary W. Brady, "National Commitment— National Asset: A Review of the Department of State International Exchange of Teachers and Scholars" (unpublished paper, 1 Jan. 1978), 1.

7. For a detailed exposition of one Fulbright program, see Appendix 6 on the U.S.–Brazil Academic Exchange Program for Fiscal Year 1989.

8. U.S. Information Agency, "The Fulbright Program," A Fact Sheet, 1988.

9. U.S. Information Agency, "Central American Program for Undergraduate Scholarships (CAMPUS)," Fact Sheet, 7 Jan. 1988.

10. The Congress-Bundestag Youth Exchange Program, one result of the President's International Youth Exchange Initiative, is discussed in the case study, "Dealing with the German 'Successor Generation,' " in Chapter 11.

11. "The U.S. Information Agency's International Visitors' Program," Fact Sheet, USIA, October 1987.

12. Winston Lord, "Commentary," *USIA World*, Vol. 8, No. 4 (May 1989), 2.

13. U.S. Information Agency, "The Fulbright Program," Fact Sheet, 1988.

5

The Voice of America

The Voice of America and Worldnet, USIA's television operation, each deserve separate chapters for several reasons. First, they are directed and operated from Washington instead of in the field, but they can and often do support individual country and area objectives. Second, the specific technological problems and opportunities they present are unique. And third, both have worldwide yet differentiated applicability as media of communication.

The Voice of America has often been called the tail that wags the USIA dog. It is the largest of USIA's elements, the oldest (launched in 1942) and best-known component of the U.S. government's public diplomacy, enjoying a worldwide reach and fame wider than its agency parent (and causing occasional turf and prestige friction between the directors of the two entities).

This chapter is not intended as an exhaustive history or manual of operations of the Voice of America.[1] Rather, it discusses how VOA functions as an important — and in some cases the only — communications medium available to serve U.S. public diplomacy objectives worldwide. In addition, VOA broadcasts often serve the objectives of a single country program particularly well, despite VOA's location in Washington, beyond the operational control of the country public affairs officer.

Winning "Attention and Respect"

The Voice of America is the one USIA element that operates under a separate charter, promulgated in 1960 and written into law in 1976 (PL 94-350).[2] This charter says essentially three things: First, to "win the attention and respect of listeners...VOA will serve as a consistently reliable and authoritative source of news." Second, VOA will represent the totality of America, rather than "any single segment of American society," by presenting "a balanced and comprehensive projection of significant American thought and institutions." And third, "VOA will present the policies of the United States...and...responsible discussion and opinion on these policies."[3] Elaborating on the charter's mandate in 1962, Edward R. Murrow declared:

> The Voice of America stands upon this above all: The truth shall be the guide. Truth may help us. It may hurt us....But we shall never be free without knowing the truth.[4]

This charter is consonant with the definition of public diplomacy discussed earlier in this book. It mandates VOA to try to bring about broad and genuine understanding of American society and of specific U.S. policies, that is, to present the American society in its diversity and to broadcast responsible discussion of administration policies. In the latter, VOA differs from its United Kingdom counterpart, the British Broadcasting Corporation — the highly regarded BBC — which has no such obligation to present or even to discuss British foreign policy, although it often does.

The news broadcasts of the Voice of America, as the charter states, must be "accurate, objective, and comprehensive." Above all, they must be independent of government control and interference if VOA is to be recognized and respected by its foreign listeners as a credible source of information. Through its mandate to provide accurate, authoritative, and credible news and information to listeners around the world, VOA fulfills one of the U.S. government's most important public diplomacy objectives.

This has not always been the case. As mentioned earlier, VOA did not divest itself of its Cold War shackles until the end of the 1950s. Since then it has made great strides to become a respected international information medium like the BBC. The latter has long enjoyed a well-deserved reputation for credibility, objectivity, and fairness in its news broadcasts, earned in World War II. Such a reputation is difficult to equal because it takes many years to achieve. Overcoming listeners' perceptions of aggressive partisanship takes even longer.

The VOA charter has codified and strengthened the independence of VOA news. Members of Congress have repeatedly emphasized the importance of the charter and especially of VOA's news independence. The seriousness with which the charter is regarded on the Hill was exemplified by Senator Charles Percy, then chairman of the Senate Foreign Relations Committee, at a Senate authorization hearing in 1976, when he cautioned the acting director of VOA that he would be violating the law if he permitted anyone to interfere with VOA news broadcasts. President Carter, in his memorandum of March 13, 1978, to USICA Director John Reinhardt on Reorganization Plan No. 2, reaffirmed this policy by reminding the director that he would be responsible "for maintaining the independence of VOA news broadcasts."

If one compared the newscasts of VOA and the BBC item by item over a period of time (something I did frequently during my years at VOA between 1976 and 1980), one may have noted differences in editorial judgment but not in accuracy, objectivity, or journalistic quality. VOA's own highly professional and experienced corps of foreign correspondents reporting from strategic spots throughout the world, its stringent rule requiring at least two sources for every news story, and its insulation from outside interference contributed to convincing many of its listeners that VOA had become a reliable source of news and information.

During the first years of the Reagan administration, VOA's managers caused some damage to this reputation by returning to stridency, oversimplification, and lack of sophistication in the writing of editorials. Crafting these editorials more subtly, more imaginatively, and less simplistically might have achieved greater credibility with VOA's listeners. That credibility would have been further enhanced if VOA had adhered more rigorously to the charter requirement to broadcast "responsible discussion and opinion" on administration policies. Something like a radio version of an "op-ed" page can provide the political breadth and maturity that credibility requires.

A related problem for foreign listeners is their frequent inability, based on their own culture and experience, to believe that VOA, which admits it is the official U.S. government radio broadcasting facility, is nonetheless independent of any government control in its news broadcasts. Many listeners — high government officials among them — cannot divest themselves of the notion that if something is broadcast over VOA, it must be official and must therefore have been at least tacitly approved by the U.S. government. A number of our diplomatic representatives abroad report receiving frequent complaints from foreign heads of state and other officials about the content of VOA news broadcasts. These highly placed listeners simply will not accept the fact that

VOA news is insulated from government control and supervision. They thus assume that offending news items are broadcast as deliberate insults or provocations instigated or abetted by the U.S. government.

Walter L. Cutler, U.S. ambassador to Zaire in the late seventies, used to report receiving early morning summonses from President Mobutu, a daily VOA listener. Mobutu would harangue the ambassador about something or other that VOA news had broadcast—"obviously" intended to offend him. Cutler's explanation that neither he nor the State Department had any control over VOA's news content met with disbelief.

Another example of the difficulties inherent in VOA's news independence comes from former Under Secretary of State David D. Newsom, who relates a disastrous experience during a sensitive mission he undertook to Nigeria at the end of their civil war in 1970, when he was assistant secretary for African affairs. Newsom writes that his instructions were to try to persuade General Yakabu Gowon, the Nigerian head of state, to accept "an international commission to survey the reconstruction of Biafra, the secessionist area....Any public mention of the U.S. interest [in this matter] was likely to kill it." At breakfast on the morning of his appointment with General Gowon, Newsom heard the Voice of America broadcasting the gist of the State Department's instructions for his meeting with the Nigerian head of state. "Had there been any chance of successful diplomacy," Newsom concludes, "it died at that moment."[5]

This news item, contends Newsom, was "broadcast to satisfy an American domestic or congressional interest in the subject."[6] Perhaps that was the reason it was released by someone in the State Department, and one could fault those who made it public for lacking sensitivity to the impact the story would make on our diplomatic efforts. One should not, however, blame the messenger. Once the item was in the public domain, it had become a legitimate news item. Whether or not VOA had included it in its news broadcast, someone else would have done so. VOA's lapse would have been noted, to its discredit as an authoritative source of international news.

Such situations present a dilemma in an open society. However, VOA's news independence and the credibility it seeks thereby to achieve is a powerful tool of public diplomacy that should not be compromised. Curiously, the BBC has rarely had this problem. Its worldwide radio operation, the BBC External Service, is entirely financed by a grant from the British Foreign and Commonwealth Office; yet the listening public abroad apparently does not associate the BBC with the British government as they do VOA with the U.S. government.

Another perennial issue for VOA has been the question of how many hours and in what languages it should broadcast. There is the view, forcefully promoted by Kenneth Giddens, VOA's director during the Nixon and Ford administrations, that VOA should be the world's leading international broadcaster, in keeping with U.S. prestige and international obligations. If Radio Moscow broadcasts two thousand hours per week in eighty-five languages, VOA should broadcast a greater number of hours in at least eighty-six languages. In his congressional testimony and public speeches, Giddens complained that in international broadcasting the United States is a second-rate power, transmitting in less than half the languages and roughly half the number of hours as the Soviets. He further decried the fact that VOA did not broadcast in some major world languages, such as German, Japanese, and Italian. Giddens found some sympathy for his views on the Hill, particularly among those members who have consistently supported VOA as a principal anti-Communist weapon.

Others have maintained a different view. Only if budgetary and technological resources were unlimited might the argument for being the biggest and the best be supportable, they say. Under current circumstances, however, VOA should serve not so much as a symbol of international prestige and power but as an effective communications tool that should be deployed judiciously and cost-effectively in the context of the U.S. government's overall public diplomacy effort.

VOA's Special Value

As a communication tool, radio is unique. It is the only medium that can transmit a message directly from the sender to the receiver without having to pass through any intermediary, human or physical, that might be able to affect the tone or content of the message. Thus, in addition to the value of its English and vernacular broadcasts as a credible source of news and information worldwide, the Voice of America is particularly effective, even indispensable, in certain parts of the world and under certain specific circumstances. Among these are the politically denied areas — where governments are able to prevent or control access to all other sources of information; inaccessible or politically unstable areas or those with widely dispersed populations — where other communications media are impractical or impossible; and countries of interest to U.S. policy that have a high level of illiteracy.

The denied areas — principally the Soviet Union, China, and the Communist countries of Eastern Europe, but also including Iran, Afghanistan, Vietnam, and Cambodia, among others — have been prime targets for VOA broadcasting. In the past, few other methods of communicating with the peoples living in China and the Soviet Union were available. Even with the opening to outside contacts in both countries, their areas are so vast, with such huge and widespread populations, that radio — VOA — continues to be the most cost-effective medium of communication.

The political and social changes taking place in the Soviet Union and Eastern Europe during the last six months of 1989 presented new opportunities and challenges for VOA as an important instrument of U.S. public diplomacy, no longer needing to concentrate its technical and editorial ingenuity on the penetration of jamming. Its East Bloc listeners, no longer starved for information or news from the West, had suddenly gained access to multiple domestic sources of uncensored news from home and abroad.

Capitalizing on this new situation, VOA turned to providing direct to listeners in these newly opened societies the up-to-date information they now required — on the opportunities and problems of establishing and operating a democratic society with representative government; on management and business practices in a market-oriented economy; on the free flow of information, unencumbered by censorship; and on judicial systems that represent the rule of law rather than the rule of dictators.

The VOA has addressed this new public diplomacy responsibility by building radio bridges in these countries with national networks and local radio stations, now permitted to cooperate with VOA and make use of VOA's worldwide network of facilities and correspondents. Such radio bridges enable foreign citizens to participate directly in discussions with American specialists and experts on subjects of interest and importance to them, relaying their conversations back and forth via the local radio station and VOA in a joint hookup.

In cooperation with Radio Warsaw, for instance, VOA started a new program on December 4, 1989, in which Polish listeners call their radio station in Warsaw with a question on market economy practices. VOA facilities relay the questions from Warsaw to VOA's studios in Washington and elsewhere in the United

States, where Polish-speaking American experts respond via VOA transmissions to Radio Warsaw, to which the questioner is listening.

Similarly, on November 15, 1989, Lech Walesa's historic address in the U.S. Congress was broadcast live via VOA to Radio Warsaw I, whence it was relayed to radio listeners throughout Poland. Following the speech a fifty-minute discussion between American and Polish citizens in Washington, Chicago, Warsaw, and Katowice was also broadcast live over the VOA-Radio Warsaw bridge. And shortly after President Gorbachev's visit to the Vatican on November 30, 1989, experts on religion broadcasting from Washington, Ottawa, and Bound Brook, New Jersey, discussed the Soviet leader's historic meeting with Pope John Paul II for listeners in the Ukraine via VOA's Ukrainian Service and Radio Kiev. Such radio bridges were already a regular feature of VOA's Hungarian Service and Radio Budapest, with Hungarian listeners participating in live question-and-answer programs on such diverse subjects as constitutional practices, business management, information technology, and marketing.

Time and again, VOA has proved to be the only medium available to U.S. public diplomacy when political upheavals abroad eliminate all other methods of communication. The American media rediscovered this fact in 1979, after the taking of the U.S. hostages in Tehran, and again in the spring of 1989, after the brutal suppression of the pro-democratic demonstrations in China. While public diplomacy professionals have fully appreciated this asset over the years and have argued during periods of budgetary stringency for retaining VOA's capabilities for just such emergencies, the U.S. public usually become aware of VOA's value only during these instances of chaos, when American television and press dramatically focus on the Voice as the sole communications link with people denied all other contact with the outside world.

Radio is also well suited to areas in Africa and Asia that lack a viable communications infrastructure, but which have huge and dispersed populations, combined with high illiteracy rates and a general availability of transistor radios. In Africa, as mentioned earlier, VOA has a second public diplomacy role: It helps fill a void by serving as a medium of cross-cultural communication, providing African news, culture, and other information for African audiences having few other opportunities of communicating with one another.

At the start of the 1990s, taking advantage of new technologies and drastically changed political conditions to address the information needs of its listeners abroad, the Voice of America represented a unique public diplomacy medium for the U.S. government.

Technological Challenges

A major consideration in radio's effectiveness as a method of international communication is technology. Radio as a medium depends on available technology for transmission of its messages. International radio broadcasting is transmitted primarily via shortwave. VOA therefore requires an audience that has, and regularly listens to, shortwave receiving equipment. Such an audience exists in the Soviet Union and in China, both of which use shortwave for their domestic radio broadcasting because of the vast distances to be covered.[7]

Longtime jamming of VOA broadcasts in Russian and other Soviet languages made listening in some areas very difficult or impossible. The jamming was expensive, however, and acted as an irritant for Soviet citizens. Many resented their government's efforts to deny them access to information from abroad, and some created ingenious ways of eliminating the grating noise, thus enabling them to hear the forbidden broadcasts. The Soviets ceased jamming VOA's Soviet-language transmissions in 1987, perhaps as a sign of *glasnost*; and on December 1, 1988, they stopped jamming Radio Liberty for the first time since the station went on the air in the early 1950s.

The United States is somewhat handicapped in its international broadcasting via shortwave because its transmissions have to cross two oceans to reach the majority of listeners. While VOA's long-distance radio signals are now transmitted via satellite with a minimum loss of quality, VOA still needs a network of relay stations in Europe, Africa, and Asia to transmit programs to its target audiences from satellite downlinks. The Soviet Union, in contrast, can place its transmitters within its thousands of miles of border and still reach all its foreign audiences except those in North and South America. Having to rely on an overseas network of relay stations is fraught with political, security, and technical problems that are lessened only through the cooperation of close allies and friends, such as Great Britain and West Germany, which have not only permitted VOA transmitters on their soil but in some cases even put their own at our disposal.

USIA launched a major technological modernization program for VOA early in the Reagan administration. This program, at first amply supported by congressional appropriations, was designed to modernize and improve existing relay stations and to build new ones (an expensive investment in transmitters, antennas, real estate, and personnel). Unfortunately, curtailment of funding in 1987 and 1988 has delayed VOA modernization. Areas that are fertile territory for VOA listenership continue to lack a good signal because existing transmitters and antennas cannot reach them adequately. One such important geographical gap for VOA is in Soviet Central Asia, Western China, and South Asia. These are largely inaccessible from VOA's relay stations in Greece and the Philippines.

Medium-wave broadcasting, as well as long wave and FM, have replaced shortwave in an increasing number of countries around the world. Many of these areas are out of reach of VOA reception because medium- and long-wave frequencies — geographically limited as they are — are nationally allocated, controlled by the International Telecommunication Union, and hard to come by. Fortunately, VOA gained access many years ago to some of these medium-wave frequencies, which it has been able to hold on to with the cooperation of the host governments, thus giving VOA access to medium-wave radio listeners who are important targets in public diplomacy terms. Most of the countries of Eastern Europe can be reached from VOA's medium-wave relay station in Munich, for example, and the Arab world is at least partially accessible from VOA's medium-wave transmitters in Greece — in Kavala and on the island of Rhodes. Southern China is accessible from VOA's powerful medium-wave transmitter in Thailand.

Much of Central and South America is also a medium-wave listening territory and would be largely inaccessible to VOA coverage were it not for the acquisition of medium-wave relay stations in Antigua, Belize, and Costa Rica.[8] In addition, over one thousand local radio stations throughout Latin America regularly carry the news reports of VOA's American Republics Division, "fed" to these stations via satellite or shortwave. VOA, however, also broadcasts directly via shortwave throughout Latin America in Spanish and Portuguese and claims an overall regular listenership ranging from 1 percent to 5 percent, except for the approximately 10 percent of adults who reportedly listen at least once a week in El Salvador.

Setting Priorities

Because both technological and budgetary limitations restrict VOA's worldwide reach, its managers need to marshal VOA's resources for broadcasting to those areas of the world where they best serve U.S. public diplomacy. Perennial opposition to introducing VOA Japanese broadcasts, for instance, recognizes, first, that Japan is media saturated; second, that VOA would have a difficult time building an audience and competing with other established radio stations there; third, that Japan, a democratic society, provides its citizens with a choice and abundance of uncensored information; and fourth, that USIA could employ its resources in Japan more cost-effectively in other public diplomacy programs.

Much the same reasons could have been applied to the introduction of VOA Europe in 1985. The argument in favor of the Munich-based VOA Europe (broadcasting on medium-wave and FM stations, in English and eventually in other Western European languages) was that young Europeans were not being reached adequately with information about the United States by their own media or by other U.S. public diplomacy programs, and that an attractive and imaginative radio program aimed at this young audience would fill this alleged information void. Even if VOA Europe were able to build significant audiences, however, one may seriously question the cost-effectiveness of a program that contains about 80 percent music — typically about ten minutes of hard information per hour and fifty minutes or more of audience-building music.

Could the considerable resources devoted to VOA Europe not be used more cost-effectively for communicating with Europe's young people, as, for example, through exchanges? Rather than scattering its resources on programs and in areas where it is not the best medium for achieving U.S. public diplomacy objectives, VOA could employ the talents of its dedicated and superb professional staff and its limited technical resources in broadcasting important information to those areas of the world and to those audiences where it is the only, or at least the most effective, medium of communication. VOA can also use its unique resources and expertise, as mentioned earlier, for training journalists in the Third World to become responsible and technically well-equipped members of a population that values, practices, and promotes democratic principles.

As noted at the beginning of the chapter, VOA is one of only two USIA media not under the control of the country public affairs officer. Yet some PAOs have always thought about Voice of America broadcasts to their countries in the terms outlined here, namely as a communications medium supporting their public diplomacy objectives. In the Soviet Union, for instance, PAOs have long considered the Voice their most important asset in conveying information from and about the United States. In other countries they have felt that VOA constitutes a strong cultural bond between the United States and their particular host country.

The working relationships between these PAOs in the field and their VOA colleagues in Washington are, in such cases, highly productive and worthy of emulation by others. The PAOs recognize the independence of VOA's news operations. They do not interfere with those operations, and they keep anyone else from interfering. Just as they would not think of interfering with any reporter of a commercial medium, PAOs do not interfere with VOA correspondents working in their countries; yet they would give those VOA correspondents the same professional attention and support as given to other American journalists.

At the same time, PAOs can communicate with VOA about those aspects of their country programs in which the Voice can help. They can suggest subjects for VOA coverage, comment, and analysis — subjects that VOA is better able to convey than other media at their disposal. Such program suggestions are particularly useful for VOA's vernacular language services since these are usually country- or area-specific, in contrast to VOA's English-language broadcasts, which must appeal to a much wider audience.

The applicable essentials here are these: that the Voice of America recognize its responsibility to convey to its audiences abroad, in a manner both relevant and comprehensible, the "balanced and comprehensive projection of significant American thought and institutions" called for in its charter; that it also present "the policies of the United States...and...responsible discussion and opinion on these policies"; and that the public affairs officers of the U.S. Information Service regard VOA as an important support element in the attainment of their country public diplomacy objectives.

NOTES

1. The most comprehensive compendium of both technical and program information about VOA — including a listing of languages in which VOA broadcasts, the number of hours broadcast in each, and the location and equipment of VOA relay stations — is contained in its yearly publication, *Voice of America*.

2. A formal statement of principles to guide VOA was commissioned in 1959 by VOA Director Henry Loomis and approved in 1960 by USIA Director George

V. Allen, who had it issued as a VOA directive. By the time Edward R. Murrow endorsed it in late 1962, the directive had become known as the VOA Charter.

3. VOA Charter, in PL 94-350, signed July 12, 1976, by Gerald R. Ford, President of the United States.

4. Speech delivered at ceremony commemorating the twentieth anniversary of VOA, USIA press release, 26 Feb. 1962.

5. David D. Newsom, *Diplomacy and the American Democracy* (Bloomington: Indiana University Press, 1988), 186.

6. Ibid.

7. In the United States, only radio buffs have radios with shortwave bands, a fact leading one to wonder why Radio Moscow and other international broadcasters spend valuable resources attempting to reach U.S. audiences via shortwave broadcasts.

8. As of early 1989, Antigua and Costa Rica were scheduled for closing, victims of budget cuts.

6
Worldnet

There is no doubt in my mind that when the annals of U.S. public diplomacy are written, the name of Charles Wick will loom largest for his pioneering work in developing the medium of television as a viable instrument of American public diplomacy. Without his energy, persistence, and political clout, USIA could not have advanced into the television age as quickly and pervasively as it did — much earlier than any of its foreign competitors and much sooner than most of the agency's career public diplomats could have imagined.

When Wick became director of USIA in 1981, he brought with him to Washington his interest in, one might even say his obsession with, television. To some career officers at the time, it seemed that television as a communications medium was one of Wick's only two interests (the other being radio), which he wanted everyone to promote to the exclusion of anything else the agency was involved in. Even as he came to realize that there might be other instruments of public diplomacy, he singlemindedly and aggressively worked to establish television as the principal new star in USIA's international communications universe.

That television would become an important information and cultural medium throughout the world, and an increasingly effective tool of public diplomacy, was clear to most of the professionals; but many had been stymied for some time by three problems. First, the international community appeared to oppose the unencumbered transmission of television signals across international borders without the consent of receiving countries.[1] Second, even if reception by private individuals of foreign transmissions were legally and politically possible, receiving antennas were still inordinately expensive for most people. And third, it was difficult to get independent, highly sophisticated television stations in Europe to accept programs produced by a foreign government, even though American commercial programs were regular and highly popular fare on these networks. (A similar situation exists in the United States, where the major networks would not normally be willing to put on a program produced by a foreign government.)

In Western Europe (and to some extent even in Eastern Europe), technology overtook politics with the advent of television transmission via satellite. Anyone with a receiving antenna — whether an independent cable television station, which would retransmit programs to its subscribers, or an individual with the wherewithal to acquire a receiving–only dish — could now receive television broadcasts from elsewhere in Europe, or even from the United States and Canada across the ocean.

The issue for USIA, therefore, was not one of overcoming technological or political restrictions, but of managerial determination and vision, technical innovation, and the availability of budgetary resources. And that is where Charles Wick led the charge. He believed in "the power of television" to sway and convince mass audiences, and he made it his personal goal to promote through television what *he* considered USIA's principal public diplomacy objectives — to have President Reagan recognized as a world leader, and to persuade the world of the evil nature of Soviet Communism.

Wick argued, cajoled, negotiated, stormed, flattered, manipulated, persuaded, and fought for his goal. His targets were the Office of Management and Budget, the Congress, the State Department, other nations' ministers of communications, American ambassadors, his own Washington staff, and USIS public affairs officers abroad. And he achieved unprecedented success in the new technology he instituted.

With newly provided funds and technical expertise, USIA established Euronet, a system — now called Worldnet — consisting of a network of television receiving–only antenna dishes located in overseas U.S. installations, including embassies, consulates, cultural centers, and USIS libraries and offices. The system was set up initially in Europe and subsequently in other regions. Its antennas receive a television signal via satellite from USIA studios in Washington or elsewhere in the United States. This one-way video-receiving circuit was coupled with a two-way audio circuit. Thus, for example, a group of journalists assembled in USIS cultural centers in London, Bonn, Paris, Rome, and Brussels could see and interview the secretary of state in Washington as though in a press conference (although the secretary could not see his interlocutors).

For the sake of historical accuracy, it should be noted that the precursor of Worldnet was USIA's "Electronic Dialogue." Begun in the early 1970s, it originally involved self-contained discussion programs in which an American participant in the United States would speak over a designated telephone circuit with a group of journalists or specialists assembled in a USIS center or American embassy abroad on a pre-announced subject of mutual interest. On special occasions, particularly if a foreign television station might share the cost, a one-way television circuit would be established so that the foreign participants could see their American interlocutor as they spoke with him or her. That, in turn, evolved into the Euronet/Worldnet system, with its USIS-controlled satellite television-receiving antennas. The new system was dramatically in-augurated in the wake of the U.S. incursion in Grenada in November 1983, when a series of U.S. policymakers, including U.S. Ambassador to the United Nations Jeane Kirkpatrick and Defense Secretary Caspar Weinberger, made themselves available for questioning by journalists in European capitals. An early newsmaking coup using this new technology came in 1983 when an extraordinary Euronet hook-up was arranged. President Reagan in Washington and German Chancellor Helmut Kohl in Athens (attending a European Community conference) spoke with the American astronauts and their West German colleague in a U.S. space shuttle circling the globe. That historic conversation, linking two heads of government on two continents with U.S. and German astronauts in outer space, was broadcast in prime time in Germany and elsewhere in Europe.

The technology was in place, but what indeed was to be its purpose?

Dissatisfied with the way U.S. policies were presented on European television networks through the allegedly distorted lenses of European journalists, Director Wick initially thought of Euronet/Worldnet as a vehicle to get American policymakers like the secretary of state directly onto prime-time European television news shows, where they could explicate U.S. policy in answer to questions posed by correspondents in the various capitals. Wick believed that an appearance by the secretary of state in such an interview would be important and dramatic enough for a lead story in prime-time network news programs throughout Europe. In other words, Wick thought of the technology as a means of making news, and he was highly critical of the European television networks and his USIS staffs in the European capitals if these supposedly headline-making interviews were not prominently included in the newscasts. In the opinion of many USIS officers serving in Europe at the time, including the author, that was an unrealistic expectation for the new technology.

The German media, by way of example, are so well endowed that they do not consider Worldnet, beyond its initial novelty value, as a major asset in producing their news. They have too many other sources of information to need this one — especially coming, as it does, from a foreign government. If we in USIS desired to get U.S. policymakers' views onto German television, several German television producers told us, all we needed to do was to have them make themselves available for an interview to one of the German network correspondents in Washington, who would make sure that their story got on the air — and it would cost the U.S. government nothing.

A number of PAOs in Europe felt that USIA had created an exciting new method of communication without, however, coming to grips with how to employ it most effectively and efficiently. It needed experimentation and creative thought. Some PAOs became convinced that the new medium could be used to best advantage in different ways in different areas of the world. What works in one place will not necessarily work everywhere, they reasoned, and, conversely, what does not work in one country might well work in another. Thus, while Worldnet may not be a cost-effective medium as a "newsmaker" on West European television, it may be the best medium for this purpose in, say, Lagos, Bogotá, Karachi, or Manila, whose television networks have no permanent correspondents stationed in Washington and, in any case, would likely find a satellite link to transmit an interview with the U.S. secretary of state too expensive.

In Western Europe, on the other hand, Worldnet has served in a uniquely effective manner by bringing together busy experts and specialists for substantive discussions. Worldnet is the only way such a discussion could take place, since the American experts would find it impossible to travel to numerous cities for personal meetings. For example, such a "face-to-ear" discussion occurred via Worldnet between the noted American heart surgeon, Dr. Michael de Bakey, sitting in a Houston studio, and heart surgeons in various European cities. This interchange was highly regarded and appreciated by the participants and could not have taken place in any other way.

Another example was a lengthy Worldnet conversation between then-Secretary of Agriculture John Block and European agricultural journalists and trade officials, discussing U.S. agricultural export policies and trade relations with the European Economic Community. What came out of this conference was not front-page or prime time TV news, but it served a valuable public diplomacy purpose, one that no other information medium could have delivered as effectively, by providing timely and significant information about U.S. agriculture from an administration official to a selected audience of gatekeepers. (Secretary Block reportedly also benefited from the discussion by learning firsthand some of his interlocutors' criticisms and problems.)

During 1988, a major expansion of technical facilities took place. By the end of the year, USIA had installed ninety-five receiving-only antennas for Worldnet — forty-six in Europe, twenty-seven in Latin America, nine in Africa, and thirteen in Asia and the Middle East. According to the agency, a total of 156 antennas were ultimately to be installed covering every continent. With the new communications system in place in many capitals and other major cities around the world, Worldnet was transmitting in 1988 five hours per day to Europe, one hour each to Latin America in Spanish and Portuguese, four hours per day to four locations in Africa, and ad hoc programs to other parts of the world.[2]

These transmissions were not all the interactive type of programming described above. Such interviews and discussions constituted only a small if significant proportion of materials transmitted. Various other materials were "fed" to USIS posts via Worldnet: U.S. network news shows, weekend network interview programs, State Department and White house press briefings (these for the information of embassy staffs only), and cultural, scientific and educational programs produced or acquired by USIA. Because the system was in place and operating, agency management believed it should therefore be used to capacity. Too little thought was given, perhaps, to whether these program feeds were useful for public diplomacy purposes, or even as a source of information to embassy staffs. Just monitoring these transmissions requires considerable staff time, and deciding on whether and how to use this steady flow of material is beyond the capability of many USIS posts.

The agency claims that Worldnet reaches "over five million households in 15 countries through 133 cable television systems, and 126 local broadcast networks in six countries with a potential viewer audience of 13 million."[3] The service, according to USIA, "is also available in over 31,915 hotel rooms in 226 hotels throughout Europe through closed-circuit systems."[4] While these statistics appear impressive, it is difficult to determine what they mean. Having 32,000 hotel rooms wired for Worldnet says nothing about the audience. And how does one evaluate a "potential" viewing audience of thirteen million unless one can determine numbers of actual viewers, who they are, and what programs they watch?

Worldnet, in 1985, was operated from Washington almost like a textbook example of technology replacing substance, of the medium constituting the message. Country public affairs officers had little input as to how this impressive new medium might specifically serve U.S. public diplomacy objectives, yet they had to spend a great deal of time and effort trying to integrate it into the totality of their country programs, lest it be deemed not cost-effective. Still, there was hope that in time the hype (and the hyperbole) would recede and resources would be more rationally focused, as the objectives, audiences, and programs might be scrutinized more rigorously and careful thought be given how best to use this new medium.

The change came about in the fall of 1988, when Congress mandated curtailment of daily transmissions of "passive" programming (regular daily transmissions not specifically requested by USIS posts) and limited the use of Worldnet to interactive programming, for which the medium is ideally designed. According to a report from Bonn in January 1989, Worldnet's offices in Washington had become sensitive to the public affairs officer's suggestions. USIS Germany was averaging three to five interactive dialogues weekly, most of them suggested by Bonn. Sometimes, the report continued, USIS Bonn would "hook up two or three branch posts with one or two other European cities and Washington to comprise a dialogue with a German flavor — or have a program exclusively for the German audience." Because Worldnet is in the German cable system, USIS staff are able to set up a dialogue at any site with a cable outlet, allowing "much flexibility in planning conferences away from USIS installations." The conclusion was that USIS Germany felt they could "justify Worldnet *now* in terms of public diplomacy objectives" and that Worldnet dialogues would "draw apace in importance with the American Participant program" in their programming mix.[5]

Until the fall of 1988, USIA management had been too involved in the creation of the new medium to be expected to regard its brainchild critically and determine how to employ it effectively. Now, budgetary necessities have mandated rationalization of Worldnet's advantages over other media in its ability to focus on specific audiences and specific objectives at a specific time. Thus Worldnet joins other USIA media as an innovative, imaginative, highly effective tool serving the U.S. government's overall public diplomacy effort.

NOTES

1. When the question was debated in the UN General Assembly in the early 1980s, the United States was the only nation to vote in favor of free and uncontrolled transmission of television signals across international borders comparable to the free and unencumbered transmission of shortwave radio signals that has prevailed throughout this century.

2. *Worldnet Fact Sheet*, USIA, June 1988; *Worldnet: Putting Satellite Technology to Work for Global Understanding*, USIA-TV, Washington, DC (undated).

3. USIA *Worldnet Fact Sheet*, June 1988.

4. Ibid.

5. Letter dated 2 January 1989 to the author from Minister Terrence Catherman, country public affairs officer in Bonn.

7

The Advisory Function

The preceding chapters of this book dealt with the "active" aspects of public diplomacy: conveying information and eliciting understanding abroad for the United States and its policies, primarily through the efforts of the public affairs officers and their USIS staffs in the field. The other integral element of the practice of public diplomacy, as spelled out for the first time in President Kennedy's Mission Statement for USIA in January 1963, is the advisory function. As noted in Chapter 2, Kennedy called upon USIA to help achieve U.S. foreign policy objectives by providing advice to policymakers "on the implications of foreign opinion for present and contemplated U.S. policies, programs and official statements."[1] As President Carter made clear in 1978, this means helping to insure that government policymakers adequately understand "foreign public opinion and culture."[2] The advisory function is thus directly related to the "learning experience" and the "two-way street," terms frequently applied to the intercultural communications process.

For a foreign policy to be effective, it should be so shaped and promulgated that it can be understood and have the best possible chance of acceptance by the foreign people toward whom it is directed. This necessitates *our* understanding and consideration of the motives, the cultural background, the history and traditions, as well as the psychology, of the people with whom we are communicating. It means, in Edward R. Murrow's words, having those concerned with public diplomacy in on the take-offs of our foreign policy endeavors and not just the crash landings.

One way in which this advisory function is carried out is in commenting on emerging administration policies. In one such instance, the National Security

106

Council called upon the director of USIA to contribute to an examination of NSC Presidential Review Memorandum no. 28 of May 20, 1977, which dealt with a major tenet of U.S. foreign policy, namely the defense and promotion of human rights. The acting director of the Voice of America, taking into account his professional experience and perspective, provided the agency's director with the following analysis:

> Both the words and the concept of "human rights" have a different meaning for us than they do for people in many parts of the world....The comprehension and acceptance abroad of our understanding of the concept pose psychological barriers which need to be overcome.
>
> If our concept of "human rights" were limited to protection of life and opposition to torture, we would have no difficulty in making it understood and accepted. But we normally include in our definition other human rights important to the American people, among them the dignity of the individual, freedom from arbitrary arrest, right to fair trial and freedom of choice.
>
> In countries where history and tradition have not laid a foundation for the exercise of these human rights — where people have never had them (in contrast to those countries where people may have had them but have lost them) — it is difficult to make people understand *our* preoccupation with these rights for ourselves and for other peoples. I dare say the majority of the world's peoples, especially those in developing countries, are in that category.
>
> For peoples who have never experienced human rights as we define the term, they are less important than other rights which they would include under their concept of the term, such as the right to have enough food for themselves and their families, the right to have shelter, the right to an education. These *we* take for granted, but many people don't and can't, and they assume a much higher priority for them than some of the political rights so inalienable to us. (The right to free choice, for instance, does not appear to many peoples as important at all. They think that it is wasteful.)
>
> The Soviet Union and other Communist countries...on the other hand, always emphasize their alleged concern with these needs and thereby strike a note of greater empathy and understanding in the non-industrialized world than we are able to do....
>
> In pursuit of the human rights objective therefore we ought to keep several points clearly in mind and act accordingly:
>
> 1. *Our* human rights are not necessarily others' human rights.

2. In order to make an international human rights campaign successful, our human rights aspirations must be compatible with those of other peoples whom we are trying to convince.

3. We must understand and be empathetic to others' human rights aspirations.

4. We must take especial care to make *our* concept of human rights understandable and meaningful to other peoples.[3]

Professional public diplomats must have knowledge and understanding of the foreign audiences with whom they deal. Furthermore, they must also have a grasp of current attitudes on the part of their foreign audience on issues affecting the bilateral relationship. This knowledge and understanding help the public diplomat in contributing to a more effective formulation and execution of our foreign policy and programs. If the policymakers, however, pursue a policy that the public diplomat knows is going to be unpopular with an audience, there is little he or she can do to prevent negative reaction. But, as W. Phillips Davison suggests, the communication professional ought to urge strongly, "Before you complicate my life by antagonizing my audience, at least give me my day in court."[4]

How does this advisory function manifest itself in field practice?

Based on their knowledge of the language, culture, and traditions of the country and their understanding of its political and social ambiance, the public affairs officer and the USIS staff read the press, listen to the radio, and watch television. Above all, they talk to many people — the gatekeepers and opinion molders — to learn their attitudes and views, their prejudices, hang-ups, predilections, and misperceptions, on issues of importance to the bilateral relationship. The PAO discusses his or her analysis and assessment of all these impressions and information with the ambassador and embassy colleagues and contributes opinions and recommendations to the embassy's reporting, negotiating, and policy formulation. The ambassador communicates with the Department of State (and nowadays, rather often, directly with the National Security Council and the White House) at his or her own initiative or on instructions from Washington, forwarding the embassy's analyses, comments, and recommendations. One such advisory message was a public affairs goal paper for President Reagan's visit to the Federal Republic of Germany in June 1982, prepared by the public affairs officer and his staff (reproduced herein as Appendix 4).

Another example was a request from the Department of State in 1984 to report the embassy's views on anti-Americanism in the Federal Republic and to suggest ways of counteracting it. The ambassador's assessment, largely prepared by the USIS staff, again demonstrated the advisory role played by the Foreign Service's public diplomats, working within an embassy's country team. USIA Washington summarized the embassy's assessment for the attention of the director, as follows:

American Embassy Bonn sees three manifestations of intellectual tendencies that are sometimes called "anti-American": (a) committed ideologues who oppose everything that America represents, including, ultimately, democracy itself—a small, relatively unimportant but vocal group; (b) people who actively oppose certain American policies or who criticize aspects of American society—these constitute a conspicuous and vocal group that considers itself no more anti-American than the loyal opposition in the U.S.; (c) persons who, because of ignorance and lack of experience, do not know America, cannot judge it properly, and are exposed to misperceptions that they parrot back to others. This group is the largest, especially among young people.

Bonn's report states that "anti-American bias among opinion leaders is rare" in the FRG, and it examines five major institutions: education, press and media, political institutions, churches, and labor unions. It focuses particularly on problems in education, where Vietnam generation teachers carry 1960s prejudices into their instruction. It also cites difficulties with two major weekly publications and some elements of radio and television, while stating that, generally speaking, German newspapers are responsible and objective. In the churches, unions and elsewhere, the radicalizing influence of small groups of "young Turks" is cited.

Bonn's report states German misunderstanding of America is the result of the "drifting apart" of our two countries. As the best remedy, it proposes increased German-American contacts on all levels, especially exchanges for students and other young people.[5]

As part of their advisory function, USIS posts routinely send to Washington summaries of editorial coverage by local press, radio, and television on issues of importance to U.S. foreign policy interests. In countries of bilateral policy significance, these media summaries are sent daily and early enough in the day for USIA Washington to compile them into world media reaction reports that are delivered to the White House, the State Department, and other government agencies.

PAOs sometimes chafe under the administrative burden of this requirement. Experienced bilingual editorial personnel must monitor the electronic and print media and come in early in the morning to prepare their reports for timely transmittal to Washington. Yet the importance of this task is impressed on them repeatedly by the number and high level of inquiries and comments they receive about their reporting, because Washington policymakers seem to accept these media reports as fairly typical and comprehensive expressions of foreign public opinion.

Only a few of the most critical posts must prepare these media summaries on a daily basis, and they usually restrict themselves to coverage of issues suggested by Washington. PAOs add to this list any topic that they consider important for Washington's attention, including internal political, economic, or social developments. Posts in some sensitive countries whose media are censored or government-controlled also have a daily reporting requirement. Posts of lesser importance to the ongoing conduct of U.S. foreign affairs send media reaction reports less frequently, when they are specifically requested by Washington or when the PAO believes they are of interest.

The PAO's assessment of public attitudes and other factors that affect the bilateral relationship are part of the annual country plan and, in some areas, of quarterly letters, such as those required of PAOs in Europe by the European area director in 1980–85. Perhaps more timely and more pertinent than the country plan assessments, these informal PAO letters described the current state of local public diplomacy issues, how the USIS post copes with them, how the agency might help in addressing them, and what worked or did not work. The letters also described the local public opinion climate as it affected USIS operations. These less formal assessments — sent in fairly regular intervals — can be particularly useful to USIA Washington headquarters in its advisory role vis-à-vis the White House, the National Security Council, and the Department of State. Thus, for instance, a PAO could discuss the post's views on an upcoming visit by the secretary of state, how the local media might treat the visit, what the public will expect from it, and what the secretary might do to help U.S. public diplomacy efforts. (One such quarterly letter is reproduced in Appendix 5.)

USIA's research capability in gauging public attitudes toward bilateral issues can sometimes benefit posts in the field. West Germany, for example, is fertile ground for public opinion surveys. The Germans conduct them and permit others to do so on practically any subject—whether to gauge their preference for cheeses or their resistance to INF deployment. The result, some claim, is that the German population is the most surveyed and probed in the world. To help USIS posts in Germany tailor their public diplomacy programs, USIA was willing to analyze German attitudes, especially, at USIS request, those of young people. It was hoped that professionally conducted surveys might provide better and more reliable information on public opinion than the posts were able to obtain through their own often imperfect means.

These surveys served their purpose with partial success. (For an example, see the case study on INF deployment in Chapter 12.) Their main drawback was that the results usually took too long to be of operational value in the short run, and they were often contradictory in their conclusions, depending on the timing of the surveys, other extraneous factors, and the way questions were asked. In general, however, although never conclusive they added considerably to USIS knowledge of German perceptions, political leanings, prejudices, and ideological convictions.

USIA's Office of Research could be of greater assistance to PAOs than it has been in the past, not only in helping them assess public attitudes, but also in measuring the effectiveness of USIS programs and media in terms of audiences and in relation to cost. In theory the Office of Research has had that capability, but it has always been handicapped in performing such valuable research and surveying, especially in a timely fashion, by personnel and budgetary constrictions.

Public diplomacy's advisory capability is an asset to policymakers to the extent that it is included not only in the execution of foreign policy abroad, but also in its planning and formulation. Whether that is done, in Washington, by including USIA participation on the level of the National Security Council is not the issue here. Rather, it has been to emphasize the importance of the advisory responsibility in the context of the conduct of public diplomacy and to explain its functioning in the field.

NOTES

1. Memorandum for the Director, USIA, from John F. Kennedy, 25 Jan. 1963.

2. The White House, Memorandum for Director, International Communication Agency, 13 Mar. 1978.

3. Memorandum dated 1 June 1977 [in author's files].

4. Davison, *International Political Communication*, 166.

5. Summary of Bonn embassy telegram, in 1984 USIA European Area Office Memorandum to the Director of USIA, Washington [in author's files].

8

A Critique of U.S. Public Diplomacy

One of this generation's most respected American diplomats, David Newsom, who during his career spent several years as a practitioner of public diplomacy, has been critical of the way it has been conducted:

> In practice, it has been extremely difficult to carry on effectively a government information program [abroad] in the environment of free American democracy. USIA has fallen far short of its basic goal of creating broad international support for U.S. interests and policies. The organizers were naive in many respects. They imagined the international public environment to be fundamentally sympathetic to the American message. Instead, USIA's message has, like official policies, encountered a complex and occasionally hostile reception, even in areas outside Soviet influence.[1]

Americans, says Newsom, see this failure in terms of their belief "that if their policies are not acceptable to others, it is because the nation has not been sufficiently effective in 'selling' the policies."[2]

Public diplomacy cannot convert unacceptable policies into acceptable ones, however. But part of the blame, Newsom readily acknowledges, must be assigned to those who oversell public diplomacy as a magic cure for the myriad foreign affairs problems that we face.

USIA directors have at times exaggerated the effectiveness of public diplomacy programs because they thought they needed to do so in order to convince the Congress to appropriate the necessary resources for the agency's activities. Realizing that USIA is not a permanent department of the U.S. government with its own domestic constituency, they sought to justify its budget and, especially, increases for new programs and technological improvements by demonstrating, statistically and dramatically, USIA's alleged successes.

Some career Foreign Service officers, both in traditional and in public diplomacy, have held the view that if USIA's aims were limited as per President Carter's memorandum to promoting understanding of America and its policies, its efforts could be justified and their effectiveness, in some cases, even documented, but that support or even acceptance of our policies by foreign publics is a goal that is overly optimistic and therefore unrealistic. If public diplomacy cannot live up to what has been promised, a disappointed Congress may then find in USIA a convenient scapegoat for others' policy failures and handicap the agency's efforts further by curtailing its resources.

During the Reagan administration, for example, the impressive technological innovation of Worldnet, as a new and potentially highly effective medium of communication, was jeopardized by USIA's inflated statistics allegedly documenting its early successes. Meaningless publicity, noted earlier, that the new service was reaching "31,935 hotel rooms in 255 hotels throughout Europe" and "over five million households in 15 countries"[3] is pure puffery and lacks credibility for anyone seriously wishing to evaluate this medium.

The ballyhoo over USIA's 1981 television spectacular "Let Poland Be Poland" is another example of oversell. The program was meant to elicit sympathy for the Polish people's loss of freedom and to gain worldwide support for their resistance against Soviet-manipulated oppression. However, USIA's director could not be convinced by his professional staff that his approach would not have the desired effect among foreign viewers but would instead be completely counterproductive, as one friendly European television producer put it, demonstrating naïveté. "You can't convince Europeans of America's seriousness and its concern for the Polish people by bringing on Hollywood celebrities and having Frank Sinatra sing a couple of songs," he told the author. Yet even eight years later, USIA's domestic publicity listed "Let Poland Be Poland" as one of its most successful achievements, claiming "...185 million people in 50 countries saw at least 30 minutes or more of the [90-minute] telecast....Three- to thirty-minute highlights were shown in 17 countries and seen by at least 200 million persons, including 100 million in China."[4]

It is natural that congressional and other critics view such hyperbole with skepticism, and that this skepticism is then transferred to other, possibly more deserving USIA programs.

Another perennial problem that confronts the career practitioner of public diplomacy is the one-dimensional ideological approach that some USIA directors have adopted both in directing the agency's programs and in selling the agency to the Congress. Such directors have represented anti-Communism as practically the only justification for USIA's existence. For them, everything else the agency did was subsidiary to this, the agency's main purpose. This way of thinking held two dangers for the agency: First, if it turned out that USIA's anti-Communist activities did not produce the desired results in diminishing the menace the Soviet Union posed to the democracies, the agency would be discredited in the eyes of many of its supporters. Second, if somehow the Communist menace were to disappear or be modified as a principal issue facing the United States, the rationale for the agency's existence would be endangered.

A serious problem in many areas of the world, for example, one that USIA is both qualified and expected to cope with, is Soviet disinformation (or "Active Measures," in Soviet terminology). These campaigns spread deliberately false information to confuse or subvert foreign publics in the interest of furthering Soviet aims and ideology. In countries where this problem exists, PAOs must concern themselves with countering these Soviet "Active Measures." With the assistance of the agency's specialists in this field, they work to counteract Soviet disinformation, usually by exposing the source of the lies, documenting their falseness, and condemning the Soviets' venality in spreading them. A distorted impression of USIA's broader purposes is created, however, when the agency launches such a worldwide publicity campaign as "Project Truth," announced in 1981 to combat Soviet "Active Measures" and designated as a central USIA objective.

Indeed, Soviet propaganda efforts, including "Active Measures," have been powerful weapons in the Communist arsenal and have posed a threat to democratic interests. That "this is a struggle, above all else, for the minds of men" has been recognized as far back as President Truman's "Campaign of Truth." But that wise president's policy advocated making ourselves known "as we really are" and endeavoring "to see to it that other peoples receive a full and fair picture of American life and of the aims and policies of the U.S. Government." That, he felt, was the best way of combating Soviet ideology.

Public diplomacy's potential for contributing to the conduct of U.S. foreign policy — and, at the same time, for solidifying its support in the foreign affairs community, in the Congress, and among the American public — could be enhanced if its announced goals were scaled down. Those enunciated in President Carter's 1978 memorandum offer a useful model, namely (to quote once again): "to reduce the degree to which misperceptions and misunderstandings complicate relations between the United States and other nations"; to achieve "the clearest possible understanding of differing points of view[;]...to encourage the sharing of ideas and cultural activities among the people of the United States and the peoples of other nations"; to have "other nations and other peoples know where this country stands and why"; and to have them "understand our values, our institutions — the vitality of our culture."[5]

These positive goals expressed in measured terms appear more in keeping with an overall realistic approach to foreign affairs. Rather than striving for ideological or political "victory" (implying defeat for the other side), these goals point toward managing and representing our interests, protecting our national security, and maintaining peace.

The communications process that underlies the conduct of public diplomacy is best maintained as a dialogue — a two-way relationship. Such a relationship suggests informing, understanding, and persuading rather than gaining superiority, making points, or achieving victory.

Dynamic USIA directors, as presidential appointees, understandably want to leave their mark. They would do well, however, to learn from the experience of their predecessors. As a first step, they ought to study and become familiar with the process that is public diplomacy, recognize its limits, and grasp its opportunities. Second, they should not confuse their personal ideological or political agenda with the objectives to be achieved through public diplomacy. Third, they ought not, in their ambition to succeed, oversell the potential of public diplomacy lest they contribute to diminishing it.

Finding understanding and support in Congress for a U.S. Information Agency with more reasonable goals and more limited expectation of effectiveness should not be as difficult now as it may have been in the past. Congressional approval of educational and cultural exchange programs has increased along with legislative familiarity with their objectives, operations, and successes. Support for exchanges has not been at the expense of such other public diplomacy programs as the Voice of America, libraries, and publications, nor of recent efforts to enter into the age of television. To keep the Congress and the American public informed about these activities without promising unattainable successes should be a priority for any director of the agency who wants to leave a personal imprint on the U.S. government's public diplomacy.

An even more basic problem facing public diplomacy in a democratic society, to which David Newsom alluded in his book, is the question whether any government program can compete with, much less prevail over, the daily onslaught of information, impressions, and perceptions to which foreign audiences are exposed through commercial or private channels such as film, television, advertising, press services, and tourism. For years the Germans have complained to their American counterparts about the image of contemporary Germany fed the American public through frequent repetition of the popular TV series, "Hogan's Heroes." If they worry about the impression that Werner Klemperer's Colonel Klink makes on American television viewers, one must surely be concerned about the cumulative impact on German audiences of "Dallas," "Dynasty," "Falcon Crest," Marlboro ads, and punk rock, not to mention Lyndon LaRouche and his partisans demonstrating in front of Social Democratic Party headquarters on the streets of Bonn.

No social scientist has yet assessed the depth, duration, and breadth of impact that all these images and signals carve into the consciousness of various audiences with different cultures and traditions, living on different continents. It is also impossible to measure accurately, except in very limited circumstances, the impact of a government's public diplomacy program on foreign audiences in the face of all the other images and signals to which they are exposed. Public diplomacy professionals have taken comfort and encouragement, however, from the realization that their efforts significantly balance, moderate, and supplement the information available to foreign publics from other sources without necessarily being able or even wanting to supplant them. The absence of the body of thought and information supplied through public diplomacy programs, one can thus argue, would deprive foreign publics of the opportunity to obtain as comprehensive and accurate an understanding of America as possible.

Some programs useful for creating knowledge and understanding of our country — or the basis of that knowledge and understanding — are not and cannot realistically be carried out by anyone but an agency of the federal government. The Wireless File, for instance, so valuable to selected foreign audiences, is a medium of information that would not be available were it not for USIA. Similarly, the Hubert Humphrey Scholarship Program serves a clear purpose not addressed by private institutions, but vital for our public diplomacy objectives. USIS libraries would not be maintained privately or commercially, yet they contribute significantly to achieving USIA's goals. Teenage youth exchanges, while customarily carried out privately by nonprofit exchange organizations, need the current U.S. government injection of funds to achieve their intended purposes.

It is incumbent on USIA's leadership, acting, one would hope, cooperatively with their professional colleagues in the field, to deploy the agency's limited resources intelligently. They should not duplicate private or commercial efforts, but concentrate on those activities and themes that would most effectively promote the achievement of U.S. public diplomacy objectives. For example, a new USIA director, in the process of determining the agency's priorities, may want to question the need for introducing a worldwide television news operation within Worldnet (similar to that of VOA) in light of the Cable News Network's plans to provide an American global television news service.[6]

Further, public diplomacy must be flexible in adjusting to major social or political changes in the internal or international conditions in a country or region. The largely peaceful democratic revolutions that erupted in Eastern Europe toward the end of 1989, to cite one clear example, appeared to signal a successful conclusion to the work of the U.S. government-financed Radio Free Europe. Indeed, the success of these revolutions in the former Soviet bloc nations, many of their own citizens agreed, was enhanced greatly by RFE's broadcasts, which served effectively for forty years as a surrogate source of free news and information to the denied audiences in Poland, Hungary, Czechoslovakia, Romania, and Bulgaria. With Eastern Europe basking in its own free radio networks, newly liberated newspapers, television, and other media, some RFE professionals who remained citizens of their former countries could even expect to be welcomed back to assist in their home nations' newly free media communities. A shift in U.S. government public diplomacy priorities in the region thus seems clearly in order for the 1990s.

Eastern Europe's students, young professionals, and creative, politically-minded intellectuals urgently need opportunities that would help them convert their countries into open, democratic societies and market-oriented economies. To address this need, the United States should follow the precedent of its successful educational and cultural exchange programs following World War II. Those programs brought thousands of Germans and Austrians, along with other West Europeans, to the United States to study, to exchange ideas, and to become acquainted with the ways of living, functioning, and creating in a democracy. This large commitment of people and resources was a major factor, together with the Marshall Plan, in the successful reestablishment of all of war-devastated Western Europe into viable, politically free, economically strong democratic societies.

And that is how U.S. public diplomacy can help again, applying the often forgotten lessons of the postwar period. The U.S. Information Agency should take the lead, in collaboration with the U.S. private sector and academic institutions, in developing exchange programs and other opportunities designed to help emerging East European democratic leaders catch up and learn what they had missed during their dark years under totalitarian rule.

Still another critical factor potentially affecting the conduct of public diplomacy by the U.S. government is the necessary preoccupation with protecting the security of overseas personnel and installations. The security concerns have their origin in the frequency of terrorist attacks on U.S. personnel and buildings abroad. An Advisory Panel on Overseas Security (the so-called Inman Panel, named for its chairman, retired Admiral Bobby R. Inman) issued a report in June 1985 analyzing how the U.S. government could better fight international terrorism and protect the security of its overseas personnel, facilities, and classified information. Although USIA joined the State Department in welcoming and supporting many of the panel's conclusions, the report had one flaw basic to the conduct of public diplomacy: It did not take into account that USIA's mission and mandated responsibilities differ in some important respects from those of the Department of State and other foreign affairs agencies.

The Inman Panel suggested, among other things, that U.S. embassies and other facilities abroad be so constructed as to make unauthorized access difficult and that they be relocated away from urban centers to make them less vulnerable to attack. The conduct of public diplomacy, however, places high priority on access to the public by the USIS staff and easy and inviting access by the public to USIS libraries and cultural centers. Anything that affects the ease and ambience of access to these cultural and information centers and removes USIS officers from proximity to their public contacts would jeopardize public diplomacy's essential mission of communicating with target audiences.

Countering the Inman Panel was the independent, bipartisan U.S. Advisory Commission on Public Diplomacy, which is required by Congress to assess the work of USIA and recommend policies and programs in support of its mission.[7] The commission issued its own report,[8] which included, among others, the following recommendations:

— That legislation on diplomatic security take fully into account USIA's public diplomacy mission, the need for relatively free access to USIA's libraries and cultural centers, and the desirability that USIA give visible evidence of the free and open society it represents.

— That the threat of terrorism not be allowed to deter the United States from conducting public diplomacy. USIA should avoid leaving the field to terrorists by closing its programs and facilities. USIA should also avoid fortifying itself against the dangers of terrorism to such an extent that it becomes isolated from its audiences....

— That there be no differentiation between U.S. employees and foreign national employees in providing security at their place of work.

The last point, especially important for USIS, implies that we treat foreign national employees with the trust and respect accorded to U.S. personnel. Much of the work of USIS depends on the dedication, experience, expertise, and contribution of these foreign national colleagues. They provide the insight, the continuity, and the knowledge that are indispensable for the conduct of public diplomacy.

The problems we confront weighing our security requirements against our professional responsibilities were illustrated by a 1988 trip to the Middle East by David Newsom. At two USIS posts he visited, new security regulations require that foreign national employees working on the premises after 6 P.M. be accompanied by an American employee. This clearly affected their ability to work on significant evening programs and to work after regular hours, as so many do. Even worse, noted Newsom, is that "this is an affront to the reliability and dignity of highly qualified professionals who often take extraordinary risks for the United States and on whom we greatly depend."[9]

The penultimate critique concerns the training of Foreign Service officers specializing in public diplomacy. Those officers who specialize in political or economic work usually have ample academic training in these disciplines before entering the Foreign Service. Those who embark on a career in public diplomacy may have training and experience in journalism, social work, or the law, or they may have an academic background as teachers; but they usually know nothing about public diplomacy, what it is and how it works, indeed what this book has tried to describe. Before these new career officers go abroad into the real world of public diplomacy, they need some grounding in the discipline — theoretical, historical, conceptual, and practical. How to do that is best left to the expert trainers in the U.S. Information Agency. Beyond the discipline itself, however, new FSOs specializing in public diplomacy need thorough language training and area studies to prepare them for their country of assignment. Unless they speak the language fluently — not adequately but fluently, so that the subtleties and intricacies of the language will not hamper their ability to communicate — FSOs are handicapped in their career aspirations, and the USIS post cannot adequately discharge its mission. Further, the officer's knowledge of the country, its history and its culture, is indispensable to his or her ability to communicate effectively and empathetically with the designated audience and to fulfill the advisory function.

It would be advantageous to the conduct of foreign affairs if FSOs specializing in other types of work also received some training in public diplomacy. It would help them in their work to know how public diplomacy functions as an element in the overall foreign relations process, how it can support them in their work, and how they can facilitate its mission. It would make them better Foreign Service officers and prepare them for occasions when they themselves may have to work on public diplomacy or supervise, as deputy chiefs of mission or ambassadors, those directly involved in it.

One final point is more in the way of exhortation than criticism. Most professionals in the field have known and practiced what political appointees who direct the U.S. government's public diplomacy also need to learn and remember: that we must present America in its diversity and in its totality. The credibility of the communications process embodied in the practice of U.S. public diplomacy overseas depends equally on truthfulness and on comprehensiveness. If we meddle with the truth or if we present only one aspect of American life while hiding another, we will inevitably be found out and suffer a corresponding loss of credibility, and thus effectiveness, as public diplomats.

NOTES

1. Newsom, "Telling America's Story," chapter 14 in *Diplomacy and the American Democracy*, 181.

2. Ibid., 179.

3. *Worldnet Fact Sheet*, U.S. Information Agency, June 1988.

4. *U.S. Information Agency*, Fact Sheet, May 1988.

5. The White House, Memorandum for the Director, International Communication Agency, 13 Mar. 1978.

6. In August 1989, Cable News Network (CNN) International signed a five-year agreement with Intersputnik, the Soviet satellite agency. Under this agreement, CNN's special news and information feed — already linked to Europe, including Moscow, via Intelsat satellites — will be "uplinked" from Moscow via the Soviet Stratisonar 12 satellite, in stationary orbit over the Indian Ocean, to reach as far as Western Australia. With its programs already carried to Central and South America and the Far East, CNN says the addition of this Soviet satellite coverage will make CNN available to virtually all countries on earth. (*Washington Post*, 10 Aug. 1989.)

7. *The United States Advisory Commission on Public Diplomacy — 1986 Report*, 4. The Commission has seven presidentially appointed members who report their findings and recommendations to the president, the Congress, the secretary of state, the director of USIA, and the U.S. public. The 1989 Authorization Act for USIA changed the composition and tenure of the Commission's membership, as discussed in the Commission's *1989 Report*, a particularly rich document illustrative of the Commission's commitment to its mandate.

8. *Terrorism and Security: The Challenge for Public Diplomacy*, U.S. Advisory Commission on Public Diplomacy, December 1985.

9. Interview with David D. Newsom at Georgetown University, 15 June 1988.

Part II

Case Studies in the Practice of Public Diplomacy

To lend perspective, color, and depth to this picture of how public diplomacy is practiced and to frame it in the context of the overall U.S. foreign affairs process, Part II presents four cases in point. Each case exemplifies the conduct of public diplomacy in a different area or context and demonstrates how its practitioners identify public diplomacy objectives, how they select target groups, and how and why they choose specific programs. The author has drawn these case studies from his personal experience, as substantiated by the written record, and begs the reader's indulgence for the frequent intrusion of the first-person narrative voice.

9

The Beginning of U.S.–Soviet Cultural Relations

U nlike a number of other nations, the United States has traditionally opposed making cultural treaties with other countries. Intercultural relations, we reasoned, flow from normal, friendly relationships between countries, and in turn contribute to the comity of nations without any need for interference or participation by governments or for regulation through agreements. In principle, the United States continues this cultural laissez-faire policy today, but with important exceptions.

In the early 1950s, we Americans learned that the Soviet Union would not tolerate any cultural contacts between ourselves and the Communist world and kept its populations in virtual isolation from the outside world. After the death of Stalin, the rise of Khrushchev, and the 1955 Geneva Foreign Ministers Conference, however, there appeared the first indication of a slight thaw in the relationship. The thaw was at least partially occasioned by Khrushchev's desire for recognition of the Soviet Union as a world power and equal adversary of the United States, one whose stature and culture deserved respect and approbation in the West. The Soviets seem to have felt that earning such recognition — and even admiration — could be furthered by exporting such notable cultural achievements as the Bolshoi and Kirov ballets and the Moiseyev Dance Ensemble, and such outstanding artists as David Oistrakh, Emil Gilels, and Sviatoslav Richter. They also sought to convince the Western world of "the superiority of the Soviet system," as they put it, by showing off their prowess in sports competitions—those they could be counted on to win, such as track-and-field, wrestling, and ice hockey.

The Soviets had apparently also concluded that certain academic exchanges would assist them in "catching up and overtaking the United States"—*dognat' i peregnat'*, so the Khrushchevian slogan went in Russian—by enabling selected Soviet scientists and engineers to do advanced study and research in U.S. institutions that had been closed to them heretofore. They must have imagined they could accomplish all this without exposing the Soviet population to too much "unfiltered free air" from the West or that they could at least control the amount and quality.

The United States in turn realized that the only way it could ever get the Soviets to open their windows to fresh Western ideas was to insist on reciprocity, that is, that they permit U.S.–Soviet cultural exchanges and U.S. presentations in the Soviet Union. These cultural exchanges and presentations, we believed, would more accurately reflect our society, our ideas, and our policies to Soviet citizens than the images they were fed by their own information media. In short, the United States wished to achieve public diplomacy objectives in the Soviet Union.

This convergence of interests led to the negotiation of the first U.S.–Soviet cultural agreement in January 1958.[1] The negotiation had been preceded two years earlier by the conclusion of an agreement to exchange periodicals, with the distribution in the Soviet Union of fifty thousand copies of the U.S. Russian-language magazine *Amerika* and an equal number of copies in the United States of the Soviet English-language magazine *USSR* (later changed to *Soviet Life*).

The negotiation was conducted on the U.S. side by the State Department, assisted by USIA and other organizations that were going to participate in U.S.–Soviet activities, such as the National Academy of Sciences and the newly-formed Inter-University Committee on Travel Grants (IUCTG; later IREX, the International Research and Exchanges Board). The U.S. delegation was headed by Ambassador William S. B. Lacy, President Eisenhower's special assistant for East-West relations, the Soviet side by their ambassador to the United States, Georgii Z. Zarubin.

The U.S. objective for this agreement was to get information and ideas from America direct to the Soviet population, practically for the first time. We hoped that through public diplomacy programs and personal contact we would be able to crack, if ever so slightly, the Soviet monopoly on information about the West and thereby counteract the pervasive anti-American propaganda and distorted information to which Soviet citizens had been exposed. One must remember that since the end of World War II there had been practically no contact between American and Soviet citizens on the nongovernmental level and that the only medium of communication available to the United States had been the heavily jammed Voice of America.

Our interest, therefore, was in information and cultural activities that might reach the maximum number of people in as many places in the Soviet Union as possible. We wanted in particular to promote a dialogue with the so-called "New Class" and with intellectuals, a traditionally privileged group in Soviet society.

A second U.S. objective in the agreement was to help quench the thirst of Americans, especially in the academic community, to learn more about the Soviet Union, its institutions, its culture, and its people, subjects that students and researchers could study closely only in the Soviet Union. At the same time, Soviet visitors to the United States would be able to absorb something of the atmosphere of a free society and realize that neither the U.S. government nor the American people conformed in reality to the stereotypes that Soviet propaganda had made them out to be.

We believed that the Soviets would try to resist and restrict U.S. activities, but would not, in the end, reject them entirely lest they fail to attain their own objectives in the agreement.

After weeks of hard bargaining, an agreement was hammered out that seemed to satisfy both sides. The "Agreement between the United States and the Union of Soviet Socialist Republics on Exchanges in the Cultural, Technical, and Educational Fields" was signed on January 28, 1958.

I was assigned to Moscow that summer as press and cultural attaché to look after U.S. interests in the agreement, to watch over distribution of *Amerika* magazine (the distribution agreement of which had been incorporated in the cultural agreement), and to serve as embassy spokesman. At the time, the Soviets would not issue me a visa as an employee of USIA. I had to resign from USIA and be reappointed to the Department of State, whence I had originally come. Officers subsequently assigned to Moscow in similar capacities were issued visas without having to resign from USIA, a sign of recognition by the Soviets that USIA was the agency with which they must deal in the administration of the cultural agreement.

Starting in the fall of 1958 the agreement began to bear fruit. The first contingent of twenty-one U.S. graduate students arrived, the majority to be located at Moscow State University and a few in Leningrad.

The students and the U.S. embassy agreed at the outset that in order to emphasize the independence of American scholarship from the U.S. government and to exemplify the nongovernmental nature of U.S. academia, the students would have as little to do with the embassy as possible and we would not interfere with their activities. Both we and the students soon discovered, however, that the Soviet authorities could not or would not differentiate between what they considered "American embassy spies" and American students, to whom they attributed similar nefarious motives. The students, some of whom were accompanied by spouses, thus found that keeping their distance from the embassy did not alter Soviet perceptions about them. They began to welcome embassy officers' proffered hospitality and availed themselves of the meager offerings of the tiny embassy commissary, the services of the embassy doctor, and invitations to film showings. They were also grateful for our frequent though often fruitless intercessions with various Soviet ministries regarding access to certain libraries and archives that appeared legitimate and harmless to us but had been declared closed to the students. Without that access, some of the students felt they were wasting their time in the Soviet Union. But Soviet suspicions were often impossible to overcome.

The Soviets treated these young American scholars harshly throughout the year — as though they were American diplomats. Perhaps the Soviets were projecting a mirror image of how they expected us to regard their students in the United States, some of whom may have had other than purely academic assignments; but their treatment of these students was surely misguided. If they had gone just a little out of their way to accommodate the Americans in their scholarly pursuits instead of hampering them at every turn, treated them a bit more hospitably instead of imposing on them the "capitalist swine" routine, and permitted them access to the people and institutions that their work required, they might have favorably influenced the attitudes of a very important segment of the American academic community, namely the future teachers of Russian history and culture and of Soviet affairs in leading U.S. academic institutions.

At the embassy we noticed a distinct change in the students' attitudes toward their hosts, resembling the cold warrior's "siege mentality" that we sometimes detected in ourselves if we had been in Moscow too long without occasional respites outside the country. Few wanted to stay even one day longer than their designated period. Only one student extended for a second year, and that ended sadly for him: Shortly before his departure from Tashkent, where he had spent his second year studying the Uzbek language and culture, all of his dissertation notes were stolen and he was denounced in the press as an "American agitator."

The reader may think that the author has digressed from the case study. The point, however, is that the United States had much to learn about dealing with the Soviet hierarchy on such matters as cultural exchanges. We found that the concept of reciprocity was one that Soviet authorities understood, practiced, and responded to quite well. We therefore let them know that without some changes in their ways, their students in the United States would receive similar treatment and the exchanges in this field might even be curtailed. The second year went much better. (That contingent of graduate students, incidentally, included two future Foreign Service officers, whose careers benefited from this initial experience of living and working in the Soviet Union.)

Tit-for-Tat Diplomacy

The United States slowly learned how useful the tactic of reciprocity could be in its dealings with Soviet bureaucratic intransigencies, security concerns, and manipulative practices, as the following example clearly demonstrates: On one occasion, the embassy found that the entire country outside Moscow had been closed to travel by American diplomats. Although large areas of the Soviet Union were permanently closed to travel by foreigners (and the U.S. government had, reciprocally, restricted travel by Soviet diplomats in certain U.S.areas), this time we could not even get permission to travel to normally open cities like Leningrad. Finding ourselves thus limited, the embassy suggested that the State Department institute similar restrictions on Soviet diplomats in Washington— knowing that Soviet Ambassador Anatoliy Dobrynin had an imminent speaking engagement in Chicago. When the department imposed the new travel restrictions, the Soviets got the point immediately. They lifted the restrictions on travel to Leningrad and other points, the State Department reciprocated, and the ambassador was able to meet his commitment in Chicago.

The graduate student exchange was paralleled by exchanges of writers, composers, and artists, who traveled in delegations. Some of the initial

American delegations did not fare well. Their members, usually well-known and accomplished personalities, found that they were prevented from having any real contact with Soviet counterparts. Instead they were herded from tedious discussions with Soviet cultural bureaucrats or cowed members of the respective "creative" unions to endless rows of Soviet monuments, culminating, if they were lucky, with a performance of the Bolshoi Ballet. The first delegation of U.S. writers—Arthur Schlesinger, Jr., Norman Cousins, and Paddy Chayefsky among them—consequently left the Soviet Union at the end of their stay in some disgust.

The fall 1958 tour of the first delegation of American composers, consisting of Roger Sessions, Roy Harris, Peter Mennin, and Ulysses Kay, also ended badly. On the last day of their visit, an embassy colleague and his wife joined my wife and me in organizing a party for the American visitors to which we invited Soviet musicians and composers whom the U.S. delegation had met or wanted to meet. We sent our invitations through the proper protocol channels, which meant they were vetted by the Ministry of Culture. To assure the Soviets that we meant nothing subversive, we also invited some of the ministry's officials who had acted as "hosts" for the composers.

On the afternoon of the farewell party, one of the Soviet officials called and stated flatly, "*Nam nie udobno*" ("It is inconvenient for us") to attend. When asked for whom it would be inconvenient, he replied, "For the Soviet guests." And, indeed, none of them showed up.

We learned our lesson from this experience: When, two years later, the second U.S. delegation of composers came to Moscow—Aaron Copeland and Lucas Foss—we asked Ambassador and Mrs. Llewellyn Thompson to host the farewell dinner at their residence. We knew by that time that it was more difficult for the Soviets to snub the American ambassador as cavalierly as they had treated mere embassy staffers. As predicted, at the appointed hour Messrs. Khachaturian, Kabalevsky, and Shostakovich showed up—in the company, alas, of the uninvited Tikhon Khrennikov, whose only claim to musical fame was his position as chairman of the Union of Soviet Composers.

The Soviets did not seem to care about the generally negative impression they left on these noted Americans, many of whom were gatekeepers in our country. Their calculation may have been that permitting meaningful contact between the American visitors and genuine Soviet writers, musicians, artists, and composers—those who craved such contact—was too great a risk, even if such a stance confirmed the widely held image of the Soviet Union as a repressive and insensitive society.

Some of the Americans' negative impressions were not directly the fault of Soviet bureaucrats. In 1960, the painter Jimmy Ernst and the printmaker Rudy Pozzatti, who constituted the first delegation of American artists under the cultural agreement, became increasingly depressed during their four-week stay in the Soviet Union. To our surprise, they wanted to leave early, explaining that, as artists, they experienced things primarily in a visual way. What depressed them so much was the absence in that huge country of anything visually interesting, original, or exciting that had been created since the Revolution. The stagnation in artistic creativity had utterly demoralized them.

Performing arts exchanges were the Soviets' trump card in their efforts to project themselves and their system to the American public. Indeed, the Bolshoi Ballet, the Kirov Ballet, the Moiseyev Folk Dance Ensemble, and several other first-rate performing groups created highly favorable impressions of Soviet culture. Most observers doubted, however, that such admiration translated — as the Soviets had presumably expected — into increasing acceptance in America of the Soviet political and social systems, especially in the face of a number of highly publicized defections by Soviet artists, which marred the intended propaganda successes. Similarly, sports exchanges showed off the excellence of individual Soviet track and field athletes and ice hockey teams, but not the superiority of Soviet Man and Soviet Woman.

The impact of American performing artists on the Soviet Union — in public diplomacy terms — is impossible to measure, even after thirty years. To be sure, the New York Philharmonic in 1959, the touring company of *My Fair Lady* in 1960, the Robert Shaw Chorale in 1961, and the New York City Ballet in 1962 made strong artistic impressions and received wide popular acclaim in the cities where they appeared. They gave ample evidence of the creativity and quality of American performers and opened many Soviet eyes to American dynamism and artistic freedom. Perhaps that is enough of an accomplishment. It is hard to tell how deeply these impressions penetrated into the Soviet psyche or how far they extended beyond the relatively few exposed to the American artists, especially if one wishes to determine their long-term societal and cultural impact. On the other hand, the University of Michigan Concert Band, which toured in 1961 and consisted of gifted and well-disciplined college students eager to experience Russia and make contact with young Soviets wherever they appeared, may have been more effective as communicators of American culture and values than their older, more famous professional colleagues.

The role that the legendary American impresario Sol Hurok played in the initial performing arts exchanges cannot be ignored. He was in many respects the man who made it happen. He often ignored the advice, and even the rules, that the State Department imposed on those promoting exchanges under the agreement. He frequently negotiated on his own with the Soviet cultural bureaucracy, yet he represented U.S. interests well. The Soviets respected him for his experience, artistic instinct, commercial acumen, and command of the ins and outs of the performing arts in the United States. He was of Ukrainian birth, spoke Russian, literally loved the great artists whom he represented, and was loved by them in return.

Hurok had what could only be called an inordinate sense of chutzpah in the way he went about his political and financial dealings with both American and Soviet officialdom. His was the grand manner, complete with bouquets of flowers, French perfume, Russian caviar, and the stiletto. By cajoling, threatening, persuading, and compromising with the authorities in both countries, he usually succeeded in making these artistic exchanges possible. He was responsible for bringing to the United States the Bolshoi and Kirov ballets, the Moiseyev, Ukrainian, and Georgian dance ensembles, and musicians such as David Oistrakh, Emil Gillels, and Sviatoslav Richter. In return he sent "his" American artists—Isaac Stern, Byron Janis, Ruggiero Ricci, Roberta Peters, Mattiwilda Dobbs, and George London to dazzle Soviet audiences. Despite the headaches he often caused officers in the State Department and the Moscow embassy, he was the one American impresario who could manage these exchanges so that they worked in both directions, satisfying both governments and the artists involved.

It was our hope that the cultural agreement would assist us in developing greater and better contact between American and Soviet citizens—individually and en masse—thereby improving and increasing Soviet understanding of American society and the issues that concerned both nations. For those of us specifically charged with public diplomacy responsibilities, making personal contacts and communicating with Soviet citizens on a one-to-one basis remained a frustrating process and usually quite impossible. The Soviets considered all official diplomatic personnel as intelligence operatives intent on either spying or subversive missions. To them, our interest in communicating with the Soviet public was subversive and dangerous—never mind that we considered it part of our legitimate diplomatic responsibilities.

The Soviets did their utmost to prevent contact between U.S. embassy personnel and the Soviet public, except for those Soviet citizens who were authorized to have such contact. They resorted to constant "tailing," electronic surveillance ("bugging"), and harassment of U.S. diplomats and any Soviet citizen suspected of having unauthorized contact with anyone in the American embassy. Our personal contact efforts were thus often more hazardous for the Soviet citizen who had or wanted to have a relationship with an American than for the U.S. diplomat.

This atmosphere of suspicion and fear presented a special dilemma for the U.S. public diplomat. He did not know — could not know — which contacts were genuine and which were provoked by Soviet authorities; worse, whether a contact that had been genuine was compromised as a result of Soviet pressure. We naturally wanted to avoid getting our Soviet acquaintances into trouble, so it was often we who ended a pleasant relationship for fear of compromising our friends.

It occasionally happened that the Soviet authorities, suspecting that an American diplomat had more contacts than they could control, would eliminate the source of their concern by declaring him *persona non grata*. That occurred with a USIS officer who was our first black colleague in Moscow to work in public diplomacy. After his arrival in 1964 he made friends quickly with students at the Lumumba Peoples Friendship University. These mostly African students liked the friendly American and he them, supplying them often with reading material and inviting them to film showings in his apartment. We warned our young colleague to slow down in his otherwise highly commendable personal contact work lest the Soviets take counteraction against him. And, indeed, his popularity with his numerous African student friends became too painful a thorn in their side, so they kicked him out, thereby eliminating the source of their problem. We lost an able colleague.

The cultural exchanges that took place under the agreement sometimes enabled us to penetrate this curtain of suspicion. By escorting and accompanying the delegations of writers and artists and the musicians who performed under the agreement's auspices, we were able to meet and get to know their Soviet counterparts. The latter, in turn, found it easier to become acquainted with us under the umbrella of the agreement. Even though the visiting Americans often complained about being kept under tight wraps by their Soviet hosts, their presence provided us a rare opportunity to communicate with Soviet citizens who genuinely desired to interact with us. That is why I appreciated the chance to serve as escort for such American artistic groups as the New York Philharmonic, *My Fair Lady*, and the New York City Ballet, which toured several Soviet cities.

The exchange of films also figured prominently in the 1958 negotiations for a cultural agreement. Virtually no American films had been exhibited in the Soviet Union since World War II. Soviet citizens were still talking rapturously in the late fifties about the last American film they had seen, *Sun Valley Serenade* (with the Glenn Miller band), and about their favorite American actress, Deanna Durbin, in *A Hundred Men and a Girl.* Soviet films in the United States were also rare, not for political reasons but because American film distributors found no market for Soviet films of that time.

Both sides were interested in having their feature and documentary films shown in the other country, at least those films that were believed to advance their respective objectives. The cultural agreement specified that both sides would encourage film exchanges and that an agreement for an exchange of commercial films would be negotiated separately.

These negotiations took place in Moscow in the fall of 1958, with the U.S. delegation led by Eric Johnston, the long-time president of the Motion Picture Association of America, and Turner Shelton, head of USIA's Motion Picture Service and a flamboyant product of Hollywood. The entry of the U.S. delegation into the conference room of the Soviet Ministry of Culture on the first day of the negotiations must have appeared to the Soviets as a scene straight from a Hollywood movie. As the Soviet delegation assembled into a stiff welcoming line-up, in marched the Americans led by Johnston and Turner, followed by assorted secretaries and bag carriers, all deeply tanned, all sporting dark sun glasses (in spite of the gray wintry weather), all looking strictly Metro-Goldwyn-Mayer.

Protracted negotiations finally brought forth an agreement to exchange ten American and seven Soviet films over a two-year period. The agreement ran into practical difficulties immediately. The Soviets wanted the U.S. government to help publicize and distribute the Soviet films in the United States. There was no way this could be done under the U.S. market economy. Further, the Soviet films at that time were, with few exceptions, not of a quality or subject matter to interest a wide American public.

On the other hand, *any* American film was going to be popular in the Soviet Union. The first American film selected for distribution by the Soviets, for example, was *Roman Holiday* with Audrey Hepburn and Gregory Peck. Before dubbing it into Russian, the Soviet film distribution agency showed the film in its English-language version at the 8,000-seat sports arena in Moscow's Luzhniki Park over a period of four days, with five showings per day. Every showing was sold out, permitting the Soviets to finance the dubbing, copying, and distribution of the film nationwide entirely from the proceeds of that initial showing.

The United States insisted on the State Department's right to approve the American films selected for distribution in the Soviet Union—a procedure, unprecedented in this country, that turned out to be unworkable. When independent U.S. filmmakers, not members of the MPAA, refused to comply, the Soviets were glad to do business with them. The right of approval had been based on the justified fear that the Soviets would mostly select films that were one-sidedly critical of the United States.

These vexing problems could not be solved at the time, and the exchange of commercial films faltered. American films thus did not at that time become a major contributor to the communications process in the way that they have—for better or for worse—in other countries.

Two other exchange activities under the cultural agreement turned out to be quite successful, in this writer's view, in meeting U.S. public diplomacy objectives. One was the exchange of periodicals, with the United States distributing *Amerika* magazine in the Soviet Union. The periodical's distribution difficulties have already been described in chapter 3, but a different challenge facing us concerned the content of the magazine.

The constant objective of *Amerika*'s editors was to present informative articles, photos, and graphics that would help Soviet readers understand the dynamism, diversity, complexity, and freedom of American society. In these efforts to project as accurate a picture of our country as possible, some of us wanted to "show America—warts and all," as the saying goes, and include discussion of our social problems and our varied approaches to solving them. Other experienced observers of the Soviet Union, including Ambassador Thompson, argued that we should not write and edit *Amerika* magazine as though it were intended for an American audience. To do so would mislead the reader. Instead, we would have to take into consideration, these experts insisted, the different background, experiences, and traditions of the magazine's intended readers. The Soviet citizen had never experienced a press free of government control and would have no way of evaluating such self-criticism, especially in a publication put out by a foreign government. If such "warts" were discussed in *Amerika*, Thompson argued, most Soviet readers would probably surmise that they must be much more disfiguring and festering than described, or they would never have been mentioned.

The magazine could not simply serve as an example of the free press, but had an obligation to explain to the Soviet reader what a free press is and how it works. The periodical had to make clear the importance of a free press in a democratic society. Without preaching or appearing to preach, it had to convince its readers that Americans consider a free press — "telling it as it is" — essential to a free and democratic society.

Glen Fisher, a noted student of cross-cultural behavior, emphasizes the need for USIA, in designing its materials, to take "into account the way that their audience will actually see and comprehend what USIA is trying to say."[2] *Amerika*'s editors learned to recognize this requirement, peculiar to publishing a magazine for readers unfamiliar with the ways of another culture and political system. They learned to explain and carefully "background" the facts they presented so that they would truly inform rather than confuse the reader.

An example of how a bare fact can cause serious misunderstanding unless it is properly explained to an audience of a different culture was a VOA news story announcing that the president had declared a disaster emergency in the face of severe flooding in California. This straightforward news item was met with both consternation and disbelief among Soviet listeners: There must be hundreds of drownings, and the disaster must have biblical proportions; otherwise there would be no emergency declaration by the president. And the flooding must be much worse, otherwise it would not be on VOA news. Every American knows that a presidential emergency order does not imply a Noah's flood, but not so a foreign audience unfamiliar with U.S. relief legislation and insurance practices. Such news, to be comprehensible to a foreign audience, needs conscientious backgrounding and context-framing, something that *Amerika*'s and VOA's editors had to keep in mind.

The other communications medium with lasting public diplomacy value in the Soviet Union turned out to be the traveling American exhibits. The impact of the 1959 U.S. National Exhibition in Moscow was detailed earlier, in Chapter 4. We did not realize until after we had mounted this monumental enterprise how effective a medium it was. What achieved so much popular appeal was the combination of choice of subjects, visual attractiveness, manner of presentation, and, above all, the presence of the Russian-speaking American guides, who translated a static show into a lasting and meaningful experience for the hundreds of thousands who attended.

During the 1960 and 1962 renegotiations of the two-year cultural agreements, the United States pressed vigorously for continuation of the exhibit exchange, against considerable resistance by the Soviet side, which did not attribute such great value to its exhibits in the United States but recognized the effect of the U.S. exhibits on the Soviet population. In the end we succeeded in sending a number of smaller exhibits, which traveled not only to Moscow and Leningrad but to provincial cities like Kiev, Tbilisi, Kharkov, and Tashkent and, later, to cities in Siberia.

The themes of these exhibits, all of which were subject to negotiation with the Soviets, were selected for their informational value. Although they were designed so as not to appear "provocative" from the Soviet point of view, there were constant hassles over inclusion of this book or that picture. Subjects ranged widely, from plastics, graphics, architecture, and industrial design, to transportation, education, medicine, and outdoor recreation. All of them included as a central feature the Russian-speaking American guides, specially selected and trained for this purpose by USIA. They served as front-line communicators with the thousands of Soviet exhibit visitors, for many of whom these guides represented their first personal contact with an American.

The renegotiations of the agreement—in Moscow in 1960 and Washington in 1962—were led on the American side by, respectively, Ambassador Thompson and former ambassador to the Soviet Union Charles E. Bohlen, both experienced and knowledgeable in U.S.–Soviet negotiations. The United States pushed for those programs that would enhance attainment of its public diplomacy goals, while the Soviets pushed for their own objectives. Compromises reached were satisfactory to both sides.

The atmosphere for exchanges improved greatly between 1962 and 1964, Khrushchev's last years at the helm of Soviet authority. In those two years, despite the Cuban missile crisis of October 1962, Americans were able to meet and communicate more freely with Soviet intellectuals and creative personalities than ever before. In my own case, during several brief visits to the Soviet Union at that time, I met more Soviet writers, painters, and theater people than during my entire three-year service in the embassy, 1958 to 1961.

When Khrushchev fell, the fresh-air windows to the West were again slammed shut. Most of the exchanges continued on their course, however.

After the Soviet invasion of Afghanistan in December 1979, President Carter suspended the agreement. Many observers considered this blanket cancelation a mistake. The United States could clearly have shown its disapproval by curtailing some of those exchanges that the Soviets favored most. But we should not have arbitrarily canceled those, like the exhibits, that were in our interest. If the Soviets had subsequently canceled them in retaliation for our dropping exchanges favored by them, it would at least have been at their initiative; but canceling all exchanges unilaterally deprived us of some effective tools in a communications process we considered vital to U.S. foreign policy objectives.

As mentioned earlier, the United States finds itself in an entirely new "ballgame" with different rules, brought on by Gorbachev's revolutionary *glasnost* and *perestroika* policies. How these policies will affect cultural and informational exchanges in the future, and what role they will play in the context of the U.S.–Soviet relationship, is something about which one can only speculate. Current discussions and plans for increased exchanges, especially of young people, lead one to hope for greater knowledge and better understanding between the American and Soviet peoples.

Postscript

That such hope is not merely wishful thinking was confirmed for the author when he returned to the Soviet Union in September 1989 at the invitation of Komsomol, the Soviet Youth Committee, for discussion of possible teen exchanges through Youth For Understanding (YFU). (The author, now retired from the Foreign Service, is a YFU trustee.)

Psychologically and politically — though not physically — almost everything had changed in Moscow since my last visit thirteen years earlier in 1976. Every conversation, official or private, started off with one version or another of "we have opened up," "don't judge us by the past," "you are facing a new situation here" "we have developed 'new thinking'," — "we have changed."

It was a complete turnaround in atmosphere, one that I had not experienced before in the Soviet Union and one that Soviets claimed they too had never experienced until a couple of years before. It was as though sunshine, for the first time, had penetrated a dark, chilling, ever-threatening cloud cover. My Soviet hosts and other contacts seemed particularly anxious to take advantage of this moment, as if to soak up as much warmth and fresh air as possible in case the icy fog and cold of winter were once again to envelop the country.

Being invited by the once ultraconservative Komsomol was the first of several surprises for a former diplomat who had been repeatedly denounced in Soviet publications as an American spy and prevaricator. The reception could not have been friendlier. There was an eagerness to engage in cooperative arrangements — in this instance, youth exchanges — and to do so quickly, before anything might happen to stop or reverse the thrust of the reform movement. The Soviets were willing and ready to arrange with YFU, a private American organization, for exchanges in which U.S. and Soviet teenagers would live with host families, attend school, and become familiar with the society of the other country.

This openness and desire for contact was almost unbelievable. It was a far cry from 1959 but a development that perhaps could not have taken place without the foundation that was put in place thirty years before.

NOTES

1. For a detailed account of the history and content of the U.S.–Soviet cultural agreements, see Yale Richmond, *U.S.–Soviet Cultural Exchanges, 1958–1986* (Boulder, CO: Westview Press, 1987).

2. Glen Fisher, *Mindsets: The Role of Culture and Perception in International Relations* (Yarmouth, ME: Intercultural Press, 1988), 32.

10

Practicing Public Diplomacy
in Brazil

Brazil in the early 1970s challenged U.S. diplomacy on many fronts, including its public diplomacy. One of the largest countries in the world, occupying one half of the South American continent, Brazil was rapidly evolving from "developing" into "developed" status. Its impressive potential in industrialization, agricultural production, and raw materials supply was far from fully realized. Over 30 million of its people, fully one third of the population, living in the arid Northeast, existed outside of the country's economic life—destitute, illiterate, unstable, emigration-prone.

Politically, Brazil had evolved from fragile democracy into rigid military authoritarianism, with a wretched human rights record. Yet the military dictatorship of this proud, bustling, and friendly Luso-American nation differed in character from those of its Latin-American neighbors. While its generals provided the ideological, political, and psychological leadership for the country, they left its management to professional technocrats. And once a general had been "elected" to the presidency—there were five in succession from 1964 to 1985—he was never again seen in his military uniform.

The United States has had a "special" relationship with Brazil ever since World War II, when Brazil was the only other country in the hemisphere whose military forces joined with the Allies in fighting the Axis powers. That Brazilian expeditionary force, which fought valiantly in the Italian campaign, counted among its officers those who became, by the 1960s, the country's military leaders, including all of its presidents. Some of the intimate relationships between the U.S. and Brazilian military had been formed during World War II, such as that between President Humberto Castello Branco, who led the coup against a tottering democratic government in 1964, and General Vernon Walters, the U.S. defense attaché in Brazil at the time. Since 1921, the United States had had a naval mission in Brazil, headed by an admiral, and maintained there its largest military cooperation mission in the hemisphere, with three flag-rank officers to coordinate strategy, tactics, training, and procurement of U.S. equipment and weapons.

Beyond the close military relationship, the two governments had been friendly partners in the Organization of American States and in their bilateral dealings. The United States had long been Brazil's principal trading partner, economic assistance donor, and creditor. Strategically, Brazil was important to the United States because of its long Atlantic coastline, its strong anti-Communist stance, and its size and influence in the hemisphere, having a common border with all but two of the countries of South America.

The people of the two nations, furthermore, have sustained an apparent affinity for each other with many and varied exchanges. In particular, the huge U.S. economic assistance program in Brazil contributed to Brazil's rapid, if uneven, development. In the early 1970s, when the author served as U.S. counselor for public affairs in Brazil, that assistance program — involving hundreds of AID officials and billions of dollars — was coming to an end.

In these circumstances, the United States sought to achieve some of its policy objectives vis-à-vis Brazil using the tools of public diplomacy. Critical of the military dictatorship, especially of its record of human rights abuses, U.S. policy aimed for an early return of democracy to the country. Shaping our public diplomacy efforts was the desire to maintain our traditional friendship with the Brazilian people and avoid alienating them, while distancing ourselves from their leaders and remaining critical of the way the latter governed the country. At the same time, we recognized the importance of maintaining good relations with those who governed, for strategic and other reasons, as enumerated above, including our wish to remain Brazil's valued trading partner and to protect our economic assets. While reassuring the people of our continuing friendship, we also wanted them to have accurate and comprehensive information about the global, regional, and bilateral policies of the United States and to understand our attitudes toward them and their neighbors.

Even though the Brazilian public and its elected representatives in the national Congress had relatively little power at the time, the military leaders did pay attention to public opinion on a number of issues, to improve their own image of legitimacy with the country's natural gatekeepers. The technocracy that actually managed the country, moreover, depended on the United States for professional contacts and accurate information.

Having identified the principal long-term and short-term public diplomacy objectives, the USIS team in Brazil addressed the question of target audiences. Among USIS officers' most important contacts were those in the press, especially the editors and columnists of the reputable newspapers — principally, *Estado de São Paulo, Folha de São Paulo, Journal do Brasil, O Globo, Correio Brasiliense* — and weekly magazines, such as *Veja, Manchete,* and *Visão*. They were the best disseminators of information and, at the same time, the best-informed people about what was going on in the country.

Brazil's print and broadcast media were then suffering under increasingly stringent government censorship. Yet government restrictions on information in Brazil had their own Luso-American peculiarity, different from the controls practiced by Communist authorities in the Soviet Union and the other countries of Eastern Europe. The extent of censorship and the penalties for violating it were severe; yet on the day new and stricter censorship rules were announced by the government, every leading newspaper had the censorship decree as its lead story and, furthermore, featured editorials denouncing it — unimaginable then in a Communist country. Indeed, not content with merely criticizing the regime for violating the nation's liberties, *O Estado de São Paulo* showed its independence and courage by filling the front-page spaces excised by the censors with poetry and, later, popular recipes. This served to inform the paper's readers that they had been denied the news, but also entertained them by substituting cultural and culinary information.

There was less censorship of foreign news, except from Communist sources. Thus, as noted in Chapter 4, even the most highly regarded Brazilian newspapers readily and regularly accepted USIS Wireless File material for inclusion as feature stories, something the press in the West European democracies would not normally do. Even lengthy articles appearing in the USIS periodical *Problems of Communism* would be translated and serialized in Brazil's major publications. The USIS Wireless File thus became a highly useful medium for disseminating information without the U.S. label, since most

Brazilian journals published Wireless File material under their own bylines or merely credited USIS as they would AP or Reuters.

After media leaders, important USIS target groups included state and federal government officials in the ministries dealing with foreign affairs, education, economics, planning, trade, culture, and information. It was also important for USIS to identify and maintain contact with federal legislators and potential legislative candidates. Although this group had little influence at the time, they were expected to play an important role if and when the promised return to democracy occurred. Another target group included leaders in the field of education, both in the bureaucracy and in university teaching positions, particularly those in American studies, international affairs, economics, and management. Some — not all — elements of the Roman Catholic hierarchy were important to our public diplomacy, especially in the area of human rights and economic development, since they represented the only organized and effective critics of the regime's excesses. (The worker-priest movement, considered too radical for U.S. interests in Brazil, was not a USIS target.)

The Brazilian military was a potentially important target group, consideration of which presented special problems for USIS. They were influential because they ran things, and thus were significant contacts for us. Yet we did not wish to appear to have too close an affinity with the country's authoritarian rulers. We needed to communicate with them, however, to help them understand U.S. policies and views vis-à-vis Brazil, in the hope that they would act upon that understanding. We were particularly interested in the officers who had passed through the sieve of the General Staff and Command School, the majors and lieutenant colonels expected to become the next generation's military leaders. At least some of these believed it was important for Brazil to regain its reputation as a society in which political and social peace reigned.

One problem faced by USIS Brazil in reaching its target groups and maintaining contact with them was the vastness of the country and the dispersal of its population into large regional centers, thousands of miles distant from each other. Brasilia, the capital, had become important as the administrative center of the country, but São Paulo was far more significant for its industrial, business, and educational communities. Rio de Janeiro was still the most important center of publishing, the print and electronic media, and cultural activities. And such regional metropolises as Belo Horizonte (with a population of 1.8 million), Salvador (1.5 million), Recife (1.2 million), Porto Allegre (1.1 million), and

Curitiba (1 million) were important centers for USIS programs and contact work. Instead of a centralized operation in Brasilia, where our targets were few, we maintained strongly staffed USIS branch posts in these cities (though some branches were closed in the early 1970s for economic reasons, Belém, Fortaleza, and Curitiba among them).

Implementing the Country Program

Having determined its public diplomacy objectives and identified its target audiences, USIS Brazil mapped out a program appropriate to both, consulted with Washington, and received approval for what became the country plan. Its long-term objectives were to be approached in two ways: through educational exchange programs and through support of cultural and binational center activities.

Educational Exchanges. In the educational exchange field, USIS Brazil concentrated on sending Brazilian academics to the United States for postgraduate and postdoctoral studies, and on bringing U.S. professors, graduate students, and researchers to teach, study, and work in Brazilian institutions of higher learning. Although Brazilian universities were well equipped for undergraduate teaching, American graduate schools had much to offer Brazilian academics in certain fields, such as American studies, business management, and some of the sciences. An example of one such program in American studies was noted in Chapter 4.

The mechanism for educational exchange was the Fulbright Commission, strengthened with new personnel and enlarged U.S. resources after its move from Rio de Janeiro to Brasilia. The Brazilian government eventually demonstrated its commitment to this bilateral program by also contributing a substantial sum to the program's budget.

The Fulbright Commission performed its mission well during that 1971–75 period: It enabled Brazilians to do advanced study and research in disciplines that were not strongly developed in their country; it advanced the cause of American studies in Brazil; and it gave American graduate students and researchers a chance to study in Brazil. The commission's chairman was the U.S. public affairs officer, its executive secretary a retired Brazilian diplomat, and its deputy executive secretary an American with long experience in education in Brazil. The U.S. members were the embassy's cultural attaché, a U.S. businessman, and the Ford Foundation representative in Brazil. The Brazilian members were the head of the cultural department of the Foreign Ministry, a representative of CAPES (the Brazilian government agency managing foreign grants and scholarships), and a Brazilian businessman. At its bimonthly meetings, the Commission set academic priorities, reviewed the budget, and monitored the selection and evaluation of participants.

The Binational Centers. Supporting the binational centers (BNCs) in Brazil seemed the most cost-effective means of acquainting Brazilians throughout their vast country with American life and culture.[1] There were seventy binational centers in Brazil, most of them indigenous institutions unrelated to the U.S. government, with approximately 85,000 students enrolled in English-language classes. USIS worked closely with sixteen of the largest centers,[2] providing USIA-produced English-language teaching materials and consultants, videotapes, films, library materials, and speakers. Teachers from the BNCs were also selected for USIA-sponsored training programs in the United States, such as the Georgetown University TESOL (Teaching of English as a Second Language) Institute in Washington, D.C., and the University of Florida in Gainesville.

The binational centers served as the principal U.S.–Brazilian cultural nexus: USIS Brazil disseminated information about the United States through their programs and libraries and found them valuable for keeping in contact with local target groups. In addition, USIS Brazil operated three reference libraries of its own, in Brasilia, Rio de Janeiro, and São Paulo, each an integral part of a network and each specialized in a few subjects geared to the interests of local target groups. Inter-library lending and exchange of information between these libraries and the USIS branch posts were facilitated through telephone, telex, and fax services and a systemwide combined catalogue.

Resources in these three USIS-operated libraries included about 20,000 volumes, over 350 periodicals, audio tapes, and back issues of publications on microfilm. The libraries published monthly annotated acquisition lists and bibliographies to support such ongoing USIS programs as conferences, lectures, and exhibitions.

Perhaps the most dramatic and visible demonstration of U.S. public diplomacy in Brazil in the early 1970s was the construction of the Casa Thomas Jefferson in Brasilia. After the U.S. embassy moved from Rio de Janeiro to Brasilia in the summer of 1971 — one of the first diplomatic missions to do so, in support of Brazil's intention to make its new capital work — USIS became convinced that it should further demonstrate American respect for Brasilia as the new focal point of the nation by establishing a representative American cultural center there. Such a center would also be useful in view of the new capital's lack of suitable fora for USIS-sponsored American cultural activities or a place to house the USIS library.

Because Brasilia prided itself on its preeminence in contemporary architecture, we wanted, furthermore, to present it with an example of modern U.S. architectural design that would stand as a permanent display of American creativity in the late 20th century, worthy of Brazil's new capital. A distinguished American architect, Romaldo Giurgola of Columbia University, agreed to design the building and supervise its construction. (When asked once why he would want to build such a center in far-off Brasilia at a relatively low fee while involved with major commissions all over the world, Giurgola had replied that as a boy in Italy he had learned English in the American library in Rome. He had always wanted to build such an institution as a matter of gratitude and happy memories.)

The Casa was inaugurated with considerable fanfare in the fall of 1974. It housed the USIS library, a multipurpose auditorium for cultural performances, eighteen classrooms for the teaching of English, and offices for USIS Brasilia and the Fulbright Commission. A long-term loan collection of contemporary American art lent distinction to the public rooms and attracted many viewers, and the Brasilia Tourist Office included the Casa Thomas Jefferson on its itinerary of Brasilia's architectural achievements.

Cash for the Casa

Readers wondering how such a project as the Casa Thomas Jefferson was financed in view of severe U.S. government budgetary restrictions may find the answer of interest: The Brazilian Government donated the land. USIS obtained a $100,000 grant and a $100,000 interest-free loan from USIA Washington. $50,000 was available from existing USIS Brasilia English-teaching income. And a $500,000 commercial bank loan was obtained — for a total of $750,000.

It had earlier been determined that a potentially profitable market for English-language teaching existed in Brasilia, in the absence of proprietary teaching institutions in the new city. After the Casa Thomas Jefferson was completed, it opened its classrooms at a market-rate fee to anyone who wanted to learn English. In short order, the Casa had about two thousand students, ranging in age from twelve to eighty. Within two years the profits from the English-teaching program were sufficient to retire the commercial mortgage and the USIA loan! Thereafter, the English-teaching program was limited to specialized target groups, but the income was still sufficient to pay for the upkeep and program activities of the cultural center.

Other Cultural Activities. The sesquicentennial celebration of Brazilian independence in 1972 provided USIS another opportunity to demonstrate American friendship and empathy for Brazil by honoring the anniversary with an American cultural festival. Brazilians appreciated our decision to hold it in the still culture-starved capital. The festival featured an exhibition of graphics by five contemporary U.S. artists from the Metropolitan Museum in New York — Josef Albers, Helen Frankenthaler, Jasper Johns, Robert Motherwell, and James Rosenquist. The U.S. Navy Show Band, popularly known throughout the hemisphere as the UNITAS Band, performed for thousands of *Brasilienses*. Lectures on the "Philadelphia Constitution as the Basis for Brazilian Constitutional Law" and "Brazil at the Time of its Independence as Seen by North Americans" brought together distinguished audiences and U.S. academics. The Pro-Musica chamber music ensemble under Noah Greenberg performed on their Renaissance instruments. The Brazilian premiere of the film *Cabaret* took place in Brasilia's largest movie theater. And American pianist Andre Watts, as the pièce de résistance, came especially to Brasilia to give a recital at our invitation.[3]

On a more limited scale, our long-term cultural objectives were aided by, among others, the noted printmaker Rudy Pozatti of Indiana University and the outstanding American violist Raphael Hillyer. Pozatti conducted week-long master workshops in graphic arts in Rio de Janeiro and Salvador, Bahia, the latter a center of both traditional and contemporary Brazilian culture. Such noted resident artists as Caribé, Calasans Neto, Emanuel Araujo, and the writer Jorge Amado were impressed by the American artist and, in turn, left a lasting mark on him. Hillyer, the long-time violist of the Juilliard Quartet then teaching chamber music at Yale, held master classes in São Paulo and Rio and enjoyed performing with Brazilian chamber musicians in such provincial cities as Goiania, 150 miles west of Brasilia. By staying on to interact with Brazilian counterparts, rather than merely giving a single recital and flying off to the next, Hillyer made a lasting impact as a representative of American culture.

Also useful in promoting long-term public diplomacy objectives in Brazil was the USIS book translation and publication program. Through agreements with American publishers and joint ventures with Brazilian publishers, USIS was able to promote the publication in Portuguese of American books that supported country objectives. The USIS post also agreed to purchase a certain number of copies of the translated books for presentation use and for placement in USIS and BNC libraries. (Books published under this program were also made available to USIS posts in Portugal and in the Lusophone countries of Africa.)

USIS Brazil's most ambitious publishing project was *Dialogo*, the Portuguese version of USIA's magazine, *Dialogue*, which aimed for a fairly high-level intellectual audience. The post also made good use of other USIA periodicals, notably, *Economic Impact, English Teaching Forum*, and a few targeted copies of *Problems of Communism*. In cooperation with the embassy's Commercial Office, furthermore, USIS published the periodical *Boletim Comercial* to promote U.S.–Brazilian trade. The Wireless File, as mentioned earlier, turned out to be an excellent medium in meeting more immediate public diplomacy objectives, though in a manner entirely different from the writer's experience in Europe.

Bringing prominent Americans invited as speakers and conference participants into contact with Brazilian counterparts helped USIS to promote current U.S. political and economic objectives, including those concerned with human rights. To help make Brazilians more aware, and more supportive, of U.S. policies toward the Soviet Union and other areas of the world, for instance, we invited Zbigniew Brzezinski, at the time head of the Trilateral Commission, to come for two weeks of lectures and discussions on U.S. foreign policy. Similarly, we invited William Griffith of the Massachusetts Institute of Technology, to give an American academic's appraisal of Watergate, a subject that fascinated and concerned many Brazilians. Both did excellent jobs and were, in turn, helped by USIS in making contact with interesting Brazilians. As first-time visitors to the country, both Brzezinski and Griffith were intent on learning more about it, recognizing its growing importance in international affairs and, incidentally, demonstrating the two-way benefits of U.S. public diplomacy.

Such expert visitors enhanced the embassy's own communication efforts on current bilateral and multilateral issues. In Ambassador John Hugh Crimmins the U.S. government already had a first-rate public diplomacy resource: He spoke Portuguese fluently, was an expert practitioner in personal communication, and enjoyed "mixing it up" with Brazilians.[4] Other embassy officers fluent in Portuguese also served as front-line communicators.

Speaking personally, I felt somewhat handicapped by my imperfect knowledge of Portuguese, especially in the subtleties of political dialogue. It was not difficult, for instance, in conveying the U.S. position on nuclear nonproliferation, to make clear to the Brazilians that we would not permit U.S. firms to bid for construction of nuclear power plants in the face of Brazil's refusal to sign the nonproliferation treaty. But when it came to discussing the intricacies of current Brazilian politics and expressing our concerns regarding the bilateral relationship, I was often forced into explication in English, a handicap in the communications process.[5]

I was also critical of at least some of my bilingual USIS colleagues whose interests were almost exclusively cultural, with too little attention to the political or economic issues of the day. Others at USIA in Washington shared this criticism of what became known, perhaps unjustly, as the Latin American syndrome. It has since been largely corrected. Those who were effective political communicators at the time — among them our embassy press attaché and several branch PAOs and information officers — have now risen to positions of responsibility in the USIA hierarchy and are able to insist on the required motivation, training, and language expertise of officers assigned to public diplomacy duties.

The Voice of America's daily two hours of short-wave Portuguese-language broadcasts did not seem to enjoy a wide listenership in Brazil, except perhaps in the frontier regions of the country. Accordingly, they were not an important element in our country plan considerations or a primary tool in our communication efforts. The post did supply local Brazilian radio stations with VOA Portuguese-language "package" programs that smaller broadcast entities seemed to use regularly, although it was difficult to monitor their impact. (In the 1980s, Brazilian radio stations were reportedly recording daily satellite-transmitted news briefs from VOA Washington for rebroadcast over their medium-wave transmitters, a development VOA considered a major breakthrough in its communication efforts.[6])

USIS Brazil experimented with its own television productions, producing a current events program that was broadcast by one of the Brazilian TV networks. This was, of course, before Worldnet. The post was able to claim a pioneering success, in part because the Brazilian television industry was at the time in a somewhat chaotic state, preoccupied with sports and popular entertainment rather than serious information programs.

The Brazilian motion picture industry was amply served from the United States. As in many countries on this and other continents, however, the most popular American films and television programs are not always those conveying the accurate and objective picture of American society that a U.S. public diplomat might have wished. That is an endemic problem for public diplomacy in a democracy.

It was impossible, certainly in the short term, to evaluate the effectiveness of the public diplomacy program in Brazil or its impact on the total U.S.–Brazil relationship while actively engaged in it. USIS did try to evaluate the cost-effectiveness of individual activities and program techniques, assisted by USIA's Research Service, though not always with conclusive results. Such analysis did help to fine-tune USIS Brazil's operations, a necessity forced on the post by persistent budgetary pressures.

In 1976, shortly after the end of the period covered by this chapter, U.S.–Brazilian relations suffered temporary deterioration. The Brazilian government, stung by persistent U.S. jabs about human rights violations, shut down the entire U.S.–Brazilian military cooperation program under a barrage of mutual recrimination. The underlying cordial relationship between the two societies was not permanently derailed, however, and undoubtedly contributed to easing the tensions that had built up.

With Brazil's gradual return to democracy and its need of U.S. assistance and understanding in overcoming its economic and financial problems, the relationship returned to its former level — aided, one hopes, by U.S. public diplomacy efforts. (See, for example, Appendix 6, containing significant portions of the fiscal year 1989 USIS country plan section on cultural and educational programs.) From the subjective hindsight of a former public affairs officer, it is clear that the apparent effectiveness of our public diplomacy in Brazil during 1971–75 grew out of the cooperation, understanding, and personal involvement of the ambassador and embassy staff, as well as the sympathetic assistance of USIA area and media specialists in Washington.

NOTES

1. Chapter 4 briefly describes the history and development of binational centers.

2. Those in Rio de Janeiro (IBEU), São Paulo (Alumni Association and *União Cultural*), Campinas, Santos, Curitiba, Porto Allegre, Victoria, Belo Horizonte, Brasilia (Casa Thomas Jefferson), Salvador, Recife, Fortaleza, São Luis, Belém, and Manaus.

3. Watts had to play on the only available concert grand in Brasilia at the time, an inferior instrument from the American ambassador's residence. He did so with skill and good humor, retuning the piano during intermission. In the end, he refused to accept even the previously arranged reduced fee, explaining that he was happy to contribute to this American cultural program in gratitude for what America had done for him in helping develop his career.

4. Crimmins was also a public servant who took the term seriously and personally. On one occasion he literally had to put his career on the line to save the life of a U.S. citizen who had been imprisoned and tortured by the Brazilian military in Recife. Crimmins never hesitated. He personally protested to the foreign minister — in this case, appropriately, in a confidential and not public manner — in such strong terms that the Brazilians came close to terminating his assignment as ambassador; but his action helped save a man's life. See Jeffrey D. Merritt, "The Ford Administration Response to Human Rights Violations in Brazil," in *The Diplomacy of Human Rights*, David D. Newsom, ed. (Washington, DC: Institute for the Study of Diplomacy and University Press of America, 1986), 111–15.

5. My own experience in Brazil persuaded me to insist strongly, frequently over USIA's objections, on having officers with adequate language capability assigned to USIS missions where I later served as public affairs officer. I sometimes lost that battle–to the detriment of the officer's career advancement and the post's communication mission.

6. "Country Data Sheet for Brazil," 1 October 1985, U.S. Information Agency, 12.

11
Dealing with the German "Successor Generation"

I n the late 1970s and early 1980s, both Americans and Germans concerned with U.S.–German relations began to recognize a problem posed by the gradual passing from positions of power and influence of a generation of Germans and Americans, many of whom had formed a network of human relationships linking the two nations since World War II. The network included many German emigres of the 1930s, half a million German prisoners of war who had spent years in the United States, tens of thousands of American and German officials who cooperated in the rebuilding of Germany, and the numerous participants in the large educational exchange programs of the early postwar years.

The generation taking their places had no similar formative experiences, observers in both countries realized, and consequently no comparable commitment to the German-American relationship. The younger they were, the less they remembered or even knew about the Marshall Plan, the origins of the Cold War and the NATO alliance, the Berlin airlift, Hungary in 1956, U.S. disarmament after World War II, or the rebuilding of Germany as a democratic, economically and socially viable society through the vision and dedication of its then-young citizens.

This gap of knowledge and understanding was perceived as posing a danger to the future cohesion of the German-American relationship. Furthermore, an alienation from their elders had taken place on the part of young Germans and young Americans alike, an alienation that consequently affected mutual understanding between the two societies.

Both American and German policymakers saw a need to intensify efforts to increase and improve intellectual contact between their young people, to rekindle an appreciation of their respective values and historical experiences, and to bring about better understanding of their spiritual, cultural, economic, and political interdependence.

German youth, according to our analysis, were suffering from a growing anxiety about the world in which they lived. Among the components of this angst were:

— the seeming helplessness of smaller nations and their citizens to moderate superpower confrontation and their frustration at being "in the middle";

— fear of war, especially nuclear destruction;

— environmental concerns;

— alienation in a highly industrial society consisting of large impersonal organizations, including government;

— the problems of unemployment in this harsher world with a shrinking social net;

— bad conscience over being part of an affluent society while millions in the Third World starve;

— absence of national identity, a consequence of living in a divided country that had been defeated and destroyed in a terrible war.

Many young Germans, observers concluded, identified the United States with the things that troubled them — especially the superpower competition, high technology, consumerism, emphasis on military build-up, and capitalistic society generally.

In the United States there had been, at the same time, an inward turning on the part of many in the younger generation, caused in large part by the events of the sixties and seventies: the Vietnam war, the civil rights revolution, and the political convulsions in our country — the assassinations, Watergate, the first resignation of a president. This turning inward resulted in a consequent lessening of interest in the world outside — in Europe, in Germany — as exemplified in school and university teaching. Foreign languages were generally no longer requirements for high school graduation or college entrance; and whatever interest in other countries still existed shifted to some extent to Latin America and Asia as U.S. involvement with those continents grew along with an influx of refugees from these lands.

By 1980, the political and intellectual leadership in the United States and the Federal Republic of Germany had become alarmed over the increased misunderstandings, misperceptions, and plain ignorance about each other's ideas, beliefs, and objectives, especially among the very generation succeeding to the reins of power and influence in our respective societies. It was agreed that this weakening in the net of associations and understanding was deleterious to the interdependence that had become a reality in our existence as free, democratic, and economically viable societies.

Those concerned with public diplomacy in the American embassy in Bonn asked: How *does* one go about rebuilding cultural and sociological bridges, not only between societies but also between generations, where structural differences exist, where tradition, history, national interests, and current political, economic, and security questions persist in complicating our efforts?

In addressing this question, we determined first that when we spoke about the so-called successor generation, we were dealing with what is essentially the post-successor or, perhaps, the successor-successor generation — the young people currently attending high school or entering their trades and professions as apprentices. They were the sons and daughters of those who had had their formative experiences in the 1960s. Second, as American public diplomats we had to concentrate on affecting the attitudes and prejudices of the youth in Germany, even though we knew we could not ignore the views of American young people.

Consequently we focused our attention on two objectives: better education about the United States in German high schools and colleges, and educational and cultural exchanges of young Americans and Germans.

As it is almost impossible to transmit experience and emotion direct from one generation to the next, it is the educational system in our democratic societies that has the responsibility to compensate for young people's lack of direct personal experience by teaching them ethics, history, languages, and political science. Only through a profound understanding of the history that had created the German-American relationship, through a grasp of the shared basic values, a feel for each other's culture, could we instill in our young people an understanding for our interdependence.

We determined that in German high schools and colleges there was a paucity of courses in contemporary history and political science. We learned that many young Germans seemed unable to differentiate between the moral and political order of the West (which, however imperfect, is capable of correcting and improving itself), and the oppressive and immutable totalitarianism of the Communist world.

On the basis of this analysis, USIS Bonn proposed to launch a program to provide accurate, comprehensive, and up-to-date information about the United States and American society to those who would lead the Federal Republic in the coming twenty-five years. The proposal was put forward in the fall of 1980, first in correspondence between USIS Bonn and the European area directorate in USIA and later more formally in USIS Bonn's country plan. The subject was vetted at length with the ambassador, Arthur Burns, and other members of the country team. Ambassador Burns not only gave it his full support but made this objective one of his own priorities as chief of mission.[1] This theme was to be a long-term public diplomacy objective, to be pursued vigorously and determinedly over at least ten years if there were going to be any prospect of achieving it.

The program that USIS Bonn devised included in the first instance a number of projects involving the teaching of American studies in German high schools and universities for the benefit of young people who would not have the opportunity of experiencing the United States personally and directly. Our targets were the teachers in teacher-training institutions and instructors in German high schools teaching English, history, and government.

Thus, since 1983 USIS Bonn has published an *American Studies Newsletter* three times a year, with a circulation of eighteen thousand, that is directed at secondary school teachers throughout the Federal Republic responsible for teaching about America in the context of their courses. In addition to supplying topical information about American society, the *Newsletter* calls attention to seminars and conferences dealing with American studies and to material available in the America House libraries and the six American Studies Resource Centers in the Federal Republic. The latter, established jointly by USIS Bonn and the German Association of American Studies, contain videotapes, film strips, slides, posters, and other illustrative American studies materials for the enrichment of instruction by secondary school teachers. (Both the centers and the *Newsletter* are discussed in Chapter 4.)

Next, USIS Bonn began to offer financial and program assistance to regional specialist conferences organized each year by the German Association of American Studies (GAAS), as well as to the association's annual general conference. The GAAS, whose membership now includes secondary school teachers, also invites to its conferences graduate students in American studies who are preparing for teaching careers.

That these efforts have a long way to go was evidenced in April 1989 when a number of eminent German Americanists complained, in a public appeal, that American history "is being dangerously neglected at German universities." The discipline of American history, they said, is represented only at every ninth university, and there is only one exclusive university chair for U.S. history in all of Germany, as compared with twenty to thirty chairs for Russian and Eastern European history. "This situation," they concluded, "is politically and academically irresponsible. Common ideological, economic, and security interests will not suffice in time of crisis to safeguard the German-American connection as a centerpiece of transatlantic relations. There is need for patient learning about the special history of the American people."[2]

USIS Bonn itself organizes approximately fifteen national and regional conferences each year for teachers of American studies and educators charged with teaching and training. USIS also cooperates with the Bavarian Ministry of Culture in organizing training conferences and consultations designed to improve the teaching of American studies in the high schools of that state. In Hamburg, as noted earlier, the regional USIS office works with the *Senator* (secretary) for education to establish teaching modules in American studies for use in the state's high schools. At the same time, USIS Bonn invites German high school teachers and *Fachleiter* (heads of departments) to visit the United States for a month — not as teachers but as important German gatekeepers. This exchange program complements those conducted by the German Marshall Fund, the American Council on Germany, the State of Bavaria, and the *Atlantik-Brücke*, a leading private German organization that promotes U.S.– German friendship. In addition, the Fulbright Commission, the German *Pädagogische Austtauschdienst* (Pedagogical Exchange Service) in Bonn, and USIA Washington cooperate in sponsoring a yearly paired exchange of about twenty-five high school teachers from each country who instruct in each other's schools for one school year.

The German and American governments have also been sponsoring a joint textbook revision project, intended to bring high school textbooks in the respective countries up to date and to correct errors, outdated provocations, or misleading statements. History and political science textbooks have been examined and reports issued. A third project has examined the textbooks and materials used in the teaching of English and German.

A second major effort undertaken to tighten the net between the two societies was in youth exchanges. We believed that by intensifying all our exchange programs we might be able to eliminate, or at least reduce, the misunderstandings, misinformation, and misperceptions that had been identified as seriously hampering the future of our relationship. It was also essential that our exchange mechanisms reinforce shared values, objectives, and ideals.

Much had been accomplished over the years through bilateral academic exchange programs — through the Fulbright Commission, the *Deutsche Akademische Austauschdienst* (DAAD, the German Academic Exchange Service), and thousands of privately organized exchanges. At this particular stage of our relationship, however, we decided to give even higher priority to official and private support of bilateral exchanges of teenagers, those in the critically formative years before university studies or working careers begin. It was therefore deemed appropriate, even necessary, for the two governments to provide these youth with better opportunities than had previously existed to become acquainted with each other's country and people.

Experience showed that a young person who spends a school year in another country, living in the home of a host family and participating in community activities, has a real opportunity to learn to understand that society. The insight and knowledge thus gained, we were convinced, could last a lifetime. One could not expect all young persons to become enamored of their partner country, but any criticism would be disciplined by first-hand knowledge.

Thus was born the Congress-Bundestag Youth Exchange Program, or *Parlamentarische Partnerschaft Programm* (PPP), as it is known in Germany. The idea originated in an exchange of correspondence in March 1982 between U.S. Senator John Heinz of Pennsylvania and Dr. Hildegard Hamm-Brücher, a Bundestag member and state minister in the FRG Foreign Ministry, and was "sanctified" in resolutions by both legislatures. Many observers see it as the most valuable legacy of the 1983 Tricentennial celebration of German immigration to America, as well as the most visible outgrowth of President Reagan's

Versailles International Youth Initiative in 1983. Simply stated, the purpose of this long-range program is to give the future leaders of the United States and the Federal Republic a genuine opportunity to know and to understand the partner society.[3]

Briefly, the program works as follows: The U.S. Congress and the FRG Bundestag appropriate funds—about $2.5 million per year for each side—to enable every member of both these bodies to sponsor one young person to spend a year going to school or learning a trade, living with a volunteer host family, and becoming intimately involved with a community in the partner country. It is the first such exchange program that ensures geographical distribution of its exchangees, that provides for a democratic selection process based on substantive qualifications rather than ability to pay, and that calls for the direct involvement of lawmakers in both countries.

Both governments have the long-term commitment to this program that is needed if the program is to succeed. For it requires a critical mass of young men and women—let us say, ten thousand—who know each other's country and people intimately and who can make a real and lasting impact on the relationship between the two societies.

Such an extensive exchange program cannot be conducted by the two governments alone. It requires the participation of such private nongovernmental organizations experienced in conducting international youth exchanges as the four nonprofit institutions first selected by both governments to administer the program—Youth for Understanding (YFU) of Washington, D.C., AFS International of New York, Experiment in International Living (EIL) of Brattleboro, Vermont, and the Duisberg Gesellschaft of Cologne (together with its subsidiary, the Duisberg Society of New York). These organizations, all with long experience in German-American teenage exchanges, had the infrastructure essential for the selection and follow-on counseling of the students and host families in both countries and for orienting and transporting the teenage participants. Without the participation of these institutions and their indispensable networks of thousands of volunteers in both countries, the Congress-Bundestag Program could not exist.[4]

There are also many privately funded German-American youth exchange programs that have similar aims and, in effect, complement those conducted by the U.S. government. Among these are the privately funded programs of YFU, AFS, and EIL, and those of Rotary International, the Federation of German-

American Clubs, and other nonprofit educational exchange institutions, as well as school-to-school exchanges like those administered by the German-American Partnership Program, financed by the FRG government with assistance from USIA.

The public diplomacy objective of this entire educational exchange program, which has been a priority in USIS Bonn country plans over several years,[5] is to develop in the German successor generation, most particularly the future leaders of the Federal Republic, a better understanding of our shared values and interdependence in the interest of a revitalized and mutually beneficial U.S.–German partnership. The public diplomacy programs enumerated in this chapter all aim at this objective.

A darkening cloud hung over this effort in 1985. USIA Washington managers who had to fight for resources for other programs — those devoted to Africa, the Middle East, and the Far East — increasingly criticized what they viewed as a disproportionate level of USIA resources devoted to the FRG program. The critics felt that the program increases in Germany, though championed by USIA Director Wick and supported by Ambassador Burns, were not justified in terms of overall USIA priorities.

USIS Bonn's argument against cutbacks was that the FRG program was justified, necessary, frugally managed, and effective, as evidenced in part by the respect, support, and funding it received from the FRG government. It was suggested that USIA use the successful German example as evidence justifying funding increases for other high-priority countries, rather than cutting the German program to the level of other programs. As of the fall of 1989, the U.S. public diplomacy effort in Germany, particularly the youth exchange program, continued at a slightly reduced funding level (caused by inflation), but still adequate for the purpose.

NOTES

Some of the material in this chapter first appeared in Hans N. Tuch, "The Problem and the Solution," *Atlantic Community Quarterly*, Vol. 23, No. 4 (Winter 1985–86), 367–73.

1. See Tuch, *Arthur Burns and the Successor Generation*, 1–12.

2. As quoted in a letter to the author dated April 10, 1989, from Professor Dr. Reinhard Doerries, University of Erlangen-Nürnberg.

3. For details on the Congress-Bundestag Exchange Program, see Tuch, *Arthur Burns and the Successor Generation*, 61–65.

4. Youth for Understanding has completed a study measuring the impact and effect of U.S.–German youth exchanges over the past thirty years. The German Marshall Fund of the United States provided support for this study.

5. See, for example, Appendix 2.

12

INF Deployment in the
Federal Republic of Germany

On December 2, 1987, Secretary of State George Shultz, commenting on the U.S. government's success in reaching an agreement with the Soviets on reduction of intermediate-range nuclear weapons (INF), called it "an illustration...of the tremendous impact and importance of public diplomacy."[1]

In his speech, Shultz sketched the background of the Reagan administration's "zero option" negotiating position implementing NATO's 1979 dual-track decision. That decision called for negotiating with the Soviets to remove their SS-20 nuclear missiles, but proceeding to deploy NATO intermediate-range nuclear missiles if the Soviets did not go along. As Secretary Shultz put it, the zero option suggested "that the Soviets take all of [their missiles] out and initially...we wouldn't deploy ours. But as ours became deployed then we'd take [them] out."

The secretary went on to explain:

As we came up to the time when, according to our schedule we would deploy the missiles, the Soviets got very nasty about it, intervened in the politics of Europe as best they could and said if you deploy those missiles, we would walk out of these negotiations.

We said we are going to deploy them according to our schedule and there's only one way you can stop us — that is agree to take yours out....

Now, I don't think we could have pulled it off if it hadn't been for a very active program of public diplomacy. Because...the Soviets were very active

161

all through 1983...with peace movements and all kinds of efforts to dissuade our friends in Europe from deploying. I shouldn't say they tried to persuade. They tried to bully, and they tried to threaten and intimidate....

[The U.S.] public diplomacy effort was very intensive, very well organized, and, as it turned out, very effective.[2]

Shultz's laudatory assessment of public diplomacy warms the heart of this former career public diplomat, who has at times been critical of the Reagan administration's understanding, or misunderstanding, of the term. Yet, one wonders whether the secretary of state, or even the director of the United States Information Agency, was aware of what went into the thinking and planning of their ambassador in Bonn, his advisors, and their Washington colleagues in devising the public diplomacy program the secretary praised so effusively.

Simply put, the challenge to U.S. public diplomacy was one of effectively supporting the governments of the basing countries (West Germany, Belgium, Holland, Italy, and Great Britain) in their determination to comply with the NATO decision to deploy INF weapons on their soil in the face of considerable domestic political and social opposition. That opposition, stimulated in part by a concerted Soviet campaign to influence European public opinion against deployment, was so strong in some of these countries that it threatened the continuation of the governments in power and, in some cases, the security and social order of the countries themselves.

In developing an appropriate public diplomacy program in support of the Bonn government's efforts to achieve the necessary political consensus for INF deployment in Germany, the U.S. embassy had to consider several aspects peculiar to the local situation. It also had to convince Washington that these factors were important to the success of our efforts. Our analysis included the following factors:

— A new center-right coalition government (Christian Democrats and Free Democrats) under Helmut Kohl — subsequently confirmed by a general election — that stood firmly behind the NATO decision;

— An opposition Social Democratic Party (SPD) deeply divided but opposed to deployment — even though the previous chancellor, Helmut Schmidt, now discredited but still recognized as the SPD's "elder statesman," had been the initial European promoter of the NATO double-track decision;

— A massive German "peace movement" uniting a number of disparate groups (environmentalist, women's rights, antinuclear, antiestablishment) of mostly young, well-educated, middle class people, spearheaded by the Green Party, newly elected into the Bundestag;

— Widespread anti-nuclear sentiment, fed by fears of nuclear holocaust or of nuclear accidents on their territory and by concern over the huge number of nuclear weapons already in their midst;

— Lessening of the German public's fear of Soviet aggression;

— Mistrust of American motives, especially of the Reagan administration's policies vis-à-vis the Soviet Union ("the evil empire"), but also in Central America, the Middle East, and South Africa; and

— Large-scale Communist, mostly East German, monetary and other support for the anti-deployment forces — but not direct from, and therefore not traceable to, the Soviet Union.

Under these circumstances, we in the U.S. embassy adopted the following approach in our public diplomacy support for INF deployment.

First, the Germans must always be seen to be in the lead. Our activities were to be strictly back-up and assistance; we must not be viewed as coercing the Germans into INF deployment. The double-track policy was a NATO alliance decision; the Federal Republic and the United States are members of the alliance; we Americans were guests on German soil; and it was therefore, in the first instance, the Germans' responsibility to implement the alliance decision in the Federal Republic, a responsibility they were willing and able to assume. Those in the FRG government were best qualified to communicate with their own citizenry.

Though they were appreciative of our support and advice, it would have been counterproductive for us to be seen as leading the campaign for deployment. We would not, for example, accept invitations to debate nuclear arms control issues with Soviet officials or with German opponents of deployment without the participation of German officials or politicians supporting the NATO double-track decisions. Such invitations came often and from all kinds of organizations — sometimes from those genuinely interested in information and ideas, and sometimes from those who wanted not debate about facts and opinions but confrontation, if possible with television coverage to generate publicity. We had to take care, through consultation with FRG authorities, not to fall into such traps.

As a second aspect of our approach, the U.S. ambassador, Arthur Burns, established the firm position that in any use of force by opponents of INF deployment against those protecting NATO installations, no U.S. troops would be involved. The Germans were responsible for the protection of NATO installations, and U.S. soldiers were instructed not to get involved in any confrontation with German citizens. Again, radical opponents of INF deployment might have sought such confrontation to create television publicity showing American troops "clobbering" German citizens on German soil.

Third, it was also important to prevent the tumult over the INF debate from obscuring the historical and emotional ties that served as the basis of the U.S.–German partnership. These other vital aspects to our relationship had to be maintained and not endangered by a troubling temporary issue.

There were some in Washington who wanted us to take a more aggressive approach. The president had appointed his ambassador to Ireland, Peter H. Dailey, as public diplomacy "czar" to coordinate the U.S. government's policy. Dailey's efforts were beneficial in sorting out and coordinating the sometimes conflicting public messages emanating from Washington. Yet we advised against a personal visit by him to Germany, believing that his presence would "draw fire" unnecessarily. There was also a strong suggestion from Washington, resisted almost unanimously by U.S. ambassadors and public affairs officers in the basing countries, for another television spectacular like "Let Poland Be Poland."

Ambassador Burns's influence in Washington was instrumental in helping his PAO turn off some of the more aggressive attempts to dramatize the INF deployment issue in Germany. Burns persuaded Vice President Bush, for instance, to permit adjustments to a major speech he was to deliver in West Berlin on U.S. arms control policy. Even more significant, he persuaded the vice president to speak at the opening of a museum wing dedicated to the works of German-American artist Josef Albers in the Ruhr city of Bottrop, the artist's birthplace. In this way we aimed to demonstrate that Bush had come to take part in the June 1983 tricentennial celebration of German immigration to America not for political reasons alone, but to express America's deep commitment to the cultural ties that bind the two nations.

In the event, the vice president delivered a short but eloquent speech at the dedication in Bottrop that was widely welcomed. On the same day, the radical opposition took advantage of the vice president's presence in Krefeld to dramatize its contempt for U.S. policies in general by permitting, perhaps even instigating, hundreds of imported "chaotics" — anarchistic troublemakers and punks — to launch a vicious stone-throwing attack at the vice president's motorcade that disrupted the festive atmosphere of the tricentennial occasion.

USIS Bonn's approach to the INF deployment issue involved all pertinent embassy elements under the ambassador's personal direction. Plans were discussed between the PAO in Bonn and the European area director at USIA in Washington, primarily by letter, telegram, and telephone. It was a relatively short-term issue that required expeditious action to succeed. The country plan process would have taken too long. (For the record, USIS Bonn did present and rationalize its program on this issue more formally in the subsequent country plan exercise.)

The target audiences for dealing with the INF issue in the Federal Republic were the print media, those writers and editors of the major responsible newspapers and journals whose writings had a multiplier effect; the political sector — members of the federal and state legislatures, the political foundations, and the think tanks, who voted, or influenced the voting, on the issue in legislative bodies; and a number of social, religious, and educational institutions whose members, though possibly opposed to INF deployment and nuclear arms in general, were amenable to intelligent discussion and debate as part of the democratic process. USIS Bonn expressly did not concentrate on the electronic media, convinced that they tended to radicalize the issue and contribute to mass emotion rather than rational disputation. The subject of INF deployment, furthermore, was too complex to be clarified and discussed in sound bites and brief visuals.

It should be noted that the parliamentary-type FRG government places a much greater emphasis on party discipline than does the U.S. political process. In the INF deployment case, the government coalition had the votes to win, or else it would have fallen. Yet it would debate the issue in the Bundestag and in public fora to build grass roots support and make its policy more widely understood. It was in this public debate that respected and knowledgeable Americans would be asked by USIS Bonn to weigh in in support of the NATO decision.

Washington responded quickly to the Bonn embassy's requests for support. Under the guidance of Assistant Secretary Richard Burt, the State Department prepared a comprehensive publication in pamphlet form entitled *Security and*

Arms Control: The Search for a More Stable Peace, describing the history and rationale of U.S. efforts to achieve nuclear arms control, particularly in intermediate-range nuclear forces. USIS Bonn immediately translated the pamphlet into German and distributed ten thousand copies. This valuable publication was then supplemented by a weekly distribution of translated Wireless File material following up on the pamphlet with authoritative statements and background information for the use of individuals in the target groups listed above.

In both the pamphlet and our discussions with German audiences, our public diplomacy emphasized certain themes: (1) that the U.S. was earnestly pursuing an arms control agreement with the Soviet Union in Geneva and, despite Soviet polemics to the contrary, the U.S. goal was to achieve a balance of INF forces on a lower level or, better still, to eliminate them; (2) that the INF dual-track strategy was in the interest of *all* members of the alliance, and decoupling the United States from European security by permitting a Soviet monopoly on intermediate-range nuclear forces would be disastrous for Europe; and (3) that nonviolent protesters were exercising their rights of free speech and assembly — rights that missile deployment was designed to protect — but violent protest endangered the very democratic institutions of the country.

The public diplomacy effort, while coordinated by USIS, involved the ambassador and all available officers who felt qualified, linguistically and substantively, to speak, discuss, and debate these themes. The USIS office, often in consultation with German authorities, evaluated all speaking invitations. Ambassador Burns was used judiciously in public fora, such as the German Armed Forces' *Führungsakademie* and the Loccum Evangelical Academy. He also met frequently with editors and reporters on defense and foreign affairs issues. (Ambassador Burns, on principle, never spoke off-the-record or on "background" when he met with representatives of the media; he always insisted on speaking *on* the record.)

We could not have done the job, however, without the assistance of volunteer speakers from the American Participants (AmParts) Program, who discussed these issues with German audiences selected by USIS Bonn.[3] USIA in Washington sent us the speakers we requested or selected others who would contribute to our objectives.

Some of these speakers were much abler than we to alleviate the concerns of many Germans that the Reagan administration might not be serious about arms control. (Earlier visits to the Federal Republic by a few administration officials had helped sow such doubts.) Several AmParts speakers — sometimes in the face of hefty opposition — effectively underscored for target audiences that the United States was sincere regarding its arms control aims and that reaching solid, verifiable agreements involved more than trusting in the good will of one's negotiating partner.

These discussions with high-level German decision makers involved both current and former U.S. government officials, among them Paul Nitze, Maynard Glitman, Richard Burt, Helmut Sonnenfeldt, Mark Palmer, Lynn Hansen, and Sven Kramer. Among the many nongovernment experts who assisted us in addressing this issue were William Griffith of MIT, Michael Novak of the American Enterprise Institute, and Gregory Flynn of the Atlantic Institute in Paris.

The Mothers of Filderstadt

The emotional grip of the nuclear weapons issue on the German citizenry was epitomized in early 1982 by the grassroots activities of a tiny group of politically committed women in Filderstadt, a bedroom community near Stuttgart. The "Mothers of Filderstadt," as they called themselves, addressed an appeal to President Reagan and Chairman Brezhnev expressing their fears about nuclear weapons on German soil and the attendant dangers.

Deftly exploiting Moscow's quick, sympathetic reply, the Soviet ambassador invited the women to Bonn to receive it in front of the television cameras. When the women complained, mildly, that they had received no response from Washington, USIS Bonn realized they had missed an opportunity to explain U.S. policy to a grassroots group of German voters and launched a friendly if sometimes intense dialogue with the group, including visits back and forth in Bonn and Filderstadt.

On the occasion of President Reagan's first visit to the Federal Republic on June 9, 1982, USIS Bonn suggested that he include in his speech before the Bundestag a reference to the concerns of the Filderstadt mothers and thereby accomplish two objectives at once: to make up for the previous lapse and to give, as he so often did, a humanizing spin to U.S. policy. This embassy suggestion was initially ignored by the president's speech writers. In a last-minute appeal to White House communications director David Gergen, however, Ambassador Burns effectively conveyed his sense of the value of "letting Reagan be Reagan" vis-à-vis the German public, and the Filderstadt reference was included.

It turned out to be the right touch: The American president had considered a group of German women from a little-known hamlet important enough to address them personally in a major speech before the federal parliament on an issue of global importance about which he and the American public also felt deeply. Fascinated no doubt by the president's addressing German women living in a place hardly any of them had ever heard of, the German media pounced upon this human interest element, which thereby added immediacy, increased relevance, and the all-important personal touch to the president's significant statement of U.S. policy.

The speech remained on the front pages for days, aided in part by correspondents who searched out and interviewed the surprised, but pleased Filderstadt women. Subsequently, the "mothers of Filderstadt" became the German equivalent of Reagan's "lady from Dubuque."

Because of the year-long commemoration in 1983 of the tricentennial of German immigration to America, we practitioners of U.S. public diplomacy found many natural opportunities to emphasize the historical, ethnic, ideological, and traditional bases of the U.S.–German partnership. The numerous occasions for talking about the values, the culture, and the institutions that bind us permitted us to place the sometimes tumultuous INF debate in its proper context, namely the firm foundation on which our partnership rests, notwithstanding frequent differences in policies and views. The public affairs officer alone gave eighteen such speeches during 1983. Other embassy officers and many noted speakers from the United States also contributed to this effort.

Vice President Bush made this point eloquently when he spoke at Krefeld in June 1983 in the presence of the president and chancellor of the Federal Republic on the occasion of the principal tricentennial event. At Schloss Hambach in the Rhineland-Palatinate, at another commemorative event, Senator Richard Lugar delivered the keynote address and the noted American historian Gordon Craig traced the major themes in the 300–year old German-American relationship . And Ambassador Burns, to cite just one more of many examples, delivered a widely reported address to the distinguished Overseas Club in Hamburg in March of that year on the subject, "The Human Side of German-American Relations."[4]

If these efforts illustrate, as Secretary Shultz concluded in the speech cited earlier, "the tremendous impact and importance of public diplomacy," then one could cite the actions of Embassy Bonn and USIA Washington as evidence of effectiveness. From a wider perspective, however, the success of INF deployment and the eventual conclusion of the INF Treaty are more fairly attributable to the cohesiveness of the NATO alliance, an alliance that was strong and capable of making its decisions stick over a concerted Soviet psychological campaign to disrupt NATO. It was an alliance victory — to which U.S. public diplomacy contributed — over the efforts of the Soviets and others to marshall public opinion against NATO cohesion.

USIS Bonn's assessment at the time, in April 1984, also struck a cautionary note:

> The [INF deployment] victory...does not come without some serious losses, the principal one...being the loss of a security consensus among the FRG's major political parties and on the part of a large element of the German public. This loss is all the more serious because it is part of, and contributes to, steadily growing negative public perceptions of U.S. foreign policy. These negative perceptions are summarized in USIA Foreign Opinion Note of January 30, 1984, which states, 'The prevailing view is that U.S. policies endanger peace, and lack of confidence in U.S. foreign policy prevails.' These perceptions are shared by both younger and older better-educated members of the population.[5]

In light of this chapter's attempt to describe the public diplomacy dimension of an important foreign policy objective, the reader may find it useful to examine the findings of an earlier USIA public opinion study, conducted in the fall of 1983 to help USIS Bonn assess German attitudes:

> By a better than two-to-one majority (66% to 28%) the German public exhibits pro- rather than anti-American sentiments. But they are no better than evenly divided (46% and 49%) in their perception of shared values with the U.S.
>
> Predominant pro-American sentiment and a fairly widespread, though not prevailing, identification with American values do not prevent a majority (59% to 35%) from expressing little confidence in U.S. handling of global problems.
>
> And more disturbingly, a narrow plurality (50% to 43%) has little or no confidence in the U.S. commitment to defend the Federal Republic if the safety of American cities would be at risk. This prevailing lack of confidence exists alongside a fairly widespread belief that U.S. leaders think a nuclear

war can be won in Europe. This often-reiterated theme of INF opponents is apparently accepted by 44% of the German public, almost as many (51%) as reject the notion.

In fact, the Soviet Union enjoys greater credibility than the U.S. on the limited nuclear war issue. A solid majority (62% to 33%) do not believe that Moscow thinks a nuclear war can be confined to, [or] is winnable, in Europe. This is the only indicator where the German public rates the Soviet Union better than the U.S. It contrasts sharply with the predominantly negative overall Soviet image and particularly with the majority's (60% to 22%) lack of faith in the Soviet Union to dismantle its West Europe-aimed SS-20s even if "an agreement were reached that required the USSR to do so."[6]

Whether this or other surveys are conclusive or even useful is often disputed, because too many extraneous factors affect the accuracy and objectivity of the polling. Although such surveys cannot by themselves be considered definitive, they do, however, contribute to the body of information that the policymaker and the program manager need in order to make intelligent decisions. In the view of USIS Bonn, the findings reported above indicated trends that could not be addressed by public diplomacy measures alone; they deserved serious consideration by both Bonn and Washington, because German perceptions of America and its foreign policies affect the long-term U.S.–German relationship.

Finally, the reader may find noteworthy, in the context of this case study that, four months after the cautious April 1984 assessment noted earlier, USIS Bonn was able to cite an *International Herald Tribune* poll that confirmed what many of us had already suspected: The angst level in the Federal Republic had diminished markedly. Only 14 percent of those surveyed in May 1984 listed "the threat of war" as a major concern, while six months earlier 23 percent of respondents had placed the threat high on their lists. And, finally, only five months after INF deployment began, "concern over weapons" had fallen sharply from 38 percent to 15 percent.[7]

NOTES

1. Speaking at the annual meeting of USIA's Private Sector Committees at the Department of State (*USIA World*, February 1988, 13).

2. Ibid.

3. See Chapter 4 for background on the AmParts program.

4. This speech appears in its entirety in Tuch, *Arthur Burns and the Successor Generation*, 21–34.

5. Letter from Hans Tuch, Minister for Public Affairs, Embassy Bonn, dated April 2, 1984, to Charles E. Courtney, Director, European Affairs, USIA Washington.

6. *USIA Research Memorandum*, Office of Research, 21 Dec. 1983.

7. Letter from Hans Tuch, Minister of Public Affairs, Bonn, dated August 13, 1984, to Marlin Remick, Acting Director, European Affairs, USIA Washington.

Epilogue

The reader of this book might conclude that the author attributes to the USIA public affairs officer the qualities of a deity who did not rest even on the seventh day. By placing the public affairs officer in the center of the public diplomacy universe, the book attempts to describe the actual conduct of public diplomacy in the field — the process of why, who, what, and where. That, the author acknowledges, may project an egocentric — or, from the reader's perspective, a possibly lopsided — viewpoint, suggesting that PAOs have greater responsibilities, greater wisdom, and greater powers than they do in reality.

Those sitting in Washington, near the seat of power or embedded in the bureaucracy, may disparage the author's "puffing up" the importance of the PAOs and their USIS colleagues or glamorizing their role. They would point out that PAOs *recommend* to Washington — they do not determine priorities; PAOs *advise* the ambassador or the USIA area director on foreign public opinion — they do not make policy. The PAOs direct programs in a relatively limited segment of the public diplomacy spectrum. They may think that their daily or monthly reports on public attitudes or on the effectiveness of their post's information and cultural programs will be awaited and heeded by the powers in the capital, but Washington skeptics will question their impact on those making policy.

In describing specific public diplomacy programs — youth exchanges, libraries, publications — or in detailing certain public diplomacy experiences, the author may appear to have exaggerated their significance or effectiveness in the overall foreign affairs process. That was not his intent. What he tried to do was describe one important aspect of the foreign affairs process that is less than adequately understood in the United States and, in the process, may have indulged his enthusiasm for the profession. He wrote primarily from the field practitioner's perspective to lend this account practicality, reality, and immediacy.

Public diplomacy is only one element in what makes up the conduct of foreign affairs, and the public affairs officer, the field practitioner of public diplomacy, is only one piston in the foreign affairs engine. But without that one well-oiled piston, the engine would cough and sputter on its uphill drive.

Appendices

Appendix 1

Directors of the U.S. Information Agency

Theodore C. Streibert	8-5-53 *to* 1-15-56
Arthur Larson	12-18-56 *to* 10-27-57
George V. Allen	11-15-57 *to* 12-1-60
Edward R. Murrow	3-15-61 *to* 1-20-64
Carl T. Rowan	2-27-64 *to* 8-31-65
Leonard H. Marks	8-31-65 *to* 12-12-68
Frank Shakespeare	2-7-69 *to* 2-7-73
James Keogh	2-8-73 *to* 11-30-76
John E. Reinhardt	3-23-77 *to* 1-20-81
Charles Z. Wick	6-9-81 *to* 1-19-89
Bruce S. Gelb	4-17-89 *to*

Appendix 2

USIS Germany Country Plan Fiscal Year 1986

OVERVIEW:

Although the United States and Germany were adversaries in two world wars within this century, in the postwar period the United States and the Federal Republic of Germany (FRG) have forged a close and valued relationship. Indeed, the FRG is today the nation on the continent that is closest in structure and basic philosophy to the United States. Many of the fundamental institutions of the Federal Republic, including the federal system itself, were consciously based on American models. Commitment to and faith in democracy, devotion to the rule of law, and respect for individual human rights are values basic to both societies. Beyond that, the leaders and much of the citizenry in both countries understand the importance of their inter-dependence for their economic prosperity and their political security.

The FRG is economically the strongest nation in Western Europe. It is a pivotal nation in the Atlantic Alliance and in multilateral approaches to global problems. Retaining Germany as a close and respected partner is essential to our vision of a free and democratic world. In turn, FRG governments during the past 35 years have acted upon the recognition that Germany's security is based on the NATO shield and ultimately on the U.S. commitment to its protection.

German foreign policy interests, however, are not always automatically identified with those of the U.S. — witness differing assessments of and approaches to the Polish situation, Soviet expansionism, the Middle East conflict, the economic demands of the Third World, arms control and disarmament, trade relations with the East, West-West economics, overall East-West relations and Central America.

The FRG's actions and policies are shaped and governed by a series of factors: first, its vulnerability (owing to its geographic location) in the event of a war, which has given rise to the fear among many Germans that their land might end up a nuclear graveyard; second, the fact that it is a regional rather than a global power; third, its hope for nuclear arms reduction agreements; fourth, its deep desire to preserve detente and perpetuate what it sees as its benefits (among them, continued

178

contacts with the other Germany, the stability that keeps Berlin secure under the Quadripartite Agreement, and the economic gains from extensive trade with the East Bloc); fifth, its determination to keep alive at least the vision of a reunited Germany; and sixth, the image it wishes to portray in the Third World as a progressive country that is opposed to far right regimes and is prepared to tolerate political experiments on the democratic left-of-center.

But despite the image it seeks to portray to the world and its standing today, the FRG remains a nation beset with contradictions and "internal fears"; a nation experiencing structural economic problems; a nation seeking to reconcile the growing desire for a national identity with the realities of world politics.

The transition from a left-center SPD/FDP [Social Democratic Party/Free Democratic Party] coalition to the conservative-center coalition of the CDU/CSU/FDP [Christian Democratic Union/Christian Social Union/Free Democratic Party] that took place in 1982 demonstrated again that the West German political system is able to accommodate change within its democratic framework. Yet, for the first time in the postwar period, a leftist-oriented fringe group, the Greens (an amalgam of anti-establishment, anti-nuclear, environmentalist, radical pacifists) is now represented in the Bundestag. Although the Greens have not been a major parliamentary power, there is sufficient public interest in the diverse elements of their political program to command adherence, or at least engender a sympathetic hearing, from a number of educated, young, urban Germans. Partially as a result of the Greens' successes, the SPD has been reassessing its own policies with the hope of recapturing some of the young voters who have turned toward the Greens. In the process, the SPD has shifted its policy from one of support of NATO's dual-track missile deployment decision to its rejection, thereby reneging on its former Chancellor's previous commitment.

Despite the SPD's shift in security policy and the Greens' current success in attracting voters in state and municipal elections, Germany's foreign policy continues on a steady course. As under the SPD/FDP government of Helmut Schmidt, the CDU/CSU/FDP coalition under Helmut Kohl pursues a foreign policy that is firmly anchored to the Western defense alliance (NATO) and to a partnership with the United States.

CURRENT ISSUES:

The following details the most important of those issues with which we must deal in the foreseeable future.

One of the most significant differences in the perspectives of the two governments concerns how best to deal with the Soviet Union. Continuity in the German approach toward Eastern Europe, for example, is expressed by the Kohl Government as a policy of "the outstretched hand." In keeping with this policy, the FRG government regularly extends economic credits to the GDR [German Democratic Republic] with the understanding, not stated publicly, that the GDR will in turn make concessions involving eased access of FRG citizens to the East or the relaxation of rules governing the emigration of GDR citizens to the West. These arrangements, callously mercenary as they may be on the part of the GDR, have special meaning for citizens of the FRG as they continue to strive for a closer relationship with the 17 million "other" Germans.

We will continue to reaffirm U.S. support for the FRG's desire for closer ties to its fellow Germans in the east and for a free and democratic Germany reunited by peaceful means—a goal which most responsible Germans agree will not be achieved in the near future.

U.S. support for the status of Berlin continues to be an important theme. Whenever appropriate, we will repeat the January 1985 message of President Reagan to the people of Berlin: that our "commitment is unshakeable."

Although most Germans did not blame the U.S. for the Soviet walkout of the arms negotiations in late 1983, many asserted that a more conciliatory posture on our part might have prevented that action and could even have resulted in positive movement. A year later, skepticism about the earnestness of the Reagan Administration's desire for arms reductions was revised somewhat when the president's strategy succeeded in bringing the Soviets back to the negotiating table without the concession of slowing the pace of missile deployment in the FRG or dismantling missiles already in place.

Now that the talks have reopened, the public affairs challenge will be to explain the U.S. position clearly to German audiences without building exaggerated expectations for early resolution of the fundamental differences in the stands of the two superpowers.

Almost two years after it was first articulated on March 23, 1983, the president's Strategic Defense Initiative (SDI) has generated heated debate in the FRG media and among politicians and security experts of all political parties. It is likely to be vigorously discussed throughout the period of its preliminary research phase. Some German commentators credit the SDI with getting the Soviet Union to return to arms control negotiations, but many others consider the initiative destabilizing and are concerned about its potential for "decoupling" European security from that of the United States. Soviet propaganda is certain to capitalize on these reservations about the SDI in the months to come. We should state and restate the basic purpose of the program: to seek a viable defensive system that would render offensive strategic weapons useless. We should also emphasize that at this time the United

States is only undertaking extensive research into the feasibility of such a system and that development and deployment are still years away.

While the German GNP is growing at a healthy but measured rate, unemployment is still unacceptably high, particularly in the heavy industries. Investment, one of the economic engines that has driven the U.S. recovery and created so many new jobs in the process, has lagged behind in the FRG. Many Germans blame high U.S. budget deficits and the accompanying high interest rates for drawing off capital vitally necessary for the growth of the FRG's economy. Though they appreciate the surge in American imports that has made the U.S. the second largest market for German goods, some German economists look beyond that immediate gain to the darker side of the American trade deficit: increased domestic pressure in the U.S. for protection from European goods made cheaper by an over-valued dollar.

The U.S. position on the Coordinating Committee (COCOM) issues has been criticized by the German economic press for placing too stringent export controls on "high tech" trade, not only with the Eastern Bloc but with our closest allies. Some journalists claim we are exercising "extra-territorial powers" over our European trading partners by insisting that users with access to certain sophisticated computer equipment be subject to security checks in conflict with local law. Others have argued that, under the guise of concern for national security, the U.S. computer industry is being unfairly protected from foreign competition. We need to counter these arguments by emphasizing that COCOM involves our European allies in the decision making and that, in certain cases, Alliance security must come before East-West trade.

The conservative American view that many domestic and international economic problems can be solved more efficiently by the strengthening of free market forces, is regarded by some Germans as an insensitive economic philosophy which benefits the rich and leaves the poor to fend for themselves. The U.S. social services system, and the Reagan approach to it, are misunderstood here; these are issues we must continue forcefully and urgently to address. Unhappiness about U.S. economic policies also reinforces a critical posture vis-a-vis American defense and security policies. And it spills over, eventually, into the entire range of other issues in which we need — and seek — German understanding and support. The task before us is to demonstrate that American policies serve not only American interests but are also largely congruent with and supportive of German interests — economic, political and military.

It would be wrong to let ourselves be lulled into complacency by the fact that all serious polls show that America's popularity is still strong in Germany; that the vociferous "Peace Movement" does not seem to reflect mainstream thinking; and that there is no significant revival of neutralism or pacifism among responsible elements of German society. The concerns expressed by an articulate minority — the fear of war, especially nuclear destruction; the feeling of resentment and frustration at having little control over events that will determine their fate; the anxiety that Germany is becoming a pawn in the struggle between superpowers; the perception of U.S. actions in Central America and in Grenada as aggressive, reactionary and imperialist in nature; worries about the environment, particularly in regard to nuclear power; and psychological alienation in a highly industrialized society — all of these must be addressed because such fears, if left unchallenged, could grow eventually to pervade the consciousness of all segments of our audience.

Those in the FRG most susceptible to these fears are the young. Today, more than half of the German population has no personal memory of the horrors and terrible aftermath of World War II. They also missed the positive experiences of that generation of Germans and Americans who were part of a network of human relationships linking the countries in the postwar era.

This "successor generation" has largely formed its view of America through the prism of Vietnam, the civil rights movement, the protest explosion of the late sixties and early seventies and Watergate — which it considers to be *its* history lesson. Members of this age group tend to look upon the United States as a conservative society, the defender of the status quo, and as less advanced in social policy than most European nations. Many of this generation believe that the best long-term policy for the FRG would be to steer a course midway between the two superpowers. Their rhetoric makes no distinctions between the totalitarian East and the democratic West. In short, they tend to see the U.S. and the USSR as morally equivalent.

We must try to persuade this younger generation of Germans that the ties that have been established between our two societies over three centuries, but especially since World War II, are beneficial for both countries and indeed necessary for the preservation of our democratic systems and peace. A practical way to accomplish this is by encouraging greater knowledge and understanding of each other's institutions, culture and ideas through programs at our America Houses and German-American Institutes and through meaningful exchanges among young people of our two countries.

The president's Youth Exchange Initiative, particularly the Congress-Bundestag Teenage Exchange Program, promises to become a major vehicle for allowing young Germans and Americans to know and understand each other better. These exchanges, which will wherever possible be long-term and include homestays, school attendance and community integration, are vital if the peoples of our two countries are to avoid some of the misunderstandings and misperceptions that have proliferated during the past 10–15 years.

The Congress-Bundestag Exchange Project, for which funds have been appropriated by both governments, will include up to 500 high school students and apprentices from each country in 1985.

Since it is not feasible to give more than a small minority of young people a direct experience in the United States, it is important that we concentrate our efforts on the schools, where students receive most of their basic information about the United States and form their earliest impressions. Their information about American society is often superficial and confused, their social science courses frequently taught by teachers who are themselves products of the sixties and often hostile to America and what it represents to them. Because political attitudes and opinions in Germany are usually formed before young people reach the university level or embark on working careers, our American Studies program efforts are directed mainly at *Gymnasium* [academic high school] (last three years only) and university students in the fields of English, history, political science and social science. In addition, special emphasis is placed on high school teachers in the above disciplines (particularly American Studies and English), on universities/colleges where high school teachers are trained, and on teaching materials used in the upper high school classes. USIS library collections and reference services are heavily used by German students and teachers of American Studies at all levels.

ASSESSMENT OF THE QUALITY AND FLOW OF INFORMATION AND EXCHANGES:

The Federal Republic is an information-saturated society connected instantaneously with all corners of the world. Scores of U.S.-based correspondents from the press, radio and television file sophisticated reports about the U.S., on international and domestic issues alike, as the events are taking place. Evening radio or television news broadcasts invariably include one or more important stories from the U.S. Documentary items on foreign policy and security issues involving the U.S., as well as entertainment and human interest stories, are almost daily features of the German media scene. While television reporting on the U.S. can be tendentious at times, it is no more so than the coverage on the U.S. networks. Indeed, the German media often follow the lead of their American counterparts in setting the tone on a given subject. USIS Germany has cordial relations with the media in the FRG. Through personal contacts, printed materials, cooperative projects, facilitative assistance and Worldnet, USIS makes its influence felt among important members of the media community. As is the case in the United States, however, news media will seldom publish or broadcast materials produced or distributed by foreign governments or their agencies.

Exchange Mix:

We see no need to alter our current mix of allocations for Fulbright and non-Fulbright programs. Approximately 32% of our program is allocated to youth exchanges, 56% to the Fulbright programs, 12% to international visitors. (These figures exclude the Congress-Bundestag Youth Exchange Program, which we treat as a separate item.) We think this breakdown of percentages is appropriate to our mission goals.

The following are the principal immediate *issues and concerns* which we identify for USIS concentration in FY 1985:

1. *FOREIGN POLICY/SECURITY*

A. *INF/Arms Control*

Nuclear arms control remains the most critical public affairs issue for the U.S. in West Germany. The task of persuading public opinion that deployment under current circumstances is in Germany's best interest remains primarily a German responsibility. It is important, however, that the U.S. support and complement this effort. We should focus on convincing Germans that even as deployment progresses at its pre-arranged rate, the U.S. is actively and earnestly pursuing the first track of the double track decision: arms reduction.

OBJECTIVE: SEEK TO PERSUADE BOTH GENERAL AND SPECIALIZED PUBLICS THROUGHOUT THE FRG THAT THE U.S. IS STRIVING FOR PEACE, WITH FREEDOM, AND FOR GENUINE AND VERIFIABLE ARMS REDUCTIONS AND IS DEDICATED TO EASING EAST-WEST TENSIONS.

B. *East-West Relations*

There are differing perceptions in the U.S. and the FRG on East-West political and economic relations. We should convey to our German audiences (particularly young Germans) that the U.S. approach to the Soviet Union is to have a relationship based upon mutual restraint and reciprocity. At the same time, we must remind the Germans of the threat of Soviet expansionism, making clear that the conduct of the USSR in Poland, Afghanistan, the Middle East, and other pressure points cannot but affect East-West relations and that the transfer of certain high technology goods aids the Soviet military build-up.

OBJECTIVE: INCREASE UNDERSTANDING THAT THE U.S. SEEKS A STABLE AND CONSTRUCTIVE RELATIONSHIP WITH THE SOVIET UNION WHILE MAINTAINING A CREDIBLE MILITARY DETERRENCE, CONVENTIONAL AND NUCLEAR.

- Remind both general and specialized publics throughout Europe that the United States stands ready to negotiate, has walked out of no talks, and has accepted negotiations with the Soviets even while the latter continued both INF missile deployment and its many-year massive and offense-oriented military buildup.

- Develop an understanding of, and support for, SDI among FRG political, defense and media specialists.

- Remind all German publics as frequently as possible of Soviet actions in Afghanistan.

C. *NATO Alliance*

While accepting that in a democratic alliance divergent perceptions on certain issues are inevitable, we should aim to underscore the shared interests and values (which go way beyond the military and security issues), and to demonstrate that a unified and strong NATO is a vital element in the preservation of peace in Europe.

OBJECTIVE: DEVELOP AN UNDERSTANDING AMONG WEST GERMAN SPECIALIZED PUBLICS OF THE MILITARY REASONS FOR STRENGTHENING NATO'S CONVENTIONAL FORCES.

- With the help of those specialized publics, convince West German general publics of the need for increased investment in defense and of the benefits (military and economic) that would ensue from the rational resources strategy which the U.S. has proposed.

- Seek to persuade West German general and specialized publics, that the U.S. commitment to the NATO Alliance is strong and enduring and will not be uncoupled.

D. *Central America*

German public perceptions of American policies in the Third World — particularly in Central America — are frequently critical and negative. We must make an effort to correct false perceptions of U.S. motives and goals.

OBJECTIVE: CONVINCE GERMAN GENERAL PUBLICS THAT THE U.S. IS RESPONDING IN A CONSTRUCTIVE MANNER TO CENTRAL AMERICAN DESIRES FOR POLITICAL AND ECONOMIC REFORM, AND IS DISCOURAGING EXTREMES OF THE RIGHT AND LEFT.

E. *Unified Europe*

No European nation is more deeply committed than the Federal Republic of Germany to strengthening the sense of community within the Continent. The FRG sees its own security and economic future inextricably tied to NATO, the European Community, and the European Parliament. While the U.S. may take exception from time to time with the positions taken by European nations in these organizations, we, too, believe that our own future depends to a great extent upon European unity.

OBJECTIVE: DEMONSTRATE TO BOTH GENERAL AND SPECIALIZED PUBLICS IN WEST GERMANY THAT THE U.S. HAS, AND FULLY RECOGNIZES, A STAKE IN A STRONG AND UNIFIED EUROPE. SEEK TO CONVEY TO WEST GERMAN SPECIALIZED PUBLICS OUR RECOGNITION THAT THE PACIFIC BASIN *IS* IMPORTANT, BUT THAT EUROPE REMAINS OUR PRINCIPAL DEFENSE PARTNER, AN IMPORTANT TRADING PARTNER, AND A FUNDAMENTAL PART OF AN INCREASINGLY IMPORTANT TRILATERALISM IN AMERICAN FOREIGN POLICY.

2. *U.S. ECONOMIC POLICIES*

Differing U.S.-European Community (read also German) approaches toward free trade — especially with regard to agricultural exports — have led to strains which, if not abated, could lead ultimately to the most serious rift within the Alliance. It is important, therefore, that we persuasively advance the proposition that America is not pursuing a policy of confrontational selfishness, but that U.S. and European needs and concerns are essentially compatible.

OBJECTIVE: CONVINCE WEST GERMAN SPECIALIZED PUBLICS THAT THE U.S. IS COMMITTED TO A VIABLE, OPEN GLOBAL INTERNATIONAL TRADE AND FINANCE SYSTEM THAT EASES DEBT PROBLEMS, PROMOTES LDC [less developed countries] GROWTH AND REDUCES UNEMPLOYMENT IN THE WORLD, CALLING ADDITIONAL ATTENTION TO THE CONTRIBUTION THAT FREE-MARKET ECONOMICS CAN MAKE IN REDUCING CHRONIC UNEMPLOYMENT AND STAGNATION OF INDUSTRY IN WESTERN EUROPE.

3. *AMERICAN SOCIETY IN A CHANGING WORLD*

In view of the almost apolitical revolt among an articulate and growing minority of young people against the institutions of a modern society (in which the U.S. is again the "anti-model") — an important task is to present evidence that the U.S. is indeed a dynamic, creative, vital and, above all, a just and democratic society. This is the rationale for providing balanced information on American political, social and cultural processes, and for encouraging the more effective teaching of American Studies in upper high school grades and universities.

We need to address the concerns and misconceptions of many of our target audiences, especially the youth in Germany, in regard to the extent and nature of the U.S. social net, and to correct the misperception of those who regard the U.S. as the "anti-model," a society in which the rich get richer and the poor poorer.

OBJECTIVE: SEEK TO STRENGTHEN A PERCEPTION AMONG ALL GERMANS, BUT ESPECIALLY AMONG THE YOUNGER GENERATIONS, THAT THE U.S. REMAINS A DYNAMIC AND CREATIVE SOCIETY WITH A STRONG COMMITMENT TO PROVIDING EQUALITY OF OPPORTUNITY FOR EACH OF OUR INDIVIDUAL CITIZENS, AND A COMPASSIONATE SOCIETY WHOSE SOCIAL AND WELFARE SYSTEMS *DO* TAKE CARE OF THE UNFORTUNATE.

- Develop an understanding by broad German publics of the bases of American culture and social institutions.

4. *BERLIN*

The American presence in Berlin is a tangible and symbolic manifestation of the U.S. commitment to the security of Western Europe, as well as to the security of the city. Berlin both affects and is affected by the overall state of East-West, U.S.–USSR relations. The nature of our commitment to that city — as expressed in part by USIA investments and activities — is noted in the FRG and in the East as a barometer of our continuing will and ability to meet our Alliance obligations.

OBJECTIVE: REMIND THE PEOPLE OF BERLIN AND THE CITIZENS OF THE FEDERAL REPUBLIC THAT THE U.S. COMMITMENT TO THE SECURITY OF THAT CITY IS UNEQUIVOCALLY FIRM.

Appendix 3

USIS Budget (10/1/88) — Colombia

EMPLOYMENT CEILINGS:

Americans   6

FNE (Foreign National Employees)   31

GOE (General Operating Expenses):   [in U.S. dollars]
PROGRAM FUNDS:
Radio   374
Mopix/TV   23,625
Press and Publications   21,178
Centers (USIS and/or BNC Lib., Eng. Tchg. & Cult. Prog.) . .   84,791
Exhibits   5,308
Book Programs   2,059
Exchanges and Cultural Presentations   0
Research   0
Presentations   0
Representation   0
Program Direction   9,611
                                                                    ─────────
Subtotal, Programs **146,946**

GENERAL SUPPORT FUNDS:

Training   1,325
F.S. [Foreign Service] Allowances   7,622

Foreign National Salaries   371,542
Administration   183,276
ORE [official residence expenses]   0
ADP [automated data processing]   0

Subtotal, General Support **563,765**

Total, GOE **710,711**

(Current non-add GOE travel ceilings Dols 22,268)

DIRECT SUPPORT ALLOCATION (DSA) (paid to State Dept.) 132,318

TOTAL, DIRECT PAO RESOURCES   843,029

INDIRECT PAO RESOURCES:

DISTRIBUTED ADMINISTRATIVE SUPPORT (DAS)   **82,526**
AMERICAN SALARIES **437,707**

TOTAL, INDIRECT PAO RESOURCES **520,233**

**GRAND TOTAL, DIRECT AND INDIRECT
PAO RESOURCES** **1,363,262**

Appendix 4

Public Affairs Goal Paper for President's Visit to the Federal Republic of Germany, June 1982

The German public mood that the President will face during his visit is rife with ambivalent cross-currents.

On the plus side, the Government and the Opposition are firmly committed to the Western Alliance, and all serious polls register a high positive image rating for the United States.

Yet, there is an increasing public perception — magnified by the media on both sides of the Atlantic — of a state of uneasiness, and "drifting apart" in the bilateral relationship. We therefore must not be lulled into complacency by poll results, nor by governmental expressions that the silent majority holds a positive attitude toward the U.S. and supports a close U.S./FRG bilateral relationship.

Beset by political and economic uncertainties and faced with an erosion of what was perceived to be the emotional security of the detente era, Germans appear to be searching for a role not necessarily opposed to the United States but more independent of it. German foreign policy interests are no longer automatically identified with those of the U.S. — witness the differing assessments of and approaches to a host of international issues, among them Central America, Poland, Afghanistan, North-South concerns.

In our continuing dialogue, however, we face a much more serious challenge than a "yearning for identity." The anti-nuclear peace movement — temporarily stilled by the President's bold arms reduction proposal in his November 18 address — is reemerging and on June 10 plans an anti-Reagan demonstration, involving thirty-seven different organizations. We must not dismiss lightly, nor underestimate the challenge posed by this shrilly articulate movement. (And the spreading "nuclear freeze drive" in America will provide additional credibility and stimulus to the German peace movement. We can anticipate an ever widening ripple-effect as the two movements interact and feed on each other.)

It behooves us to "understand" if not to agree with the root causes of this movement. We must, however, in particular, address in positive terms the concerns and fears of the articulate and critical young Germans, who, conditioned by a highly politicized educational and media atmosphere, swell the ranks of the "peace movement."

These young Germans—in some respects similar to the generation of young Americans in the late sixties and early seventies—are deeply troubled by the society and the world in which they live. Their concerns have coalesced into a generational "Angst." Located on what they see as a potential battleground and nuclear cemetery, they deeply fear a nuclear catastrophe. They feel a sense of frustration and resentment at being "caught" between the superpowers, with no control over their own destiny. In their perceptions, the world has grown more dangerous, and the increased danger has coincided with the advent of the Reagan Administration. The new assertiveness with which the U.S. assumed its role as a world power and leader of the Western Alliance has, rather than creating confidence, bred fear that the growing superpower rivalry will result in disaster. These young people further genuinely worry about the environment, particularly in regard to the use of nuclear power, and they are concerned about the plight of the poor nations. They feel psychologically alienated in a highly industrial society which extols consumerism and material benefits. At the same time, they confront serious economic and social problems—problems of unemployment and careers, and the prospect of a reduction in the level of government largesse to which they have become accustomed.

This "successor generation," which has formed its view of America through the prism of Vietnam, the protest explosion and Watergate, unlike the previous generation, no longer looks upon the United States as a cohesive, creative, vital society worthy of emulation.

Obviously, the Soviets are active in nurturing this general malaise for their own purpose, primarily by trying to appear as the sole champion of peace. (The latest example is the Brezhnev ploy on freezing deployment of SS-20s west of the Urals. Although dismissed by the FRG Government, this proposal may well fall upon fertile ground in the peace movement.)

The "negative image" of the President and his Administration among many young and some not-so-young people in this country—magnified by the media—adds to our problem. Confronting us in some of the German media—especially in the weekly press and on TV—is the portrayal of the President as a callous, uncaring person, willing to sacrifice the social net to the demands of military expansion; as a "cowboy," willing—even eager—to resolve problems in a confrontational manner. The President's vision of the world is generally characterized by the German media as being naive and negatively motivated, with foreign affairs problems generally viewed in the framework of the East-West conflict. According to interpretations in the press, the "harsh rhetoric" and "aggressive" tone emanating from Washington have given impetus to the German peace movement. And, as incredible as it may seem, the U.S. is often equated, especially by younger

Germans, with the Soviet Union in amorality or immorality as regards its motives and objectives.

Thus, the priorities of the Presidential visit should be: to reiterate that the U.S. is second to none in its quest for world peace, justice, economic security and human rights — in that effort, we insist on indeed being "number one"; to address in sympathetic and positive terms the "hopes and fears" of the critical younger generation of Germans; to give lie to the canard that the U.S. advocates only military solutions to world problems, while the Soviets are the "bearers of peace;" and to sustain and give encouragement to those elements in German society who are supportive of the United States and its goals.

These objectives, we feel certain, can best be attained by a *positive* approach to German public opinion. The point is to underscore the shared philosophical and ethical principles that form the foundation of the U.S.–FRG relationship; to stress that the U.S. is the champion of mankind's aspirations for peace and prosperity; to reaffirm that American foreign policy is *for* a vision of international order that encompasses human rights and not merely a *reaction* against an alien ideology or against Soviet imperialism....

We should strive, given the proven effect upon the public of the President's personal approach, to garner maximum exposure for the President through "controlled" media events. Thus, the President should make an airport arrival statement, and accept the anticipated formal invitation to address the Bundestag. (Should the visit to West Berlin materialize, then the President should make "appropriate remarks" there, as well, but the public focal point should be the Bundestag speech.)

The "Bundestag address" will afford the President an appropriate platform to speak to the "deficit of information" which prevails on both sides of the Atlantic, and which contributes to the absence of understanding and appreciation of the commonality of the goals of our respective democratic societies....

USIS
American Embassy
Bonn
January 1982

Appendix 5

Quarterly Analysis from USIS Bonn to the U.S. Information Agency, January 4, 1983

United States Information Service
Embassy of the United States of America
Deichmanns Aue
5300 Bonn 2

January 4, 1983

Mr. Leonard J. Baldyga
Director
Office of European Affairs
U.S. Information Agency
Washington, D.C. 20547

Dear Len:

The issue that agitates German minds above all others as we begin the year 1983 is the deteriorating state of the German economy, with its continuing growth of unemployment, the unabated flurry of business failures, increasing polarization in the relationship between labor and industry, and the reluctant realization that there is a limit to the social benefits which German citizens have taken for granted for as long as most of them can remember. What this means, in terms of our bilateral communications climate, can be readily deduced: disappointment, disillusionment, fear, uncertainty, the shock of recognizing that the German "economic miracle" has disappeared. All these combine to create a mood conducive to a hectic search for scapegoats. The United States is vaguely suspected of following egotistical, self-centered policies that produce problems for less powerful countries, including the Federal Republic of Germany. Interest rates, budget deficits, disregard of the poor, defense spending, restrictions on East-West trade, incipient protectionism in West-West trade are seen as manifestations of a selfish U.S. attitude toward the rest of the world. Unhappiness about U.S. economic policies also prepares the ground for a critical posture vis-a-vis American defense and security policies. And it spills over, eventually, into the entire range of other

193

issues on which we need — and seek through USIS activities — German understanding and support.

The task before us, then, is to provide persuasive proof that American policies do not only serve American interests but that, on the contrary, U.S. and German interests — economic, political, and military — are congruous and mutually supportive. These policies, more than even the Polish crisis or the Afghanistan war which in the FRG are already issues of high public attention, are those to which we need to devote our primary energies, talents and imagination in the FRG.

This is not an easy task, given the present emotional state of the German public. But, fortunately, the picture is not entirely black. The lifting of the Siberian gas pipeline sanctions, the temporary resolution of the steel import problems, the drop in U.S. interest rates and the fall of the dollar against the D-Mark have tended to ease somewhat the bilateral tensions — at least on the economic front.

On East-West issues such as arms control, however, suspicion persists that the Reagan Administration's emphasis is on "arms" rather than on "control." The Andropov proposal was obviously designed to appeal to the large constituency in Germany (and other European countries) that professes to harbor doubts regarding U.S. sincerity in the Geneva negotiations. As our media reporting must already have shown you, the latest Andropov ploy is seen here as only the first salvo in what is likely to be a complicated period in the US–USSR battle for the allegiance of German public opinion on the arms control issue.

The government-to-government relationship between our two countries may have become more fraternal, in tone, with the accession to power of the CDU/CSU/FDP coalition on October 1, 1982; but we must be aware that the issues that were perceived as contentious before have not changed fundamentally. The new Kohl Government has moved quickly to emphasize "continuity" in foreign policy: it has stressed its determination to maintain close relations with the United States, as the leader of the Western Alliance, and with its European neighbors; it has firmly endorsed the 1979 NATO decision to deploy INF in Germany unless the Soviets agree in Geneva to do away with their missiles targeted on Europe. But — lest we get euphoric over these supportive statements — the FRG Government couples this policy with what it publicly calls "the policy of the outstretched hand" to the East which, of course, has a special meaning for Germans as they continue to grapple with the problem of their relationship with the 17 million Germans in the GDR.

At any rate, the Kohl Government is still going through a phase of consolidation which we must expect to last until after early March when it hopes to win a clearer popular mandate through national elections. At the same time, the SPD, having regained self-confidence after its clear victory in the Hamburg Land elections in

December, promises to carry out an aggressive campaign to regain control of the government; while the FDP will battle for its 5% of political life. There is little doubt but that the relationship between Bonn and Washington—always a key factor in FRG foreign policy—will be an issue in the election campaign. USIS activities during that sensitive period will have to be particularly discreet and must, even more than at other times, avoid any hint of favoring one side or the other.

One USIS/G[ermany] theme that should help us steer clear of any hidden political rocks as we navigate the difficult currents and counter-currents of 1983 is the "Tricentennial." It has the unstinted support of all established political entities in the Federal Republic of Germany. The "Tricentennial" idea is seen as unobjectionable, from every point of view, and will therefore provide us with an effective vehicle for a wide range of USIS-activated bilateral events, throughout the year, addressed to all segments of the German public. We also expect that the fact that the Director of the U.S. Information Agency was named by the President as the Chairman of the U.S. Inter-Agency Committee for German-American Contacts to be beneficial to our program efforts here inasmuch as it will tend to heighten the level of receptivity, generally, for USIA activities in Germany. We shall, of course, utilize that new factor to the fullest.

The Tricentennial will give us the opportunity—the "peg" if you will—to concentrate on the long-range issues which will affect the US–FRG relationship. It will permit us to emphasize the basic common values on which the relationship rests—respect for individual liberty, freedom of choice, the rule of law and efforts to secure a peaceful existence for all of us. It is vital to restate again and again these basic truths and to persuade particularly the younger generation of Germans that the ties that have been established between our two societies over three centuries, but especially since World War II, are beneficial for both countries and indeed necessary for the preservation of our democratic systems and peace. A practical way to accomplish this is by encouraging greater knowledge and under-standing of each other's life styles, institutions, culture and ideas through mean-ingful exchanges among young people of our two countries, exchanges which will give them the opportunity to inform themselves in depth and detail about each other. The knowledge and information thus gained will, I am certain, serve the citizens of our two countries during their lifetime in enabling them to interact intelligently with one another to their mutual benefit and to the benefit of their respective nations.

Among the post's program activities addressing U.S. priority concerns in this area, the following were of particular value and impact:

The theme of U.S. leadership for the 1980s was stressed by the American participants in a three-day seminar November 29–December 1 at the Berlin

Amerika Haus under the heading "The US and the USSR — Conflicts and Conflict Management." Sponsored by USIS, in cooperation with the Berlin Department of Education and the German Association of History Teachers, to examine the political, security and economic issues of the East-West relationship, it brought together eight American and German specialists on East-West affairs from such prestigious think tanks as the Congressional Research Service/Library of Congress, the German Orient Institute of Hamburg, the Science-and-Politics Foundation of Ebenhausen and the Berlin Science Center. They analyzed the changes that have occurred in the global power structure since 1947, differing interpretations of "detente" by American, Soviet and European policy makers, the Reagan Administration's policy concepts toward relations with the Soviet Union, Western response to events in Afghanistan and Poland, and the significance of recent developments in areas of global sensitivity such as the Middle East, the Horn of Africa and Central America.

More than 70 German teachers of history and political studies rated the seminar "highly successful" in offering a framework within which to order complex issues of East-West relations, in giving new insights and intellectual stimuli, and in providing access to very practical printed materials for classroom use. Such materials included USIA publications, American library book displays and selected German textbook displays. The three-day event generated considerable press attention as well as praise by the Berlin Senator (Minister) for Schools. It should have a major — and long-range — impact on the teaching of U.S.-related subjects in Germany.

The Poland Initiative was reflected in the programming of Prof. Ivan Volgyes, East Europe specialist at the University of Nebraska, in several major German cities just prior to the martial law anniversary. His timely presentations on the obstacles to liberalization in Eastern Europe stimulated lively discussions on the lack of political, economic and social freedom as a function of Soviet hegemony at the Ost-Akademie of Lueneburg, the Free University, Berlin and several Amerika Haus facilities.

The post's other activities in connection with the "Poland Initiative," including electronic media utilization, special exhibits and the production of an updated German version of the Agency's *Poland* pamphlet, were reported in Bonn 28021.

U.S. Foreign Policy and Security Objectives were authoritatively explained at Amerika Haus Cologne and in a WDR-TV appearance by NSC Soviet Affairs expert Richard Pipes and State's Robert Dean.

At the annual Haus Rissen (Hamburg) conference on "International Politics," John Kornblum of State/EUR/CE [Europe/Central Europe] and Minister William

Woessner of the American Embassy Bonn effectively presented strong arguments against the polemics introduced in the debate by a high-level Soviet delegation.

USIS Frankfurt organized two regional colloquia on US security policy: one, sponsored by the GAI [German-American Institute] Saarbruecken at the European Academy of Oetzenhausen, engaged 50 participants from the southwestern states of Germany in a productive debate on NATO, arms control and the congruity of German and American security interests. The second, held at the SPD-affiliated Friedrich-Ebert-Foundation in cooperation with the GAI, addressed "The Atlantic Alliance in Time of Trial" and offered teachers, students, media representatives and party politicians from southern Germany a serious discussion of U.S. security goals and the state of the INF negotiations. In both events, USIS-provided AMPARTS — Gunnar Nielsson of USC and Maurice Eisenstein of Georgetown — cogently argued the necessity of implementing the NATO two-track decision with peace movement leaders and other critics of American military policies. The latter event was taped for broadcast by Radio Saarbruecken, thereby reaching a broad German audience.

USIS Stuttgart and the German-American Institutes in Freiburg, Heidelberg and Tuebingen helped assuage apprehensions and correct distortions regarding U.S. security policies by programming CSIS [Center for Strategic and International Studies] President David Abshire with influential area journalists.

American Political Processes and Values were the subject of programs in Bonn, Frankfurt, Berlin and Munich by AMPARTS June Willenz, Midge Decter and Ronald Boster, giving graduate students, young political leaders and the media a rare insight in American election procedures, the meaning of neo-conservatism and the ethical basis of American political thought and action.

AMPART Loren Smith, Chairman of the Administrative Conference of the U.S., in the first-ever USIS program conducted in the Baden-Wuerttemberg State Ministry, articulated persuasively the main points of U.S. domestic policies for his high-level audience of state government officials and politicians. This, as well as Smith's impressive presentation on the significance of "Regulatory Reform in the U.S." before jurists, administrators and legal scholars at the Berlin Amerika Haus documented, once again, the importance and effectiveness of U.S.G. officials' participation in the AMPART program.

Economic Concerns, very much on the mind of all German audiences these days, were the subject of discussions arranged by USIS Munich, Stuttgart and other branch posts for AMPART Carlos Campbell, Asst. Secretary of Commerce for Economic Development. He was able to correct media distortions of the impact of Reaganomics on America's poor (eliciting a letter of thanks from the editor of an influential church magazine who vowed to take a more critical look, in the future, at media-generated myths regarding U.S. social policies) and managed to disabuse at least the more rational ones among his listeners of the notion that whatever ails the German economy at this time is the result of selfish, callous American trade policies.

American Society is the rubric under which we might put some, though not all, of our activities in connection with the "Tricentennial." The role of German immigrants in America was a subject that met with considerable interest when Duesseldorf BPAO [Branch PAO] Ralph Ruedy discussed it in his area (which includes the town of Krefeld from where the first German settlers came in 1683). Thus, even before the Tricentennial year has started, we have made good use of the opportunity to get beyond the day's headlines with our audiences and remind them of the enduring character of the American-German relationship.

THE PRESIDENT'S YOUTH EXCHANGE INITIATIVE was helped in a highly visible way, by a three-day symposium on U.S.–German youth exchanges, under the aegis of the German Ministry of Youth, Family and Health, in Bonn. It brought together more than 100 representatives of 35 German and 42 American organizations engaged in the exchange of young people, USIA's E/YX [Educational and Cultural Affairs/Youth Exchange] and USIS Bonn prominent among them. Highlight of the program was a visit with FRG President Karl Carstens who, seconded by American Ambassador Arthur Burns, praised the concept of youth exchanges as a most effective instrument for furthering the friendly and cooperative relationship that exists between Germany and the United States (see Bonn 28124 and 28246 for details).

Youth Exchanges and the Tricentennial were also the subject of a tele-press conference, broadcast by RIAS Berlin, with Director Wick and his new German counterpart as Coordinator of U.S.–German contacts, the State Secretary of the FRG Foreign Ministry, Berndt von Staden.

Looking ahead, I see — as I mentioned at the outset — a number of imponderables to come our way, as far as the bilateral communications environment is concerned, particularly in connection with the political campaign leading up to the March '83 national elections. A major public diplomacy problem on the horizon remains the question of how best to coordinate among the Western nations — in a practical way — the public affairs handling of the INF deployment issue which also involves, of course, the treatment of the Geneva negotiations issue, particularly in the light of an expected stepping up of the Soviet side's playing to the West European (mainly German) galleries.

[signed]

Hans N. Tuch

Appendix 6

USIS Country Plan (Brazil) — Fiscal Year 1989
Academic Exchange Program

Name of Country: Brazil
Commission Status: Commission
Budget for Fulbright Programs:

USIA — Direct Funding	1,157,000	1,200,000	1,332,000 *
USIA — Regional Funding	319,725	256,125	141,625
Brazilian Government	550,300	789,328	914,100
Partners/AID	150,000	150,000	150,000
	2,177,025	2,395,453	2,537,725

* Based on FY-88 initial allocation of US$1,200,000 plus anticipated allocation of LASPAU [Latin American Scholarship Program for American Universities] grants of US$132,000

1. Overview of Proposed Program

As Brazil's Constituent Assembly moves towards completion of its work, there are indications that the new constitution may result in some significant changes in the form and style of government in Brazil. Nevertheless, after having emerged a little more than three years ago from over twenty years of authoritarian, military rule, Brazil's desire for an open, pluralistic, and democratic society is the hope for the future.

In serving the objective of promoting mutual understanding, the Fulbright program proposed for 1989 seeks to make Brazilian and American participants, and the persons and institutions with which they interact, more aware, on the one hand, of the common values and common areas of interest and concern which draw our two societies together and, on the other hand, more aware of national characteristics, interests and aspirations which distinguish our societies.

In pursuing its goals, the Commission believes it should continue to concentrate its resources on grants to Americans and Brazilians whose projects are designed to strengthen the already well-established programs of graduate education in

199

Brazilian institutions, where future professors are being trained, and to develop and improve undergraduate American studies in Brazilian universities.

Having concluded that it has made a significant contribution to the teaching of the arts in Brazilian universities and to training in the arts in general — some seventy faculty members having received graduate training in the U.S. over the past twelve years — the Commission has terminated this successful project. Recognizing the importance of the arts, however, a new program being initiated this year will provide a short-term grant for a distinguished Brazilian artist.

In view of the difficulties encountered in implementing the new professional exchanges initiative, this project has been dropped from the 1989 program.

In recognition of Brazilian needs, the Commission has included in its 1989 program two new projects, Journalism Education and Management of Science and Technology. The former seeks to instill more professionalism and an emphasis on journalistic responsibility in Brazilian university programs in journalism; the latter seeks to induce and facilitate the social use or application of advances in science and technology. The journalism education initiative also will include an International Visitors (IV) project for Brazilian journalism educators and grants to U.S. lecturers.

Although the objectives and goals of the Fulbright program are best served by projects in the social sciences and humanities, the Commission proposes devoting more resources than in recent years to projects in the sciences, in response to an increasing amount of interest among Brazilian board members in responding to the Brazilian Government's self-ascribed priority, to increase substantially the number of grants to Brazilians for graduate studies with special emphasis on science and technology. Although there are strong reasons why it would not seem wise to duplicate Brazilian efforts in the hard sciences, we do feel it may be possible, however, to identify unmet educational needs in what may be referred to as human sciences, i.e., nutrition, urban development, and environmental management. This move could satisfy the wishes of our Brazilian colleagues and still contribute to our desire to invest our money where it can have its own impact and not be subsumed within a larger program. To this end, some of the USAID resources made available to the Commission through the National Partners of the Americas (NAPA) could be used for such projects.

The Commission's program has retained its project for Brazilian legislative staff training, although little used thus far, believing that with the new role foreseen in the draft constitution for federal and state legislatures, there will be an increasing demand for training in this field. Resources also are reserved for assistance, through institutional grants, to American and Brazilian initiatives which are in keeping with program objectives and goals.

The current exchange program mix provides an acceptable level of resources to the post. Both the Fulbright Program and the post's non-academic exchanges, principally the International Visitors Program, however, could absorb considerable increases in the number of grants, if funding were to become available.

The wide range of Commission projects, as well as Agency resources available to the post, such as Academic Specialists, AmParts, English Teaching Officers, and the International Humphrey Program and USIA-sponsored university affiliations, such as the current program maintained by the Colorado School of Mines with universities in northern Brazil, provide the potential to complement the Commission's new project in Management of Science and Technology.

The USIA University Affiliations Program is of special interest to the post in view of the key role universities in Brazil play in the development and shaping of ideas of influential members of the society and, most important, of future leaders. Therefore, the ten affiliation grants sponsored by the Agency over the past four years to U.S. universities for programs of mutual interest with Brazilian counterparts have provided exceptional opportunities. The post's proposal for the FY-88 program to assist the National School of Administration (ENAP), together with the University of Brasilia, to carry out an exchange program with an appropriate American center of public administration studies is especially relevant at this time for Brazil; it would establish a two-year graduate course with emphasis on public policy and management to produce top, career-tenured public managers in all government sectors with expertise in policy formulation. This most valuable, potential component of the post's exchange program, if not funded this year, should be a priority for Agency support in FY-89.

The Commission believes that seminars such as those on Brazilian culture and language sponsored by the U.S. Department of Education and supervised in Brazil by the Commission and the South America Today seminars, should have a counterpart for Brazilians. It is therefore proposed, pending availability of funding, to sponsor another seminar on current issues of American democracy in 1989, similar to the successful pilot seminar held at the University of Texas at Austin in 1985.

The branch posts and the Commission continue to interact well in recruiting and monitoring candidates for the Hubert H. Humphrey Program. Five Brazilian Humphrey grantees are currently in the U.S., and a slate of candidates was submitted for the 1989 program.

The FY-89 program foresees the following categories and numbers of grants:

For Americans:

Senior Lecturers/Researchers	25-Full grants, co sponsored
Serial grants for senior scholars (new and renewed grants)	03-Full grants with co-sponsorship
Participants in workshops/seminars	03-Full funded with co-sponsorship
Travel grants for institutional linkages	15-Travel-only (PanAm courtesy tickets)
Regionally-funded graduate students	05-Fully funded by regional USIA funds
Regionally-funded U.S. researchers	05-Fully funded with co-sponsorship

For Brazilians:

Post-doctoral studies/research	20-Fully funded with co-sponsorship
Study/research in the U.S. to complement doctoral programs in Brazilian universities	03-Fully funded by Commission
Study/research in the U.S. to complement M.A. programs in Brazilian universities	02-Fully funded by Commission
Short-term faculty development in American Studies	03-Fully funded by Commission
Distinguished grant in the arts	01-Fully funded by Commission
Preservation and dissemination of culture	05-Fully funded with co-sponsorship
Grants for sequential contacts with U.S. scholars/U.S.universities	02-Fully funded with co-sponsorship
Short-term, non-degree awards in mutual interest fields	16-Fully funded by NAPA/USAID
Iowa International Writers Program	01-Partial funding by Commission
American Chambers of Commerce awards (new and renewed grants)	08-Partial grants
Travel grants for institutional linkages	25-Travel only (PanAm courtesy tickets)

Faculty development in the arts	04-Fully funded with co-sponsorship & some tuition waivers
Faculty development in American Studies (new and renewed grants)	06-Fully funded by Commission with some tuition waivers
Faculty development in journalism education (new and renewed grants)	12-Fully funded with co-sponsorship
Legislative staff training (new and renewed grants)	04-Fully funded with co-sponsorship
Management of science and technology (new and renewed grants)	04-Fully funded with co-sponsorship

2. Program Feasibility

Although the Fulbright Program is better known than ever and well regarded by the Brazilian academic community, the number of requests from the Brazilian universities for American lecturers/researchers for 1989 was disappointingly small. This is attributed not to a lack of interest on the part of the universities but to their general disarray this past year caused by numerous, and sometimes prolonged, strikes by faculty, students and administrative staffs. Nevertheless, a sufficient number of acceptable requests for U.S. professors was received from a wide range of universities.

Another point of concern has been the difficulty in recruiting U.S. professors for all projected assignments in Brazilian universities. This is particularly puzzling at a time when the Agency has indicated that Commission grant benefits are competitive, interest in Brazil is growing in the United States, and the maturity of many Brazilian university courses and faculties presumably is making grants to foreign scholars more attractive professionally. Hopefully, more U.S. professors will apply for the announced projects for 1989.

While science and technology are not the Commission's priority fields, the Commission intends, as noted in the Overview, to devote more resources to them, thereby increasing the number of grants to U.S. professors, directed to projects in the human sciences.

Visa problems and restrictions on the entrance of computers into Brazil continue to complicate the participation of American grantees in the program. The Commission will persist in efforts to overcome these difficulties.

Despite the difficulties cited above, the Commission's proposed program for 1989 appears to be entirely feasible, particularly in view of the current and anticipated support being given to the Commission by Brazilian agencies and authorities.

3. Cost Sharing

Although there is still potential for growth in the level of Brazilian cost sharing of the Fulbright Program, there is also the concern that, because of the increasingly difficult economic situation in Brazil, and especially that of the Brazilian Federal Government (of which two agencies, CAPES [Educational and Research Grant Giving Agency] and CNPq [National Research Council], are still the Commission's main sources of outside support), cost sharing will remain at the current level or perhaps even be reduced after 1989. (It should be noted that because of its non-juridical status, the Commission continues to be ineligible to receive funds directly from official and most private sources in Brazil.) In FY-89 an estimated Brazilian input of the equivalent to US$914,700 (compared to the estimated US$789,328 for FY-88) is expected from Brazilian official agencies (CAPES, CNPq and FAPESP, the last a São Paulo State agency which signed an agreement with the Commission in May 1987); this may be the high water mark of Brazilian official contributions to the Fulbright Program in the foreseeable future.

While financial contributions from Brazilian federal agencies possibly might be reduced, the FAPESP contribution could increase since the financial situation of the progressive state of São Paulo has far better prospects. A drawback to this seeming advantage, however, would be the Fulbright Program becoming too "Paulista" in a country where there already exists a very heavy regional imbalance.

Most in-kind contributions by Brazilian official agencies are in the form of airline tickets for American lecturers and Brazilian grantees, all being purchased from VARIG, the Brazilian airline. PAN AM continues to offer yearly round-trip courtesy tickets to the Commission for short-term exchanges, and, as of 1987, has increased the number to forty. Although efforts to obtain a similar in-kind contribution from VARIG have not yet been successful, the Commission will make new attempts. The Commission currently is negotiating for different types of contributions from Brazilian official agencies, instead of almost exclusively VARIG tickets, in order to increase its own purchase level of tickets from PAN AM.

Another important in-kind contribution — salaries paid to Brazilian grantees by their home institutions — is losing weight; the dollar equivalent to salaries paid in cruzados is diminishing as salary adjustments do not accompany inflation. This trend may become even more troublesome in 1988 and 1989 since prospects for increasing higher education funding in Brazil over the next few years are bleak.

In-kind support provided by Brazilian institutions to U.S. grantees (office space, clerical help, etc.) appears to be adequate. Other types of in-kind support, such as specialized selection review panels and detailed planning information, are expected to continue to be available for the foreseeable future.

The American Chambers of Commerce in Brazil, a private sector source of funding, are anticipating a significant increase in their contribution for FY 1989 (US$124,000 compared to US$93,701 in 1988). Even so, that contribution will mean a decrease in the number of grants, from six to four per year, in view of rising costs. A substantial increase is expected in the contribution provided by NAPA, utilizing USAID funds. It is estimated that in both 1988 and 1989 their contribution could be increased to US$150,000 per year, almost doubling the 1985–1987 US$80,000/year level. Although there are restrictions for the use of these funds which must be applied to grants to Brazilians for post-doctoral projects, as a result other funds would become available to support additional American grantees in Brazil.

If the Commission obtains juridical status under Brazilian law, there will be new possibilities of fund raising from private sources in Brazil.

4. Program Balance

The Fulbright Commission's FY-89 Program Proposal still foresees many more grants for Brazilians than for Americans, reflecting various factors: the high cost of grants to Americans in contrast to grants to Brazilians; the fact that the contributing Brazilian official agencies fund the major portion of most grants to Brazilians and that American grantees are usually reluctant to receive part of their grants in "soft" local currency from Brazilian agencies; some sources of co-sponsorship, such as the American Chambers of Commerce and NAPA/USAID can fund grants only for Brazilians; and the expected continuation of the low level of regional funding for American researchers and students.

In the last five years, however, a better balance between Brazilians and Americans has resulted from the Commission's policy of giving priority to grants for American lecturers in the reprogramming of leftover funds, including savings in administrative costs. The rationale for this policy is the fact that the Commission is, for the most part, the exclusive channel for funding grants for U.S. lecturers, U.S. students and now possibly also for regional U.S. researchers as well.

The Commission continues to strive to reflect a mutuality of interests between the U.S. and Brazil, and the post feels the Fulbright program in Brazil responds positively to this important goal. Since the membership of the Commission's Board includes the director of CAPES, a leading member of CNPq, and a representative of the Ministry of External Relations, there is ample opportunity for these host country representatives to voice their opinions and to advise the board on host country interests. Likewise, the official U.S. board component, with the CPAO [country PAO] serving as chairman and the CCAO [country cultural affairs officer] as treasurer, is able to shape program direction with emphasis on mission goals, to a large extent. Of note is the Board's recent, unanimous decision to include in the FY-89 Program Proposal, pending availability of funds, a special project, the Seminar on Contemporary Issues of American Democracy, to be administered by a U.S. university, repeating the successful 1985 pilot program.

As noted last year, the Commission, as well as host institutions, would welcome additional U.S. lecturers in the applied and natural sciences, giving emphasis to quality host graduate programs rather than specific fields. To compensate for the lack of satisfactory response from the pre-selected university graduate programs in preferred fields, the Commission has extended invitations to the best university graduate programs in the fields of sciences with social consequence, which has resulted in a limited number of approved openings in the sciences in the FY-89 Program Proposal.

Focusing on possible professional participation, in addition to the traditional academic base, the Commission's latest announcement for the Humphrey Program, reflecting this new possibility, resulted in a record number of 131 applications for 1988–1989, with six principal and three alternate candidates having been selected and nominated. Although the Commission and the post had looked forward to the prospects of the new Professional Exchanges Program, this initiative has fallen short of expectations. Other opportunities for exchange of professionals are a felt need in Brazil and should be addressed.

5. Other Exchange Activity in Brazil

As noted in item 3, there are good prospects for a substantial increase in USAID-funded training opportunities for Brazilians, in fields related to the improvement of the quality of life in urban areas through the NAPA/Fulbright agreement and also through NAPA's own university program in Brazil. National Science Foundation (NSF) programs continue at the same limited level, but substantial progress achieved in bilateral negotiations during 1987 may lead to an increase in scientific cooperation between the U.S. and Brazil and, as a result, expansion of programs in Brazil by the NSF and other U.S. scientific agencies.

The U.S. Department of Education (USED), in addition to continuing to fund research grants to U.S. scholars (including doctoral candidates) in Brazil, has indicated that while it would like to reinstate its Summer Seminars Program, it has cancelled its 1988 Summer Seminar because of program fund reduction and weak response from prospective applicants. Peace Corps activities were discontinued in the early 80's when the program in Brazil was phased out.

One year ago President Sarney announced a daring and ambitious plan to increase the number of scholarships for Brazilians to study abroad, moving from a previous level of 2,500 grants to 10,000 new grants annually by 1989. Received with much skepticism in view of the Brazilian economic crisis, this initiative, being administered by both the Ministries of Science and Technology and Education, already has fallen short of the originally stated goal of 6,000 new grants in 1987 (only 2,800 grants were awarded which most probably include many renewals of previous grants), 8,500 new grants for 1988 (5,500 revised figure), and the 10,000 goal, now projected for 1990. A minimum of 10% of new grants each year are designated for specific, high tech fields, including computer science, refined chemistry and materials sciences. Most of these new grants in the sciences are being directed toward the U.S. The Commission already has responded to CNPq's request for information on appropriate U.S. graduate programs in the sciences, especially the new fields, and CNPq is directing potential grantees to use the Commission's advising network (see item 7). There is much uncertainty concerning the 1989 program, however, and, the GOB[Government of Brazil]'s plan most probably will not reach the announced level by 1990.

There is no significant change in the nature and the level of exchanges with other Western countries, Germany, France, and the United Kingdom, Brazil's main European counterparts, which coordinate their exchange programs with Brazilian government organizations and receive some cost-sharing, both funding and in-kind. The Eastern Bloc, however, is pressing hard to increase its share of exchanges, including an emphasis on new opportunities in the arts and some in sports. The renewal of diplomatic relations with Cuba has opened the door for exchange. Film is a favorite field offering training opportunities for Brazilians in Cuba, as well as several festivals which featured prominent Brazilian participation. Three recently signed cultural agreements, a first between Cuba and Brazil, provide for exchange of publications, films for didactic purposes, and grants for the exchange of Cuban and Brazilian students and professors, as well as for a major Cuban film festival to be held in Brazil in 1988. There is a marked emphasis on popular music, also, Cuban orchestras and singers having toured Brazil during the past year. Inexpensive package tours to Cuba are accessible to the Brazilian middle class, and the flow of Brazilian tourists tends to grow.

The American Chambers of Commerce in Brazil will continue to offer their International Fellowship Program, sponsoring grants for master's degree studies in the U.S. (see item 3). NAPA has expanded considerably its own university linkage program in Brazil and also administers a small program of short-term professional training opportunities sponsored by the Atlantic Richfield Oil Co., with which USIS branch posts and the Fulbright Commission have cooperated. Of note is that ITT, in 1987, excluded Brazil from its fellowship program. The Commission looks forward to cooperation from the Ford Foundation, as their Brazil Representative, once again, will attend Board meetings, now as an ex-officio, non-voting member.

Private student exchange programs continue to do well in Brazil, with larger demand than openings available in the U.S. These exchanges take place almost exclusively at the high school level. English language courses in the U.S. also have become very popular among the Brazilian upper middle class. This interest may decline rapidly, however, in view of the loss of purchasing power by Brazilians as the economic crisis continues.

An interesting and noticeable change last year was the initiative by upper middle class students for placement in American colleges and universities, a consequence of the higher education crisis in Brazil. This may not continue since personal funds available during the past "Cruzado Plan" era, as with the increased interest of Brazilians to attend intensive language programs in the U.S., could decline dramatically with the new financial reality in Brazil.

6. American Studies Programs/Centers

There are a number of significant programs and professional organizations in Brazil involved in American Studies. Several federal and private universities have instituted academic majors and area studies programs around different aspects of American Studies, although English language study and American literature remain the single most extensive area of study in which these programs function. Another key resource in American studies is the network of 61 binational centers in Brazil, 36 of them first and second-tier. In the stronger of these centers, courses, special programs and seminars frequently offer different aspects of American Studies. The two main professional organizations involved with American Studies are the Brazilian Association of American Studies (ABEA) and the Brazilian Association of University Professors of English Language and Literature (ABRAPUI). ABEA, affiliated with the American Studies Association, has some 225 members from all academic areas. Founded in 1985 through the support of USIS Brazil, ABEA remains the single most active and academically influential area studies organization in the country.

ABRAPUI is a 280 member group of higher education professionals with whom USIS Brazil works quite closely. Both ABEA and ABRAPUI sponsor major annual conferences, usually through the support of the federal or private universities chosen to host them, which normally attract strong national and international participation, especially British and American academics, and for which the post counts on Agency support to provide Academic Specialists and/or AmParts. The informal BNC network has also given birth to a national association, the "Coalition of U.S.–Brazilian Binational Centers", which while still in its formative stage may eventually prove to be a major resource in promoting greater emphasis on American Studies at binational centers. Brazilian government and private secondary schools do provide English language courses but, in general, their offerings in American Studies range from nonexistent to frivolous and marginal.

USIS Brazil and the Commission are actively engaged in a number of projects which enhance and encourage American Studies in the venues mentioned above. The Commission, for example, has dedicated a significant amount of its resources to this end, financing the visits on the average over the past three years of four to eight U.S. university professors to teach or consult in the area of American Studies at a Brazilian university for a semester, as well as at other Brazilian institutions and organizations for periods ranging from two weeks to a full academic year. Through the Fulbright/PANAM Travel Grant Program, from three to five U.S. and Brazilian professors have travelled yearly to teach, research, consult or to attend special conferences in Brazil and the United States. In FY-88, the Fulbright Commission is sponsoring six grants enabling Brazilian scholars to study and research for an extended period of time at American universities, including one degree candidate and five non-degree scholars involved in short-term projects. During FY-89, the Commission anticipates offering two degree and three short-term grants, as well as maintaining its exchange professor and PANAM grant program at traditional levels. In addition, the Commission has offered modest but highly effective institutional grants which have made possible travel to members and officers of ABEA and ABRAPUI for important planning projects. The Commission will continue to follow this policy, with an eye toward broadening the focus from American literature to include greater emphasis on political science, history, economics and other aspects of American Studies.

Post programming and support activities in American Studies have expanded steadily during the past three years and will continue in the same direction during the foreseeable future. Recognizing the great potential for the extensive number of binational centers in Brazil, the post has organized highly successful American Studies seminars for Brazilian BNC faculty at the University of Florida. In July 1988, the post plans to offer the fourth annual seminar, the academic portion of the program to be expanded from two weeks to three weeks.

On the university level, the post has supported numerous projects by providing AmParts and Academic Specialists. The post also offers resource materials to selected BNC and university libraries, ranging from core collections to periodical acquisitions.

The recent announcement of the forthcoming establishment of an English Teaching Office (ETO) position in Brazil will fill a long-felt need by assisting the post country-wide with English language training programs at BNCs, universities, and also secondary schools, as appropriate. Depending on developments in Brazil regarding the production of secondary school curricular materials and the receptivity of the Ministry of Education, the post is considering expanding its requests for E/AA [Educational and Cultural Affairs/ Academic Affairs] support for special programs in the area of American Studies, short-term workshops and a possible project in the U.S. for Brazilian curriculum developers.

7. Educational Advising

Several agencies in Brazil provide some information about studies abroad, the most important of which are the federal agencies, CAPES and CNPq, which cooperate closely with the Fulbright Commission and refer many inquiries to the Commission-supported services. Most Brazilian public universities also provide some information, however, based on limited and usually outdated resources. Therefore, the Commission-coordinated, advising network is by far the best and most reliable source of information about U.S. education, and its services are available to a wide and diversified audience in Brazil.

The Commission's own educational advising office is located at the U.S. Consulate General in Rio de Janeiro and provides materials, research services and training to the thirteen other advising offices throughout Brazil. Eleven of these offices are located in binational centers, four of which receive financial support from the Commission to assist with advisors' salaries. The sole student advising service still provided directly by a USIS branch post (Recife) hopefully will be transferred by 1989 to the new binational center currently being established in Recife with USIS assistance. An additional service provided by the Fulbright Advising Office is an Agency-funded quarterly newsletter, with a mailing list of 360 recipients, more than half located outside of Brazil. Because of the already noted increased interest in studies abroad (see item 5), 1987 was a very busy year for the advising network, whose public consisted of some 36,000 users, approximately a 25% increase over the previous year. The Commission, with the cooperation of the U.S. Consulates in Brazil, currently is conducting a study through questionnaires to determine how many Brazilians seeking visas for study in the U.S. are users of the Commission-supported services. The Commission's educational advising office also provides consultancy and support to similar services in South America (see item 9).

8. Teacher Exchange

The Commission, although interested in the Teacher Exchange Program, has encountered difficulties which, thus far, have prevented its participation. Although the Agency offered Brazil two proposals for FY-88, neither was appropriate. The Commission would welcome opportunities for Brazilian teachers to go to the U.S., taking into consideration the need for English language capability, as well as the Commission Board's directive that Brazilian participants' teaching assignments include a component about Brazil. Likewise, U.S. teachers, more appropriately with English language teaching experience and a stated preference for Brazil, would be placeable in selected Brazilian schools.

9. Regional Cooperation

The Commission makes available to other Commissions and to USIS posts in South America lists of current U.S. grantees and, likewise, receives similar information from other Commissions in the region. There have been several cases of U.S. grantees in Brazil's program being shared as lecturers at the request of other Commissions and, occasionally, of U.S. grantees from other countries being utilized in Brazil.

Brazilian historical, cultural and linguistic differences have limited the Commission's participation in regional projects. The Commission has participated in the "South America Today" seminars and remains willing to do so, again, when this program is reactivated. The Commission continues to cooperate with the regional study on inflation sponsored by the Commission in Peru and would be pleased to cooperate with similar projects.

The most active, ongoing regional initiative of the Commission is in educational advising. During the past year Brazil's Director of Educational Advising consulted with the Commission in Peru and the USIS post in Caracas, at their invitation. The Commission's Educational Advising Office in Rio de Janeiro maintains a directory of all educational advising offices in South America and produces a newsletter which is circulated widely. Training sessions and workshops have been conducted by the Commission for educational advisors in Brazil and in other countries of South America.

10. Fulbright Program Benefits

American Fulbright grantees in Brazil represent a most valuable resource as lecturers for the post and for Brazilian universities and institutions, which may draw from a comprehensive list of U.S. lecturers/researchers prepared by the Commission twice yearly and sent to over 800 Brazilian addresses. Through this

Commission-sponsored "speakers bureau," which has become an important spin-off benefit, the Commission provided in 1987 the opportunity for 32 U.S. grantees, in addition to their primary assignments, to lecture and contribute to professional events in some 90 institutions throughout Brazil. A U.S. grantee, assigned to the Catholic University in São Paulo, established a record last year by successfully giving 54 lectures over a ten-month period in 15 Brazilian cities, including participation in two seminars for teachers of English at major BNCs. Another example of the post's successful use of this resource was the University of São Paulo/BNC co-sponsored regional seminar on Southern American Literature for Brazilian professors of American Literature and American Studies at which a U.S. professor, assigned to the Federal University of Minas Gerais, was the featured lecturer. The annual ABEA conferences also have relied heavily on the Commission for speakers. As program opportunities develop, the post will continue to use this readily available Commission service.

Several Brazilian returned grantees, having benefitted from their Fulbright experience in the U.S., are now in positions of greater responsibility, examples being a professor of American literature, now the department coordinator at the Federal University in Rio de Janeiro; the director of the graduate program in education at the State University of Rio de Janeiro; and the program director at the "Paco Imperial," Rio's new and important arts complex; the current vice-rector of the prestigious University of São Paulo; the Municipal Secretary of Culture of Campinas (São Paulo), and the current president of the International Cooperation Commission of the University of São Paulo; and a professor of American literature who is the new dean of the Graduate School of the Federal University of Minas Gerais and current president of ABEA.

The Commission's Educational Advising Office in Rio maintains current a file on Fulbright Alumni and uses these former grantees as a resource for advisees seeking information about U.S. institutions, as well as for outreach programs for Brazilians interested in special fields of study in the U.S.

The Commission constantly updates and expands its records on former grantees, information which is also available to the post's DRS [distribution and records system]. Of note is the on-going outreach to former grantees through selective mailing of USIS publications. To commemorate the Commission's 30th anniversary in Brazil, former Fulbrighters in Brasilia, Rio, São Paulo and Porto Alegre were invited to attend an ARNET [Worldnet/American Republics] featuring Bureau Director Mark Blitz and distinguished Brazilian educators and former grantees, which was followed by receptions in those major cities. Of special importance was the presence at the event in Brasilia of the Ambassador, Honorary

Chairman of the Board, who together with the CAPES director, offered toasts of commemoration.

The Commission looks forward to the participation on its Board of the newest member, an American lawyer, long-time resident in Brazil and former Fulbrighter, whose past experience with the program should prove to be a great asset. In Recife former grantees are being supportive in establishing a new binational center in that city; three of the five members of their new board are former Fulbrighters.

11. Commission Post Evaluation

The post considers the Commission's activities an important aspect of the country program and devotes considerable time and human resources to the Fulbright Program in Brazil.

The post is pleased with the over-all direction of the Commission's current program and the program plan proposed for 1989. The increase in the initial funding from the Agency for FY-88 is encouraging and makes it possible for the Commission to take advantage of additional monies from Brazilian co-sponsoring agencies, which now include FAPESP, thereby increasing the number of cost-shared grants.

In the absence of a sufficient number of acceptable proposals for U.S. professors in the preferred or priority fields from Brazilian universities, the Commission rightly sought out a select group of other quality graduate programs in fields of mutual interest, such as forestry and food science, thereby increasing the numbers of proposals to a more desirable level.

The Commission, maintaining its impressively low level of cost of operation, further reduced its administrative costs from the previous 12% of the budget to approximately 11% in FY-88.

The post will look closely at the results of the study in progress regarding the ratio of Brazilians requesting student visas to the U.S. to the cost of maintaining the present level of services through the Commission's educational advising office and advising network, especially in view of the large numbers of advisees who seek information from this extensive network throughout Brazil. Direction concerning this aspect of the Commission's budget will be determined once the results of the study are known.

Relating more closely to the post's interests and objectives, the Commission has two new projects in its program, journalism education and management of science and technology, the former a joint venture with the post, the latter also of great interest to the Ministry of Science and Technology, which has proposed co-sponsorship through the CNPq.

The participation in the Commission's program of the Brazilian federal agencies, CAPES and CNPq, as well as the São Paulo state agency FAPESP, both financially and in decision-making, is a solid indication of the mutuality and binationalism that the Commission enjoys.

The best news for FY-88 is that relief is in sight to alleviate the overcrowding of Commission quarters, in view of the recent, but much delayed, acquisition of the land for the construction of the Casa Thomas Jefferson annex. It is expected that the new quarters will be ready by 1989.

Bibliographic Note

Recorded here are publications that have been helpful to me in writing this book and some that may be useful to the reader in understanding public diplomacy — its origins, purposes, potential, and limitations and its organization within the U.S. government. An extensive bibliography on public diplomacy, prepared by USIA archivist Martin Manning and updated periodically, is available at the library of the U.S. Information Agency, 301 4th Street, S.W., Washington, D.C. 20547.

Other bibliographies on public diplomacy include those in Lois Roth's *Fletcher Forum* monograph, listed below, and in my own "Murrow Reports" monograph, *Public Diplomacy: What It Is and How It Works*, (Medford, MA: Tufts University, Fletcher School of Law and Diplomacy, Fall 1985). A superb annotated bibliography on political propaganda is part of Paul Smith's profound and scholarly study, *On Political War*, also listed below.

Bardos, Arthur. *Afterthoughts on Cultural Diplomacy.* Murrow Reports. Medford, MA: Tufts University, Fletcher School of Law and Diplomacy, April 1989.

Chatten, Robert. "Wrong Division." *Foreign Service Journal* 65 (April 1988):38–43.

Davison, W. Phillips. *International Political Communication.* New York: Frederick A. Praeger, 1965.

Fisher, Glen H. *Mindsets: The Role of Culture and Perception in International Relations.* Yarmouth, ME: Intercultural Press, Inc., 1988.

— — —. *Public Diplomacy and the Behavioral Sciences.* Bloomington: Indiana University Press, 1972.

Hansen, Allen. *U.S. Information Agency: Public Diplomacy in the Computer Age.* 2d ed. New York: Frederick A. Praeger, 1989.

Hitchcock, David I., Jr. *U.S. Public Diplomacy.* Significant Issues Series, Vol. X, No. 17. Washington, D.C.: Center for Strategic and International Studies, 1988.

Kellermann, Henry J. *Cultural Relations as an Instrument of U.S. Foreign Policy: The Educational Exchange Program between the United States and Germany 1945–54.* Department of State Publication 8931. Washington, D.C.: U.S. Government Printing Office, 1978.

Malone, Gifford D. "Equal but Separate." *Foreign Service Journal* 65 (April 1988):32–38.

— — —. *Political Advocacy and Cultural Communication: Organizing the Nation's Public Diplomacy.* Lanham, MD: University Press of America, 1988.

Roth, Lois W. "Public Diplomacy: 1952–1977." *The Fletcher Forum* 8 (Summer 1984):353–96.

Smith, Paul A., Jr. *On Political War.* Washington, D.C.: National Defense University Press, 1990.

Index